The Commodification of Childhood

Daniel Thomas Cook

The Commodification of Childhood

THE CHILDREN'S

CLOTHING INDUSTRY

AND THE RISE

OF THE CHILD

CONSUMER

Duke University Press

Durham & London   2004

© 2004 Duke University Press

All rights reserved

Printed in the United States of

America on acid-free paper ∞

Typeset in Cycles by Keystone

Typesetting, Inc.

Library of Congress Cataloging-

in-Publication Data and permissions

information appear on the last printed

page of this book.

To the memory of

my grandfather,

JOHN COOK *(1898–1983),*

my grandmother,

JOSEPHINE C. COOK

(1902–1997),

and my mother,

JOSEPHINE L. COOK

(1927–1997).

Their sacrifice for me
and faith in me have made
all things possible in my life.

They supported me in my
educational and intellectual
endeavors without hesitation,
even without much of an
understanding of what I
was trying to accomplish.

They gave me only
unconditional love.

Contents

Acknowledgments

This book derives from my dissertation work undertaken in the Department of Sociology at the University of Chicago, which I completed in 1998. Navigating graduate student existence can be tricky as one confronts the tension between one's own need to seek models of scholarship and professionalism that are worthy of emulation and the tendency of most mentors to create protégés.

Fortunately for me, I did not have to face this dilemma working with Gerald Suttles. He exhibits a grace, a genuine concern, which allowed me to find my own way without having to do so alone. His kind directives, combined with hard-hitting critiques, offered needed encouragement without coddling. His impact on my life, professional and otherwise, is large and everlasting. I am fortunate to know him and to enjoy his continual friendship.

Jean Comaroff put her faith in me and in this project long before I knew that I had an idea worth the effort. The time, support, and careful criticism she gave me is in itself flattering. She has helped make me a scholar because she treated me like one from the start, something for which I am grateful. William Sewell is a master of listening with patience. His gentle manner and quiet demeanor offered me a way to find agency within structure and to combine rigor with imagination.

Andrew Abbott was vigilant that I remain empirically grounded, standing guard when I wandered to warn me back to the trail of purposeful, disciplined engagement with the materials at hand.

Beyond my committee, a number of people have helped me along the way. Norman Denzin has again given unselfishly of his time to encourage and comment upon this work. I thank Gary Cross for his valuable support. The anonymous reviewers offered valuable comments for which I am grateful.

Yu-Ling Chen provided indispensable editorial assistance and was a constant source of enthusiasm. I thank the Larkin family of Larkin, Inc. in Newton, Massachusetts, who assisted me in my initial forays into this topic by giving me access to their resources. Jim Girone, editor of *Earnshaw's*, provided needed early assistance with access to back issues. I also recognize the numerous runners and reference librarians who helped me find various obscure publications from the Library of Congress, the National Archives, the National Museum of American History, the J. Walter Thompson Archive at Duke University, the New York and Boston public libraries and the Regenstein Library at the University of Chicago. Their work often goes unacknowledged.

The Finnigan family not only took me into their house in Washington so that I could do research, they offered me the warmth of their home. Debbie DeYoung, Sudhir Venkatesh, and Alford Young listened patiently and lent a hand in the way that true friends do.

Diane Nelson supported me in this endeavor in many different ways and on many different levels since its inception. Without her encouragement, I may never have had the will to continue past the difficult times to enjoy the better ones.

Jessica Clark continues to give me the reason to care.

1

Introduction

A consumer culture of childhood stands as a ubiquitous fixture in public life. Daily, even hourly, one is confronted with images of children posed to capture the consuming gaze. Children—or, rather, carefully fabricated commercial personae of children—hawk most any kind of ware in advertisements, from automobile tires to breakfast cereal, from hotels and vacations to refrigerators. In addition to regular sections in newspapers, dozens of magazines, web pages, television shows, and networks presently vie for children's attention and allowances.

Children's products, and the accompanying images, promotions, and meanings, have a secure place among other items in the commercial panorama of consumer goods. Free-standing stores, retail departments, internet sites, and mail-order catalogues for children's goods abound. At grocery checkouts, gas stations, convenience stores, and highway rest stops "something for the kids" dangles enticingly and purposefully at children's eye level. Previously disparate industries now cooperate to create tie-ins between products, knitting together greeting cards, fast food, action toy figures, websites, television shows, films, and clothing into a singular promotional strategy. Estimates of the monetary value of the overall children's market (including the "influence" that children exert on household purchases) run into hundreds of billions of dollars annually for the United States alone.[1]

The market-culture of childhood represents a monumental accomplishment of twentieth-century capitalism. The rise and expansion of a child-world of goods, spaces, and media over the last century signifies a development above and beyond the opening of merely one more market similar to others. The child market stands apart from others because childhood is a *generative* cultural site unlike any other. Childhood generates bodies as well as meanings which grow, interact, and transform to the point of creating new childhoods, new meanings, and quite often new markets, and in the process effectively ensuring the movement and transformation of exchange value beyond any one cohort or generation.

In this book, I contextualize the rise and proliferation of a children's consumer culture throughout American society during the twentieth century, arguing that the child consumer is its enduring product and legacy. Specifically, I describe and analyze the rise, growth, and segmentation of the children's wear industry in the United States from 1917 to 1962. This industry serves both as a historical entrée into the formative dynamics of the child consumer and as a point of departure into theorizing about the relationship between childhood, consumer culture, and modernity more generally. The study begins in 1917 when companies first began to organize and recognize themselves *as* an industry with the publication of their first trade journal, the *Infants' Department*. By 1962, just about when the Baby Boom ends, the internal age divisions of childhood, especially girlhood, had essentially completed a transformation from only grossly differentiated a few decades before to finely graded, with age distinctions nuanced by clothing choices and retail spaces.

The 1930s stand out as a turning point in the institutional adjudication of the child consumer. Despite depressed economic conditions (or perhaps because of them), merchants, manufacturers, and advertisers began to target children directly as individual consumers as a matter of business strategy. Before this time, the merchandising, marketing, and manufacturing of most children's goods, including especially their clothing, had been undertaken with the assumption that mothers in particular, and parents generally, were the primary market. Retailers believed that children's economic influence was limited mainly to the candy counter and the toy department.²

The change in this regard encompasses something beyond the capitalist drive to expand markets and to extend "consumer citizenship" to all, and something beyond merely changing the target for marketing from the mother to the child. What took place on the floors of clothing departments during this time was a change in perspective—from seeing the world as a mother would to the beginnings of seeing the world through children's eyes. What I term "pediocularity" today goes almost unnoticed as the child—better, the child's view—is routinely represented in and adjudicated by the commercial sphere, as well as in legal contexts and in everyday life. The argument put forward here is that this cultural change took strong root early in the children's clothing industry and informed other consumer goods and contexts.

The change in perspective encodes and enacts the beginnings of a large-scale transformation in the cultural construction of "the child" and "childhood." This transformation can be understood as a partial (that is, non-exhaustive) and progressive process of extending to children the status of more or less full persons, a status most concretely realized when children gain recognition and adjudication as legitimate, individualized, self-contained consumers. Consumer recognition and adjudication for children, as we will see, has taken many forms over the twentieth century: treating children as "real customers" on the retail floor, designing clothing and other goods with children's "needs" and "desires" in mind (rather than or in addition to those of the mother), structuring retail spaces and fixtures to "child scale," making use of popular culture characters and icons in decorating age-graded, gendered retail spaces, and asking children directly about their preferences for goods.

AGENTS AND STRUCTURES, EMPOWERMENT,
AND EXPLOITATION

In the 1990s the social study of childhood underwent an upheaval, what some might rightly call a paradigmatic shift. Led by European scholars, the shift entailed questioning both the place of childhood in social relations and the kind of social beings that children have been assumed to be.

The first of these positions took issue with the widely held views of both developmental psychology (that childhood is a transient stage having no importance except as a bridge to adulthood) and standard sociology (which approached childhood as essentially a derivative category of "family studies"). Childhood historically has been rendered "structurally invisible," observes the Danish sociologist Jens Qvortrup, often ignored in national statistics and sidestepped in national policy. Every individual loses child status, Qvortrup argues, but childhood is retained collectively as a structural element regardless of how many individuals enter or leave it at any one time. Childhood must be seen as an identifiable, somewhat bounded social location which exists as part of the social fabric, and children not as somehow "outside" of society to be brought in through "socialization." To attend to childhood as a social fact, and not merely as a conceptual artifact, requires a recognition of children as historically subjugated beings, in some ways like women, and a recognition of childhood as social phenomenon akin to a minority category.[3]

Accompanying the structural invisibility of childhood has been a systemic indifference to children's voices and perspective. The new childhood studies encompass an epistemological break from previous, dominant conceptions of children as passive recipients of adult culture. Championed by the British researchers Allison James, Chris Jenks, and Alan Prout, the emergent view engages children as social beings in their own right who are active in their construction of the world, including for instance the creation of space and the use of media. No longer in need of completion by the seemingly inevitable processes of "development" and "socialization," the agentive child stands on its own as a competent social actor at any given moment, transforming into new instances of completeness at various points along the life journey. Understood in this way, children are best approached ethnographically as co-participants in the research process, rather than being subjected to it.[4]

Those challenging the structural invisibility of children and their accompanying voicelessness offer welcome and long overdue correctives to generations of social and psychological scholarship which had ignored or otherwise minimized the place of children in social relations. The place of children and childhood in commercial relations in general, however, continues to be overlooked relative to the immensity of the children's market and the efforts of corporations to capture their share of it. In the 1990s other scholars not directly attuned to the new paradigm began to address children's consumer culture as a phenomenon worthy of inquiry. In general, the work on children and contemporary consumption falls in one of two familiar frames of thought. There are those who tend to take a structural approach, seeing business, advertising, and other adult institutions as "taking over" or "invading" childhood, essentially exploiting children through promotions, advertising, and media. On the other hand, some academic writers emphasize children's agency and active participation in consumer culture, characterizing their relationship to it often in terms of "empowerment." Ellen Seiter puts this view well: "We know that children make meanings out of toys that are unanticipated by—perhaps indecipherable to—their adult designers . . . Children are creative in their appropriation of consumer goods and media."[5]

It is evident that children are active in making meaning out of the world, including the world of goods. It is also clear that "adult" industries, structures, and economic arrangements temporally and structurally precede and encompass any one child or any particular historical manifestation of childhood. Each view emphasizes— some overemphasize—a position along a continuum, oftentimes to the point of enforcing a dichotomy: the child often is either exploited or empowered by the market. News media tend to emphasize the former, marketers the latter, with parents often stuck somewhere in between.

The chapters that follow reject this dichotomy from the outset, and in its stead offer a view of the child consumer as always, already embedded in market relations, both historically over the twentieth century and ontogenically, before birth. In this book, I tell a story, a history, of the social production of the child consumer. This is a discursive figure that animates children's culture with its insatiable desire for things, its knowledge about products, its tastes, its conspicuous display, and its seemingly unquestioned identification of self with commodities. It is referred to as "it," rather than as a she or he, to emphasize that the child consumer I investigate is not a sentient being with a unique biography but a discursive construct with a history. The defining features of the child consumer examined in this work have been molded and re-molded over the twentieth century on the pages of dry goods and advertising trade journals, in women's and mothers' magazines, in marketers' focus groups and eventually on television commercials. Never singular or universal, the child consumer construct I strive to make visible nevertheless has gained something of a set of identifiable characteristics, boundaries, and social and commercial locations.

This book also interrogates the flip side of the child consumer, what I call the commodification of childhood, which arguably describes a more fundamental historical process. Essentially, the commodification of childhood refers to the ways in which this phase or stage of the life cycle has taken on economic exchange values. The term focuses attention on how the imputed "nature," boundaries, and exigencies of childhood have become market segments in and of children's culture—for example, in the particular styles and goods produced and consumed around the persona of "the toddler" (see chapter 4). As I argue and demonstrate, commodification is not merely some process imposed upon independent, individualized children which has turned them into consumers, nor is it something which soils pristine, autonomous childhood, but instead forms the basis of latter-day children's culture. In the process, I challenge both the idea of purely oppressive markets which invade childhood (or adulthood, for that matter) and the notion of "the child"—and thus consumers and people generally—as essentially independent, free, self-creating beings. By concentrating on the dynamic interplay between constructions of childhood, expressions of children's desire as reported by merchants and others, and the interests and problems of those creating an industry through time, I hope to make evident the ways in which "children's" consumer culture has come to be central to the ongoing reproduction and transformation of consumer culture generally.

In taking aim at what may be called the "invasion" theory of commodification—that commodities have invaded previously untouched social realms—this work also adds to the chorus of those who deny the pragmatic separability of culture on the one hand and markets on the other.[6] Without belaboring a point argued in great and eloquent detail by others, I take it as a point of departure that markets arise within and are (in)formed by specific, historically embedded social relations which impart meaning to commercial activity. This view rejects the contention made in neoclassical economic thought that markets exist as free, independent entities which sort value with a blind eye and an invisible hand, without regard to persons, meanings, or context.

Markets and market mechanisms indeed sort and create value, but not indifferently. Rather, the cultural view of markets which I espouse underscores the moral basis of value and valuation. In this view, economic exchange invariably and inevitably encodes precepts of good and bad, of right and wrong, thereby sanctioning certain kinds of activities over others. As Igor Kopytoff puts it succinctly,[7] all goods reside in a "moral economy." The sorting and creating of value is itself thus a morally infused undertaking. Economic value never stands alone unaccompanied by socially imparted meaning. To contend that markets and culture interweave, however, is not to ignore their mutual tensions.

When attention turns to economic action undertaken with regard to or in the name of children or childhood, another dimension of morality (and thus of meaning and value) comes into play. Children and childhood, as generally understood in the cultures historically referred to as "Western," stand as distinct cultural and semantic domains which privilege the moral aspects of economic value over the monetary, calculable components. Childhood disrupts the simple, economic calculation of costs and benefits, of profits and losses, because it continues to represent, in different ways, a negation of or a challenge to the valuation of persons exclusively in monetary terms—the extraordinary rise of the children's market notwithstanding. In various ways discussed immediately below and throughout this book, childhood stands apart from the market even as children are born, live, and grow in tandem with commercial culture.

ON THE SACRED AND PROFANE

The dichotomous construction of the exploited child and the empowered child arises from a lingering tension between markets and moral sentiment; it is a tension which, at least since the beginning of industrialization, continues to inform considerations of childhood. Here, two opposing forms of value come into contact and conflict. There is, on the one hand, the kind of value embodied in the singular, sentimental "nature" of children and, on the other, that which is enforced by the equalizing, rational aspects of market calculation. Their intermingling is the actual historical process producing a moral tension in the social valuation of children. Viviana Zelizer identifies the historical foundations of this tension in her study of the rise of the sacred, "priceless" child in the early 1900s.[8]

Examining debates about child labor and children's life insurance, among other things, Zelizer describes a fundamental change in the economic and sentimental value of children taking place between the 1870s and 1930s in the United States. Over this time, a child's value became measured less and less in economic and monetary terms and was increasingly constituted in sentimental and emotional ones. As first middle-class and then working-class children left the workplace, clergy, reformers, and politicians rose to the defense of—and thereby helped create—the economically and productively "useless" child, whose worth was construed to be a function of moral, not instrumental considerations. The result, according to Zelizer, is that apart from bootblacks, newspaper sellers, child actors, and a few other exceptions, children essentially were expelled from the "cash nexus" of American society. They had become *extra-commercium*.[9]

The change here can be understood as a change in the locus of value. Commerce, the money economy, and economic exchange tend to generalize value, affixing it to that which is external to the child, making children, in a sense, derivative of that value. In the case of children's labor, the location of value resides in such things as the pool of laborers, the going wage, the kind of work and skills required, and so on. Any particular child, like any laborer, is quite incidental to the larger process of valuation. The emergent view of children and childhood that Zelizer documents so well sought to take the consideration of a child's worth out of the impersonal realm of exchange and place it in the inaccessible, internal realm of the "soul" of the child and the "nature" of childhood. Children— their activities, their life-worlds—in the process became excessively individualized or *singularized*, to use Igor Kopytoff's term, and thereby essentially decommodified. Children were to be valued for who they are and not for what they could do, for their emotional rather than their instrumental worth. These sentiments were closely tied to a belief in children's innocence, which I will discuss in more detail in chapter 2.[10]

Children, as we know, have not been expelled from the "cash nexus" of society. Limiting children's access to most forms of paid labor signaled not the end of their economic participation, but a fundamental change in it. As working-class children were gradually liberated from direct production over the first third of the twentieth century, middle-class childhood increasingly became a site for morally mediated consumption. During this time, a number of industries arose which produced goods specifically designed, manufactured, and merchandised for children: clothing, toys, furniture, and nursery ware.[11] Toy departments, children's playrooms, age-differentiated clothing departments, entire "floors for youth" in department stores, special sections of books about and for children—essentially nonexistent in 1900—were by the 1930s standard components of retail trade in department and chain stores. Since that time, the market for children's goods has burgeoned into multiple, intertwined industries making a child-world of spaces, services, products, and iconography into standard commercial practice today.

This book aims at investigating how the tension between "the child" and "the market" can at one and the same time be present and absent in such a way that sacred versions of childhood continue to commingle with instrumental, monetary valuation and how childhood is in many ways rendered into pecuniary expressions of value. By definition, it would seem, the sacred and profane determine each other through mutual exclusion. Émile Durkheim states the matter unequivocally: "there exists no other example of two categories of things so profoundly differentiated or so radically opposed to one another . . . the sacred and the profane have always and everywhere been conceived by the human mind as two distinct classes, as two worlds between which there is nothing in common." Despite the logical exclusivity of these domains, passage or communication between them is unavoidable in practice, making contamination of one by the other an ongoing concern. Since the "sacred thing is *par excellence* that which the profane should not touch, and cannot touch with impunity," ritual interdictions are required to render contact between the two domains rare and safe.[12] In this way, expelling children from most kinds of productive labor (not finalized legally until the late 1930s) can be interpreted as an attempt to exercise moral interdiction, that is, to minimize contact between the profane, means-ends logic of market calculation and the sacred child thought to be beyond all imposed value.[13]

Ideas of order, place, and separation form the crux of Mary Douglas's formulations about the interplay between purity and pollution. Her oft-cited dictum that "dirt is essentially disorder" addresses not hygiene *per se* but rather the attempt to maintain classificatory schemes: "Dirt offends against order. Eliminating it is not a negative movement, but a positive effort to organize the environment . . . In chasing dirt . . . we are not governed by anxiety to escape disease, but are positively re-ordering our environment, making it conform to an idea." It has proven untenable to chase the dirt of money out of the space of childhood. It has also proven equally untenable to disregard the sentimental aura of childhood and to think about and treat children as full persons or adults, although outcries that childhood has been or is being lost to the ravages of technology and self-centered parents have been commonplace since the 1980s.[14]

By "children's consumer culture," I refer to historically situated, socially embedded webs of meaning which shape definitions of both "the child" and "childhood" so as to render them more or less confluent with the world of economic consumption. Children's consumer culture has taken shape in a morally contested space, at some times more actively and explicitly contested than at others, which is located at the intersection of children and markets. It is a space where children and commerce exist, not in utter harmony but *in relation* to each other. This is a historical accommodation which has taken institutionalized forms, like those in the children's clothing industry, and which have worked to integrate children with monetary valuation through moral and sentimental means, not despite them. The consumer world of childhood—the stores, the icons and iconography, the goods and promotions—at any given time represents a temporary compromise, a historical resolution, of the tensions surrounding the sentimental and monetary valuation of children and their world. In this process, ideas of "dirt," of pollution, continue to undergo reordering as the relation-

10 *The Commodification of Childhood*

ship between childhood and commerce transforms. I take the interplay between sentiment and exchange as the engine driving the emergence and growth of children's commercial industries and culture, rather than as a foil to them.

I identify two basic ways that children and commerce commingle without much moral approbation, logical contradiction, or social upheaval. One way is to define or redefine commodities as *marketing it* beneficial and functional for children. "Beneficial" goods can fall *be -* under various rubrics, including those which are "fun" or "educa- *'educational* tional," which promote "personal expression" or aid in "development." "Child development," first popularized in the '20s and '30s with the aid of popular, national media such as *Parents* magazine, has served as the quintessential mode for the adjudication of what may be legitimized as beneficial to children. Developmentalism posits predictable movement though specifiable and sequential stages of the early life course. Its rise to prominence as a "scientific" view of childhood in the '20s and '30s has had the effect of essentially relegating mothers into what Lloyd deMause calls a "helping mode" of childrearing through the negation of maternal authority, tradition, and localism. What was "useful" or "good" for the child, mothers were told repeatedly by experts, were those things which assisted (or at least did not impede) a process of growth sanctioned by the timeless authority of "nature."[15]

Mothers thus became positioned as a middle term between child and market, softening the blow of commerce on the social and moral value of their children. As presented in chapter 3, mothers become the moral core of the early children's wear industry in the way that ideologies of self-sacrificing motherhood put them in a position to consume on behalf of their children for reasons beyond simple need or want. In this way, sentimental value, which congeals in the non-laboring version of childhood, serves more like a portal between children and merchants and less as a "bulwark against the market," as Zelizer describes it.[16]

The second general way that child and market achieve moral rapprochement is when children can be defined or redefined as full persons who are, in a relatively unproblematic way, desirous of goods. The simplified thesis of this book is that markets shape persons in and through the consumer culture of childhood. Markets make persons in their capacity as power structures to "hail" or call into being particular subjects and subjectivities, in a manner akin to Louis Althusser's understanding. The ideological process that I describe, however, consists of commercially focused institutions addressing and indeed encouraging active, agentive beings rather than state apparatuses creating subjects helplessly subjected to them.[17]

Unmistakably bourgeois in origin, this model of an agent who freely chooses, or should be allowed to freely choose, undergirds the historical construction of a children's consumer culture. Once children become treated more or less as autonomous, volitional persons, they lose part of the cloak of sacredness and are enfranchised as near equal participants in and through the marketplace. Whereas the laboring child came to embody the incompatibility of opposing values and thus eventually was removed from most wage-paying productive relations, the consuming child encodes these tensions and, at times, resolves them. It resolves them because the historical trajectory of the child consumer moves away from emphasizing the child's status as an *object* of economic activity and toward privileging its identity as a *subject* in and of market relations—a subject with desire.

Gary Cross points to how parents' desires and hopes for their children became refracted through and materialized in the emerging toy culture of the early twentieth century. The consuming child that began to materialize in the 1920s and 1930s not only desired the goods paraded enticingly before its eyes, it subsequently came to possess the social wherewithal, even the right, to want. Indeed, children's "right" to consume in many ways precedes and prefigures other, legally constituted rights. Children had been given a "voice" on the retail sales floor, in "design-it and name-it" contests, in clothing choice, and in marketers' research designs decades before their rights were asserted in such contexts as the UN Convention on the Rights of the Child in 1989. Children's participation in the world of goods as actors, as persons with desire, underpins their current, emergent status as rights-bearing individuals.[18]

Legitimating children's desire is an ongoing historical and ideological process which has the effect of unifying the disparate values of market and sentiment. To the extent that desire can be framed as originating from within the child, it can thereby be construed as natural and thus reflective of an inner person that is unique, and indeed sacred. If children can be offered "what they want," if they can enter social relations as already wanting, then a moral barrier has been erased or, at least, bypassed. How this wanting, desiring child has come to occupy such a central cultural space can only be understood historically.

Children's consumer culture then arises from, and transforms through, the working out of fundamental tensions embodied in the consuming child: sentimental versus exchange value, child versus market, person versus commodity, sacred versus profane—these represent *generative* tensions of this generative cultural site. Neither side "wins" completely. Each informs the other in reciprocal and progressive interaction.

THE PRODUCTIVE AMBIGUITY OF
CHILDREN'S AGENCY

The moral tensions embodied in the consuming child never completely resolve because they revolve around the endemic problem of "agency" which, along with children's innocence, composes the definitive problematic of modern childhood. Agency here carries the dual meaning of acting in the name of another (serving as an agent for) and exercising a certain measure of volition (being an agent of). The latter is emphasized by those contributing to the new childhood studies paradigm, whereas the former sense of agency often appears as a kind of oppression of children by adults who either do not recognize the extent of their power, or refuse to relinquish it without a fight.[19] The interplay between these two forms of agency is often understood as a zero-sum game whereby a gain on one end is compensated by a relatively equal loss on the other. The "game" is played out on the ontological plane in the process of development, where personal autonomy is thought to be acquired in a stepwise movement away from dependency. As a child gradually gains independence, those acting in its name—mothers, advocate groups, the state—are expected to step aside to favor the flowering of the self-sustaining, self-authoring person.

The trajectory of childhood, generally understood as this movement from dependence to independence, makes the extent of a child's personal autonomy indeterminate at any given point. It is never clear what the term "child" on its face signifies; at minimum, an age or age range needs to be specified. With few formal or quasi-formal rites of passage in American culture, age designations have become proxies for status distinctions in different ways during the last century, particularly for the ages of "youth." Age grading and age scheduling in historical perspective are analyzed in some detail in chapter 5. Suffice it to say here that social distinctions based on age are historically emergent and have never been able to completely equate age with status, primarily because age must be understood in relation to a host of historically embedded factors including, gender, social class, race and ethnicity, and geographic region, among others.[20]

The indeterminate relation between age and social status—particularly regarding the exercise of personal autonomy—renders the identity of "the child" ripe for multiple articulations. The child marks out a semantic space where the question of the locus of power and volition, of who has the right and wherewithal to make decisions, is continually negotiated and renegotiated. The timing and extent to which parents and others grant or deny children participation in various kinds of decisions speak to cultural assumptions about the nature of the person and the dynamics of power. Someone, usually a parent and often the mother, must routinely make decisions not only about the extent to which a child *will* participate in decisions affecting its life and well-being, but also *whether* the child has the ability to do so. As Gill Valentine and colleagues point out, however, children often ignore such parental directives, creating their own transgressive spaces and meanings.[21]

Every decision to act or not act in the name of a child—whether made by a person, like a parent, or an institution, like a school—is a political act in that it fixes on the child an identity which calls forth and favors certain kinds of responses. When, for instance, a parent discourages a child from viewing a particular type of television program because it promotes values contrary to those that the family wishes to encourage, that parent (perhaps unwittingly) invokes a construct of a child who is able to be influenced by such media but who cannot make that determination on its own. In the same vein, if a parent gives a child an allowance to be spent at will, then that parent is applying a model of the person as one who can and should make purchase decisions on its own.

Any child can be located somewhere in the play between these two kinds of agency. This imprecision makes for a particular kind of childhood politics in that children's "voices" (at least those which can be "heard" in and by larger power structures) are always already mediated through adults and organizations. For instance, Jacqueline Rose points out how "children's fiction" is a misnomer, and ultimately an impossibility, because the "child" is nonexistent in and for the text. In the case of Peter Pan, as she argues, an adult not only created the characters but also created "the child"—as both symbol and referent—as the purported addressee for the story. The child, in this sense, is nonexistent and thus so is its fiction. In a similar vein, as Lynn Spigel notes, children can view programming and websites originally intended for adults, and vice versa, without much encumbrance. Producers, programmers, and media buyers recognize that mothers and regulators are important potential audience members in addition to children and thus create their "children's" product accordingly.[22]

Those who claim to speak for children or a child can usually be refuted only by other nonchildren (adults) who compete to make similar claims. The uncertainty of children's agency renders defensible all sorts of claims and counterclaims about who children "are" and what children "want," allowing most anyone to frame the child in any number of ways—for example as a competent social actor, as deserving of rights, as needing protection and guidance, and so on.

In their passing state of dependency, young children in particular offer no initial or enforceable resistance to definition by others. Individual children, as well as the category of childhood itself, thereby serve as ready vehicles for the expression of any number of identities, values, and histories. A child can and does represent a range of meaning on a variety of levels. He or she can stand for political citizenship as well as for racial hope and ethnic continuity. A coming child can mean the imminence of a welfare check or the promise of a tax break; it can provide for family lineage and species expansion, for parental immortality and financial inheritance; it can be a blessing or a curse. "The child," at this level of discourse, is thus a conduit for meaning, a medium for significance—in short, a symbol.[23]

The relative powerlessness of children enables images and depictions of children—and, by extension, their identities—to be quite malleable. Parents and other adults dress their children when they are young, care for their appearance, and fight with them over their modes of self-presentation for many years afterward. The sailor suit, sports team uniforms, tie-dyed clothing outfitted by Grateful Deadhead parents, his-and-her Harley Davidson leather togs for tots, and infant T-shirts displaying sayings like "shit happens" are instances of imputing identity to young children who are taken as blank slates. It seems as if children can don almost any garb, portray almost any persona, play with most any identity. In the United States there is a century-long tradition of depicting children in advertisements as vehicles for the personification of commodities.[24]

An investment in the sacredness of anything related to children limits the seemingly endless ways in which children can stand for other things. In particular, how children are visually portrayed tends to provoke public response more quickly and intensely than simple verbal description. Overtly and illicitly depicting children as sexual beings, as victims or perpetrators of violence, and as dead or dying marks out some of the more morally charged boundaries informing the contemporary portrayal of children. That these boundaries are transgressed as in child pornography, or approached as in the advertisements of Benetton and Calvin Klein, serves to reinforce the distinction between proper and improper childhoods. In 1995 for instance, Calvin Klein's company was investigated by the FBI for depictions of "children" in its advertisements which were provocative enough to be thought of as "pornographic" had the models been under the age of eighteen. They were not. Equating an infant with innocence to be kept safe, on the other hand, as in the television commercials of the 1990s for Michelin Tires, seems to disturb no one.[25]

The ability to define children's sacredness arises from the same power dynamic that potentiates their rampant symbolization. Children remain something of sacred beings largely because they are dependent beings, for the most part powerless. They stand at the heart of much contemporary social controversy and moral panic precisely because their social identities are malleable, negotiable, contestable things—in a word, not under their control (or anyone's singular control). Children may never be able to successfully counter "stereotypes" about childhood and to expound their "rights" as women and sexual or ethnic minorities do because such action ultimately requires adult intervention (in everyday life, in media portrayals, in schools). Children did not pass the United Nations statement on the rights of the child in 1989, nor did they draft antigun legislation proposed to protect them, nor did they write and copyright the jingle about being a "Toys 'R' Us Kid" (although children sing it in the commercial).

Understood in this way, the realm of children and childhood unavoidably invokes a politics of identity and a semantics of morality. Issues of power, perhaps more transparently bound up with issues of morality when children are in question, are inseparable from grasping, utilizing, and deploying or researching "the child."[26] In the play between the two kinds of agency, an ambiguity arises around the identity and status of "the child" which, I argue and demonstrate, has been productive in the historical, commercially motivated constructions of the child consumer and its sartorial fashioning.

COMMERCIAL PERSONAE AND THE TRADE
PERSPECTIVE ON CHILDREN'S CLOTHING

Some final introductory remarks are necessary. I initially encountered the child consumer not on the streets or in schoolyards or in the malls, but in archives on the musty pages of old trade journals. It would, of course, be impossible to meet this child personally as it is a figment of the commercial imagination, yet it is real in its consequences, to recall W. I. Thomas's insight. No less real than a living, breathing biographical child, the discursively configured child occupies a different register of reality—it is what the anthropologist Ray L. Birdwhistell used to call a "menti-fact," as opposed to an artifact.

Scouring the pages of these journals[27] for what was originally intended as a study of the history of children's clothing fashion, I was continually confronted with statements by retailers, manufacturers, and editors about what "the child" wanted and what were "mother's" concerns, statements which were not uniform from journal to journal or from one time period to another. With no mention of research to support these early claims, it became apparent that these writers, both men and women, were performing as "cultural brokers": persons who occupy strategic, gatekeeping positions in organizations and industries and who thereby adjudicate cultural products and cultural meanings.[28] And they were doing just that—brokering cultural models of mothers and children from the interested perspective of merchants. I came to regard their statements and constructions as a certain order of "data," as entry points into the public perspectives of those who sought to create and maintain a mass market for children's clothing, and other goods.

To engage trade discourse as data brings opportunity, and demands circumspection. A bald, forthright approach to markets characterizes most trade talk, in which exchange value stands in the forefront of consideration in ways seldom found in consumer-directed publications. For instance, the children's wear industry's category of "grandma bait" refers to expensive, frilly dresses for young girls which most mothers would never purchase but which tends to open the pocketbook of "doting" grandmothers. The term is not intended for public consumption because it does not speak to the consumer's frame of mind but arises from that of the merchant—you will find no sign pointing you to the "Grandma Bait" section of the Kmart.

Trade publications represent what Erving Goffman called the back stage of social encounters—a space away from the scrutinizing gaze of the general public where the work of erecting a façade gets accomplished. Surely, no "true" trade secrets are revealed in these pages, as the readership consists of competitors. Nor is the truth value of trade members' statements any stronger or weaker in the trade world than in any other form of discourse. Rather, it is most fruitful to approach trade material as providing an entrée into a historically situated semantic domain and thus as evidence of a perspective or perspectives.[29]

My readings of these materials are made with the assumption that the meaning of a garment, image, or good is constitutive of the actions performed on it by various actors, individual and corporate—in much the same way as a piece of art is construed in Howard Becker's sense of "art worlds."[30] In the present case, these actors execute agendas in reference to localized, commercial contexts where selling garments and accessories as well as selling journal issues and maintaining a readership were arguably more immediate and tangible to the trade writers and advertisers than deploying images and meanings of childhood. Examining the agendas of the producers and sellers of children's wear allows one to problematize their portrayals of children and childhood and to see them as a form of commercially motivated depiction rather than as arising spontaneously from some collective ethos.

The "commodities," in this case, consist not only of physical materials but also of discursive materials forged by the producers, retailers, and press in and through time. These discursive materials create the context in which an item can become a commodity. Commodity production, at least in the modern, industrial period, is never exhausted with the making and selling of its good. Rather, commodity production always implicates the existence of social statuses, identities, and images, indeed their creation; in short, the creation of symbolic persons, or personae.

In this work, it is those personages arising in and from the children's wear trade press, what I call "commercial personae," which are at issue. Commercial personae are assemblages of characteristics—known or conjectured, "real" or imagined—constructed by and traded among interested parties in the service of their industry. They are the negotiable currency of a merchant class ideology which seeks to comprehend its subject, "the consumer" in the abstract, with the goal of opening new markets or of maintaining and expanding old ones. To put it another way, to "give the customer what she or he wants" implies that the merchant somewhere and somehow proffers a model of that customer. Here, the customer becomes an admixture of specified quantities and intensities of priorities, concerns, abilities, wants, needs, and motivations. A commercial persona consists of both statements and images which together give shape to these imputed characteristics.[31]

Commercial personae do not solely reside on the pages of trade publications. They occupy most every corner of popular-media culture, in commercials, advertisements, music videos, sit-coms and the popular press. Likewise, I did not confine my examination of the child consumer to trade publications but branched out into consumer magazines (mainly those for mothers and parents) and into academic journals as the child came to be an object of the market research gaze.[32] Virtually all depictions of people in the media represent an amalgam of derived characteristics—a particular configuration of age, race, gender, style, and sexuality produced to appeal to an audience. I approached the use of trade (and other) materials as a point of departure and not an endpoint of investigation, as images and meanings of children, childhood, and consumption proliferate and circulate through commercial media space over time and in various ways. This book strives to trace a single thread of these multiple trajectories.

Children's clothing however offers a particularly appropriate point of departure to interrogate the historical construction of the child consumer, the commodification of childhood, and the moral dimensions of consumption. Excellent, informative histories of the toy industry have been written in recent years, notably *Out of the Garden* by Stephen Kline, *Sold Separately* by Ellen Seiter, and *Kids' Stuff* by Gary Cross, which I draw upon heavily throughout.[33] Clothing differs from toys and other artifacts associated with children's culture along several important dimensions. In their materiality—their dimension, shape, iconography, and overall design— toys address themselves to children *as* children. They are meant to be played with *as* toys and, except in a few cases, there is little room for mistaking a children's toy for something else. In one sense— and just in this one, narrow sense—a toy, a game, or a book for that matter can stand on its own, alone without a child present, and still be recognizable for what it is or at least what it appears to be. A baseball bat, a Barbie doll, a board game, an action figure—though thoroughly infused with multiple layers of meaning which require nuanced, grounded interpretation—can momentarily appear to be somewhat self-evident. The child picks up the toy, sets up the game, or opens the book as something separate from or outside of herself.

Clothing differs from these and other objects in the way that the body becomes implicated in the life of a thing. Dress adorns the body and the body inhabits articles of dress, making the clothing being worn and the social identity of the person wearing it difficult to distinguish. "Clothing," Elizabeth Wilson wisely points out, "marks an unclear boundary ambiguously." It is at these unclear boundaries where the threat of pollution is greatest. She continues: "If the body with its open orifices is itself dangerously ambiguous, then dress, which is an extension of the body yet not quite part of it, not only links that body to the social world, but also more clearly separates the two. Dress is the frontier between the self and the not-self."[34]

Clothing speaks daily and publicly to the presentation of self. Clothing and personal display are visible in a more or less continuous manner, whereas toys, books, and other items are intermittent, less conspicuous markers of consumption, taste, and social status. When displayed on a body, clothing offers a dynamic, combined message—a dual articulation—which encompasses garment-plus-body and which thereby congeals both object and subject in a singular form. Because it is tied intimately to the body and the social self, clothing involves moral concerns in a different register from toys, books, and games. Children may be "exposed" to sexuality in electronic media for instance, but they are (or can be) sexual in certain clothing.[35]

If the twentieth century deserves the label of the "century of the child," as it was christened by Ellen Key in 1909, then it must also be seen as the century of the child consumer.[36] Any consistency granted to "the child" over the 1900s and beyond must incorporate the ways in which childhood has become understood in, and structured by, a market idiom. Child consumers grow up to be something more than adult consumers. They become mothers and cashiers, truck drivers and paralegals, professors and politicians. In short, they become us who, in turn, make more of them. Out of the particular pursuit of the child consumer, described below and undertaken according to the terms outlined above, emerges an understanding and a claim that serves to position children and childhood not on the sidelines of culture, but as indispensable to the rise, reproduction, and transformation of what has come to be known as consumer culture—a culture increasingly inseparable from "culture" in the generic sense.

2

A Brief History of Childhood

and Motherhood into the

Twentieth Century

As a social production, the child consumer is also necessarily a historical one. A number of historical trajectories converge in the early twentieth century to make the emergence of a nascent commercial world of childhood possible and viable. One trajectory speaks to the social identity of "the child" as an entity, as a being distinguishable from adults. Primary among this child's distinguishing characteristics are its naturalness, its innocence, and the naturalness of its innocence. Another historical strand configures the social location of the child within the sentimentalized, domestic sphere of the eighteenth and nineteenth centuries, directly implicating motherhood and its attendant morality in the formation of a children's culture. Middle-class mothers transformed their imputed status as moral caretakers into political action in the Progressive Era (roughly 1890–1920), mounting a number of campaigns and creating a number of institutions which sought to improve the health and well-being of mothers and children. A final historical thread to weave into this chapter addresses the rise of women as consumers, particularly in urban department stores in the early twentieth century—a development concurrent with the political action of women. These together provided some of the main supports for erecting a children's culture: a belief in the distinctiveness of the child, a private middle-class home where this child could be nurtured and kept separate and sacred, and a way to connect the child with the market.

The idea that childhood has a history—or better, histories—itself has a history, successfully launched with the publication of *Centuries of Childhood* by Philippe Ariès in the early 1960s. Ariès effected something of a paradigm shift in scholarly circles with his assertion that childhood is a relatively recent social invention. Before the twelfth century, he writes, "medieval art . . . did not know childhood or did not attempt to portray it." What was portrayed were "little men" or "miniature adults" depicted as small (mostly) males whose morphology mirrored that of grown persons. Beginning in the early seventeenth century, however, Ariès notes that children depicted in European painting began to have their own distinctive morphology (face, bodily posture, and features) as well as being marked by distinctive clothing, thereby making childhood socially visible.[1]

The crucial transformation is the eventual segregation of adults' from children's worlds. Ariès cites supporting evidence to this effect, including how medieval adults had engaged in activities now generally associated with children, like playing games and reading fairy tales among themselves. The emergence of specialized books and literature for children as well as a host of scholastic practices also emphasized the importance of age and age segregation. He concludes by arguing that the modern family has changed its focus toward full devotion to children based on the division between adult and child spheres and responsibilities.[2]

Of the four-hundred-plus pages in this widely cited study, only about one-fourth is spent on the "invention" of childhood theme, a theme which makes use of about half of Ariès's citations. But, it is the "invention" proposition which overshadows all the rest of his work and is often the only argument for which it is cited. Ariès is not without his critics. His historiography has been challenged as "presentism" and as being "present-minded," in that he took present-day practices as the standard against which to evaluate earlier centuries. His somewhat uncritical reliance on painting to reflect the real world has been taken to task especially by Lloyd deMause, who states that Ariès's "notion of the 'invention of child-hood' is so fuzzy that it is surprising that so many historians have recently picked it up." Ross Beales went in search of miniature adulthood in colonial New England but could not find it, leading him to conclude that miniature adulthood "must be seen, not as a description of social reality, but as a minor chapter in the history of social thought."[3]

Ariès is equally fuzzy in his explanations for the great change in childhood. From the thirteenth century through the fifteenth, Ariès notes something of a change in the types of children depicted in painting, toward types which appear to be "closer to the modern concept of childhood." One type is the "adolescent angel" with the "effeminate" features of a soft, round face. This type lasted through the end of the Italian Quattrocento in the angels of Botticelli and others. The second type, Ariès claims, is "the model and ancestor of all the little children in the history of art: the Infant Jesus." As late as the twelfth century, Jesus is depicted like other children—as an adult. Midway through the century, a more senti-mental representation begins to emerge: a miniature shows Jesus "wearing a thin, almost transparent shift and standing with His arms around His mother's neck, nestling against her, cheek to cheek." Here is the beginnings of "sentimental realism," as Ariès calls it, which carried this "theme of Holy Childhood" beyond de-pictions of Christ to that of other Biblical characters' childhoods.[4]

Sentimental realism took several centuries to move beyond the "frontiers of religious iconography," and it was not until the six-teenth century that a more generalized lay iconography of child-hood emerged alongside of and detached from the religious. In the sixteenth century, sentimental realism took the form of the por-trait—the depiction of a real, biographical child "as he was at a certain moment in his life" rather than as a miniature adult. Many of the child portraits were of dead children. Initially serving as funeral effigies, portraits of dead children began to be commis-sioned by families who could afford to memorialize the child in this way for home display. Parental love and emotional attachment had visible expression, at least among the moneyed classes in Eu-rope. For Ariès, the absence of portraits of deceased children indicated an absence of the feeling portrayed. Thus, their historical emergence marked a "watershed" in the history of feelings, because they dramatize the child as worthy of remembrance and its death as no longer one of the inevitable losses of life.[5]

Before the eighteenth century, historians argue, parental attitudes toward children were anything but loving. For Lawrence Stone, parents were simply indifferent toward their offspring until about the age of five or six. He explains that high infant mortality rates in England inhibited parents from becoming emotionally attached to their infant children. Parents maintained a detached stance from their newborns, Stone says, indicated by the practice of giving the same name to two living siblings, expecting that one would die. As improvements in medical science and sanitation allowed more and more children to live, Stone argues, parents were freed to offer them love and devotion.[6]

Other historians tend to locate the change in sentiments toward children in something other than a decrease in infant mortality. Edward Shorter blames unknowing mothers for what he sees as the widespread neglect of children. He explains the decrease in infant mortality as an outcome of a *prior* increase in maternal care, which occurred once "sensible" medical advice became widely available. Lloyd deMause characterizes parent-child relations at this time as involving a great deal of infanticide and abandonment. He sees these relations as independent sources of historical change, not tied to technological or social innovation, but to psycho-historical factors.[7]

Linda Pollock offers the most thorough and grounded critique of Ariès, Stone, Shorter, deMause, and others who have, in one way or another, accepted the general thrust of the thesis that childhood at one point did not exist and that parents were indifferent, perhaps cruel, to their children before about the mid-sixteenth century. Making use of diaries and autobiographies from British and American sources from the 1500s into the 1800s, Pollock finds that children were wanted, that conceptions of childhood did exist in the sixteenth century, and that the majority of children were not subject to brutality. She points to many provisions made for the "special nature" of children in the sixteenth and seventeenth centuries, such as laws regarding children and the beginnings of specialized medicine. What she finds, particularly in the sixteenth through eighteenth centuries, is great variability in the ways that diarists and autobiographers discussed birth, discipline, and affection for children. She warns historians to be circumspect about assuming a direct connection between "attitudes," as found in advice books and official doctrine about children, and "behavior," as found in primary sources.[8]

Pollock, along with Anne Higonnet, incorrectly accuse Ariès of explaining the rise of sentimental childhood in terms of a decrease in child mortality which supposedly allowed parents to emotionally invest in their children. Ariès points out that the practice of memorializing deceased children began well *before* the "demographic transition": the large-scale historical decline in infant mortality in Europe in the eighteenth century. He conjectures that "although demographic conditions did not greatly change between the thirteenth and seventeenth centuries, and although child mortality remained at a very high level, a new sensibility granted these fragile, threatened creatures a characteristic which the world had hitherto failed to recognize in them; as if it were only then that the common conscience had discovered that the child's soul too was immortal." Newly in possession of a soul, the child materializes as at once sacred and secular. It gradually emerges—in the "common conscience" of Western, Christian parts of Europe—as a dually articulated and articulable being, a member of common humanity, not because of market-like factors of "scarcity" (that is, mortality) but rather a cultural process of reconceptualization.[9]

Ariès discusses a new conceptualization in a brief chapter entitled "The Two Concepts of Childhood." One is the "coddling" conception, according to which children became regarded as a source of attention, amusement, and pleasure *within* the family after the sixteenth century. Coddling represents a fondness for children in which affection and attention are given over to children because they are children and not adults. A second conception, a "moral-development" conception, arose as a reaction to this sentimental attitude. Moralists, pedagogues, and churchman, representing institutions outside the family, "were unwilling to regard children as charming toys, for they saw them as fragile creatures of God who needed to be both safeguarded and reformed." Both conceptions recognized the "special nature" of childhood, albeit with different valences.[10]

What Ariès theorized was not necessarily the invention of child-hood per se, but the emergence of the multiple, variable child—a child which thereby enters the messy realm of history. This is a fig-ure whose meanings increasingly became subject to public scrutiny, interpretation, and contestation. The malleability of the child's identity is made possible by the dual inscription of being at once similar to adults by virtue of having a soul and separated from adults by their vulnerability. If, as Ariès claims, by the seventeenth century Christian iconography and practice recognized the child as the bearer of an immortal soul, then the child was thereby seen as sus-ceptible to influence—to being swayed toward good or evil. What made children different in this regard is their exceptional weakness, their susceptibility to "pollution." In a word, their innocence.[11]

Ariès thus uncovered not the invention of childhood but the invention of childhood innocence. Childhood innocence retains a sense of the sacred in secularized conceptions of children by the necessary insistence that it is an original and natural state of af-fairs, only to be corrupted by adult intervention or by virtue of life experience. Just as there is no unringing of a bell, there is no way to reverse innocence lost; it is by necessity a prior and primary state of affairs, like the possession of a soul. For Anne Higgonet, the Romantic Child of seventeenth- and eighteenth-century Europe remains iconic of a particular, ideological version of childhood in which "innocence must be an Edenic state from which adults fall, never to return . . . The image of the Romantic child replaces what we have lost, or what we fear to lose." Childhood innocence, in a way, makes reference to the original innocence of the Garden of Eden and, at the same time, offers a counterpoint to the Original Sin committed there by Eve in Judeo-Christian doctrine and tradi-tion. Gill Valentine, in a similar vein, finds expressions of this dual conception in the contemporary "angel/devil" construction of Eu-ropean and North American children.[12]

In the context of American Puritanism, childish innocence and weakness were an invitation for Satan to do his works. According to Stannard, the inability to read signs of Election (of eventual salvation) made Puritans err on the side of caution, assuming that the Devil was in all things, including children. Stannard quotes Cotton Mather discussing children in 1689:[13] "They are no sooner *wean'd* but they are to be taught . . . They go astray as soon as they are born. They no sooner *step* than they *stray*, they no sooner *lisp* than they *ly*. Satan gets them to be proud, profane, reviling and revengeful as *young* as they are." Children, especially infants, in this view are in a state of depravity and require *conversion*, and an early conversion at that, lest they die before they are saved. Religious conversion implies that human nature is a malleable thing, that children and others possessed the *ability* to change.[14]

Malleability cuts both ways. The innocent child may be weak and easily influenced by Satan or some other form of pollution, but it can also be guided in proper or desirable directions. For instance, Karin Calvert's study of early American material culture illustrates how beliefs about children's physical malleability indicated their spiritual plasticity in the seventeenth and eighteenth centuries. To the "seventeenth century mind," she writes, "human beings were quite literally made, not born." Infants were seen as a danger to both the cosmic and social orders, their crawling placing them in postural proximity to members of the animal kingdom: "Western culture inculcated a very powerful symbolic language of the hierarchy of things, from Hell below to Heaven above, from the crawling of beasts to the marching of kings. Children, if they were to assume their rightful place in the divine order, had to do so on their feet, not on their hands and knees." Practices such as swaddling, and materials such as walking stools and narrow cradles encouraged children to be physically straight—to be what Calvert calls the "upright child"—as quickly as possible, in order to bring the danger of animalness under control.[15]

"Shaping" children is also a central preoccupation in the work of the English philosopher John Locke (1632–1704), who sought to mold character, not bodies. Locke offered the conception of the child, and thus the person, as a *tabula rasa*, influenced not by predispositions or values but by experience. As James, Jenks, and Prout point out, however, the blank slate conception is tempered by what they call Locke's anachronistic liberalism: "children are charged with a potential, as citizens of the future and as imperfect but latent reasoners. Thus, although in Locke's view there are no innate capacities, no knowledge lodged in a universal human condition, the drives and dispositions that children possess are on a gradient of becoming, moving towards reason."[16]

The extent to which Locke influenced parental care is difficult to determine. Pollock found scant evidence among some British parents of trying to actively mold the child's character and virtually none among Americans.[17] However, for the historian J. H. Plumb, Locke's influence on the development of a "new world of children" in eighteenth-century England is enormous. During this time, parents of the newly emerging middle classes began sending their children to the increasingly numerous private academies, finding in Locke's views an alternative to Calvinist doctrines of "negative" innate dispositions, including infant depravity.[18]

This view of the child, coupled with the sort of education it implied, opened up a market in which middle- and upper-class families tried to effect social mobility by investing in the child's "future": "Few desires will empty a pocket quicker than social aspiration—and the main route was, then as now, through education, which combined social adornment with the opportunity of a more financially rewarding career for children."[19] The curricula of the new schools addressed the industrial needs of an emerging bourgeoisie. According to Plumb, this was an education of secular morals, whereby the goal was to instill Protestant virtues of sobriety, thrift, and industry, as well as serving as an education for trade, career, and social aspiration.

The Lockean view understood the child in essentially value-neutral terms; one can inscribe most anything on the blank slate and it will eventually be reinscribed in the language of reason. For Jean-Jacques Rousseau, people (including children) were born free, made initially good by God, but became corrupted by others through the course of living in society. In *Émile*, Rousseau presented a portrait of the education of a boy which valorized innocence and celebrated the "wisdom" in self-directed, natural growth and the value of play. In many ways, *Émile* was *the* child of the Enlightenment, personifying secular naturalism and paving the way for what Anne Higonnet calls the Romantic Child: "an older concept of a child born in Original sin, correctible through rigid discipline, hard work, and corporal punishment, gave way to a concept of the child born innocent of adult faults, social evils and sexuality."[20]

The influence of Rousseau's thought—as it diffused through the middle classes in nineteenth-century America—authorized a view of a child's "nature" as completely innocent and lacking of evil.

Rousseau in this way represents Ariès's "coddling" conception, located in the home, while Locke represents the more public "moral development" view. In Locke's view, the virtuosity of the child could, through education, triumph over evil; the evil, however, was still there, initially or potentially present. With Rousseau, the evil was gone and the child stood as an object of innocence and sentiment.

Mary Lynn Stevens Heininger traces some aspects of this transformation of childhood in nineteenth-century America. She argues that post-Enlightenment liberal thinkers began to prize children for who they were and not for who they would become, relying on Rousseau's assertion that children were the only true, noncorrupt example of "man's innate virtue." Heininger cites evidence of iconographic and literary associations of children with animals and flowers—that is, beings close to nature—in the mid- to late nineteenth century. As naturalness and innocence collapsed into a more or less singular description of middle-class childhood, it became incumbent on parents to "discover" the special needs embedded in the nature of childhood.

This view of children's nature laid the groundwork for a children's material, commercial culture. The large-scale manufacture of toys and games commenced during the mid- to late nineteenth century, as amusement for amusement's sake gained middle-class approval. By the last third of the nineteenth century, a children's literature industry had gained a firm foundation in the lives and education of children.[21] The stories, the characters, and the level of literacy to which these books were directed reinforced as well as created a children's culture beyond that of the local playground. This culture was and is based on the conviction that the young differ from the old in their perceptions and needs and are thus in need of "specialized" attention and goods. Heininger notes: "Young children in the mid- to late-nineteenth century were likely to awaken in a nursery with special furnishings, take meals in a highchair and from a set of dishes that differed from adults."[22]

For Heininger, the increasing disparity between the world of adults and the world of children during the nineteenth century was encountered most clearly in the changes of labor and training for work. The jobs and skills of fathers became opaque to children as they daily left the house to perform their duties. Unlike farming or trade, many of the skills that men used on their jobs, like mathematical and mechanical operations, were not easily divisible into manageable parts which could be taught to their sons. Women, who were left at home with increasing household and social duties owing to the absence of men, could much more easily divide tasks like sweeping or laundry for children, both sons and daughters, to master.[23]

Childhood had again split from the adult world. However, it was not children alone, in their own sphere over against an adult sphere. Heininger describes a double separation of children's and adult worlds: first children, initially middle-class urban children, are taken out of productive work and second, they are thereby relegated to the feminized, sentimental, "unproductive" sphere of the home. Nonproductive middle-class childhood had become "feminized" as the "feminine" virtues of gentleness and compassion increasingly differentiated women and children from the "masculine" ones of aggressiveness and competitiveness. It is here that we can see how Ariès's conception of "coddling" arose from the home: the Rousseauian view, in practice, ultimately framed childhood as "nature" in a period when industry and commerce were making incursions on the control of nature.

A WOMAN'S PLACE AND WOMEN'S POWER
IN THE NINETEENTH CENTURY

Women, however, confined neither themselves nor their children to the home or to passivity and, in the process of breaking out of the domestic realm, brought children with them into the world of commerce and consumption permanently. Under preindustrial conditions, most work was "house work" (or farm work); it was accomplished by a division of labor based on gender and age which interlaced various tasks into an interdependent, usually localized, system of women's, men's, and children's work. As new technologies such as steam power and the spinning jenny both centralized and increased production in the form of the factory, an expanding cash-based market drew an increasing number of men, women, and children out of the home to labor for wages. Those women who did not seek employment were faced with an ever larger share of household work once performed by men. By the 1840s, however, women, especially married women, found themselves increasingly unwelcome in factories and under attack by ministers, reformers, and capitalists alike for abandoning their "natural" place, the domestic sphere.[24]

The early audience for this domestic moralizing consisted of literate, upper- and middle-class urban women of industrializing New England. New England ministers of the early to mid-nineteenth century held that the virtue and character of children emanated directly from women's efforts alone, thereby placing the future of religion and the nation squarely on the shoulders of mothers. This duty required self-denial and full-time devotion to home duties and to the moral education of children. The doctrine of "separate spheres," as it is known, undergirded by the material conditions of industrialization, shifted the care of home and children to wives, mothers, and hired female labor—a burden which today remains largely intact in working women's "second shift" responsibilities.[25]

Unanticipated and unintended consequences, however, arose in the practice of this doctrine. Ann Douglas argues that essentially this same class constituency of women sentimentalized the Protestant creed through their presence as the majority of churchgoers and their influence as literary writers. Ministers and women, both marginalized in the expanding world of market relations, grasped for influence by writing for a majority female readership. The ministers, hoping to maintain their female base of followers, moved away from the traditional theological preoccupation with a rational means to salvation and toward the sentimental concerns of family morals, civic responsibility, and churchgoing. The women sought self-definition and expression by reading novels and women's magazines. The general result, according to Douglas, was that sentimentality—the privileging of emotion over reason—came to characterize popular culture and stamped both literature and its consumption (that is, its market) as feminine in character.[26]

Also unanticipated was the rise of women's public, political power. If Douglas's notion of the feminization of American culture stands as the inherited, "soft" underbelly of the separation of spheres, then the moral authority imputed to womanhood and motherhood is its armor. Middle- and upper-class women transformed their imposed status as the bearers of morality into political causes, from abolitionism (1830s–1860s) to child labor reform (1870s–1930s) to child saving movements (1890s–1930s) to the campaign for their own right to vote (1900–1920).[27] The separation of spheres provided avenues for these literate women to assert a public voice by claiming and framing moral issues for themselves.

Nancy Cott argues that the separation of spheres also gave rise to a feminist consciousness. Segregating women's activities, duties, and even "moral labors" from those of men allowed these women to see themselves as political partners. This awareness gave women an impetus for bonding together to resist the same practices which initially had grouped them together. She concludes: "Not until they saw themselves thus classed by sex would women join together to protest their sexual fate." Here, sharply defined external divisions enabled women to see the similarities internal to their shared boundedness.[28]

The unfolding distinction between women's and men's work carried with it moral, political, and cultural ramifications that extended beyond the physical locations of home and factory. The canon of domesticity—the idea that home was women's proper sphere—was propagated through religious practice and rhetoric and was enacted through women's education of the time. The logic of separate spheres superimposed moral distinctions on gender distinctions. Work outside the home required that men participate in the self-interested, instrumental world of market relations, leaving the domestic realm of women and children as the "refuge" of moral life under the care of women in their roles as wives and mothers.[29]

CHILD WELFARE MOVEMENTS AND WOMEN'S MORAL AUTHORITY

The sentimental, political, and moral fervor surrounding a distinct feminine-domestic sphere carried the lives and status of children in its wake into the twentieth century. The gradual liberation of children from direct production, combined with the arrival of compulsory schooling in the 1890s, cemented children's place in the home. A class of women had seized the reins of moral imperative to act in behalf of children in legal as well as domestic matters.[30] Beginning with the establishment of numerous societies for the prevention of cruelty to children in the 1870s, decades of activist women and mothers successfully institutionalized the sentimental status of children through numerous national and local agencies. These agencies focused their efforts on the physical health and social welfare of mothers and children. Social reformers initiated "child saving" campaigns out of which arose settlement houses and juvenile courts.[31]

Linda Gordon points out that initial concerns over "cruelty" toward children stemmed as much from reformers' class, ethnic, and racial fears in the face of a changing urban social landscape as it did from incidents of child abuse. Joseph Hawes interprets the legislative attention paid to child labor reform after 1900 as the effect of middle-class moral scrutiny on working-class behavior and lifestyle. In this context, the category of "youth" came into use as a marker of urban, lower-class juvenile delinquency, as innocence and sentimentality were once again reinforced as a middle-class ideal of childhood.[32]

Many of these efforts were animated by an ideology that attributed a child's delinquent behavior to inadequate training in the home, directly implicating mothers in the process. Child protection agencies rationalized (in the Weberian sense) mothers' responsibility for their children's moral conduct through the bureaucratic procedures followed for investigating child abuse cases. Child welfare workers thus accepted the separate spheres doctrine de facto insofar as it affirmed that a woman's primary duty was child care.[33]

Child saving acquired its most literal meaning when women organized "baby saving" campaigns to fight rising infant mortality rates in the face of increasing immigration and urbanization. Mothers organized local and state efforts to "educate" young mothers by offering courses to instruct girls of high school age on the proper care of children. Numerous female-headed clubs, agencies, and groups published child care advice in pamphlets, books, magazines, and newspapers to publicize their campaign for "better babies." State departments of health also began to acquire a female face, notably the one in New York headed by S. Josephine Baker. The National Congress of Mothers and the Child Study Association, among others, were some of the formally organized agencies operating under the banner of "baby saving" throughout the second and third decades of the twentieth century.[34]

The U.S. Children's Bureau, established by order of Congress in 1912 under the Department of Labor, gave institutional legitimacy and organizational centrality to these scattered and often grassroots campaigns. Unencumbered by existing governmental structures, the bureau was given a broad charge, its task defined only as conducting research on the health and welfare of the nation's children and disseminating the results. The presence of the first chief, Julia Lathrop, served as a wedge for the insertion of a "maternalist" ideology of child welfare into state policies and practices. Maternalism, Kathryn Kish Sklar notes, was a means by which many of the more educated, white mothers invoked their status as bearers of morality to further political ends, crafting policy in accordance with their own experiences and beliefs, and at times substituting gender conflict for class and race conflict.[35]

These women advocated health policy and health activism as much for feminist political goals as for health outcomes. The two ends were intertwined but after the First World War came into conflict with an emerging "male" model of infant care that stressed children's and women's health policy primarily from a medical, rather than a socio-economic, point of view. As Alicia Klaus points out, the "medical" model of child care had certain advantages. It could address child health issues "objectively" (in medical terms), thereby avoiding touchy political issues like access to health care. It also offered a relatively smooth route to gaining the American public's attention and participation. Eventually this model was advocated by the American Medical Association, by the Children's Bureau, and in women's magazines and advice books for parents, creating what some call the ideology of "scientific motherhood."[36]

Organized "baby saving" work directed much of its attention to the conditions of poor African American, immigrant, and rural mothers in an attempt to extend the ethos of scientific motherhood beyond its class and race origins. Local "baby contests," printed height-and-weight growth charts for infants, and the presence of trained nurses in department stores and infants' departments (see chapter 3) helped spread rational medical approaches to child care beyond urban centers. In the ideology of scientific motherhood, those childrearing practices that passed from mother to daughter—once thought to be a sound basis for a child's moral and physical upbringing—were now found insufficient and mothers were judged in need of "expert" knowledge and education.[37]

THE DOMESTIC SPHERE GOES PUBLIC

The organized onslaught of advice about and attention to children's health and welfare in the early 1900s would not abate until the Second World War. An elaborate infrastructure of governmental and nongovernmental organizations and institutions grew, it would seem, almost organically in concert with particular constructions of modern motherhood and modern childhood. Ironically, the establishment of the Children's Bureau institutionalized and reinforced the domestic realm as the full extent of a "woman's sphere." Even as its charge helped to legitimize women's political action in the public sphere, its existence tended to ghettoize that action around the traditional "feminine" concerns of children and health.[38]

Nonetheless, educated middle-class and activist women made themselves visible and vocal in the early decades of the century by advocating for children's welfare and for universal suffrage; they and other members of this class of urban women also increasingly moved out of the private world of the household and into the public realm of the newly arising consumer marketplace. In this burgeoning world of ready-made and increasingly affordable consumer goods, the department store stood as the hallmark of early consumer culture. In addition to serving as a site for the conspicuous and often lavish display of new goods, the department store also offered women a space to exercise other forms of power, as both workers and consumers, that were incommensurate with their subordinate status inside the home. Department stores provided women with many kinds of opportunities to earn wages outside the home and, by the 1920s, had become a major source of management positions for middle-class women. No less informed by ethnic and class distinctions than other workplaces, the realm of women workers inside department stores was overwhelmingly white, as working-class women often staffed the sales counters and middle-class women worked either as buyers or as assistant merchandise managers.[39]

Susan Porter Benson argues that store managers thought women to be well suited to the department store environment because of the match between its service orientation and women's supposedly innate ability to render such service. Male managers held onto the belief that "salesgirls" could be trained in docility and gentility and could learn to speak for the store as its public "emissary" to the mainly female clientele. However, the working-class saleswoman proved to be, for the most part, intractable in her attitude toward work, toward the middle-class women for whom she worked, and toward those to whom she attempted to sell goods. She resisted management attempts to control time, the workspace, and interactions with other clerks. Seeking refuge in a "clerking sisterhood" of resistance, these women remained a ubiquitous "management problem" over decades and were often caricatured in the trade press.[40]

The focus of retailing in this period shifted toward accommodating growing consumer desire for new and different goods and away from attempting to fit those desires with available stock. A manager's duty became less that of a selling agent for the manufacturer and more that of a purchasing agent for the consumer. Contributing to this shift was the importation of style into virtually all types of goods—from clothing to cars, from telephones to bathroom towels, from tableware to the advertisements themselves. A large-scale "consumption ethic," Roland Marchand argues, grew in response to the increased availability of these ever-changing goods, as a style-based, rather than a use-based, obsolescence began to drive new purchases.[41]

Responding to the changing nature of the public's tastes became the order of the day for department store managers eager to maintain or capture a share of this overwhelmingly female consumer market. The middle- and upper-class women who frequently patronized department stores continually came face to face with the clerks of a "lower social standing" who acted as arbiters of style and who were to advise them in matters of fashion. According to Benson, these daily class confrontations gave managers headaches because they disrupted the smooth flow of sales. The training of sales clerks remained a recurrent issue for management through the 1940s.[42]

However, Benson points out that it is precisely these kinds of confrontations and these contexts that allowed women to display, discover, and exercise forms of power the likes of which were often impossible to repeat in the home. The world of the department store *was* a woman's world—an "Adamless Eden" not only of goods, but of spaces and relationships. It was in this world that a female customer could send a male manager scurrying about to right a wrong order or discipline an impolite clerk, an exercise of power that was out of proportion with what she could wield in the home.

This power, however, was not exclusively class-based. In addition to the sales clerks' resistance, their income, their ability to interact with and deal with high-class women, and their access to and knowledge about fashion all combined to enhance an independence which often accompanied urban life. Indeed, fashion may have been the most public expression of this newly emerging independence for women. For immigrant women of the period, fashion and consumer items not only expressed their independence through sexuality and personal display, but also conveyed a break from their parents and the yoke of Old World tradition.[43]

In addition to the economic power of income and choice of goods, this burgeoning culture of consumption gave women a "legitimate" reason to be present in public spaces. In the latter part of the nineteenth century, their presence outside the home could be met with concern. Shopping was only a minor part of a woman's duty in the 1870s, but by the 1890s it was being decried as a female vice akin to men's drinking and smoking. Understandably, just as production gradually moved out of the home in the face of an urbanizing and increasingly cash-based economy, women physically had to leave the home to purchase the things their grandmothers used to make, and more.[44]

Women's role in the gendered, household division of labor thus became that of "purchasing agent" for the family, and shopping became a domestic chore. Predictably, as advertisers and merchants came to realize the influence that women wielded over the family pocketbook, the desires, foibles, and concerns of women took center stage. Thus, for example, in 1915 the business trade magazine *System* found it useful to inquire into the preferences of ninety-seven "housewives" (who were also presidents of women's clubs).[45]

Indeed, a "woman's perspective"—on goods, services, and advertising copy—itself became a valued commodity throughout the 1920s. The influence that women exercised over the family budget was seized on by those in the consumer goods trades with such vigor that by 1923 a writer for *Printer's Ink,* an advertising trade journal, complained of the "almost forgotten male" in advertising appeals. Not surprisingly, the persona of "the woman" that emerges out of the advertising trade press is that of an emotionally driven, impulsive creature who has an almost unhealthy (but profitable) preoccupation with the stylistic aspects of things. This "woman" or persona, in many ways, encompassed the very model of the generic, mass consumer—fickle, nonrational, and pleasure-driven.[46]

By contrast, in public, *consumer*-directed advertising women were portrayed as business "agents" throughout this period, as Roland Marchand demonstrated in his study of the rise of the modern advertising industry. The "Little Woman, G.P.A." (General Purchasing Agent) was one such portrayal. In an effort to elevate the perception of women's place in consumer society, it glorified women as "business managers" of the modern, efficient household by likening their work in the home to the "real" world of male corporate work. The contradiction between the fickle, female consumer of the trade press and the efficient modern housewife in consumer advertisements underscores some of the discrepancies between how cultural brokers—here, advertisers—transform their backstage models of "the consumer" into palatable, front-stage personae.[47]

The public attention paid to women compounded the "empowerment" present in this expanding world of goods and retailing. Yet this power remained circumscribed as court cases in the 1920s ruled in favor of men's proprietary status over their wives, particularly in terms of household money and women's allowances from their husbands.[48] Women were indeed "agents" of household money—money that often technically and legally was not theirs. Nevertheless, it is clear that the interaction between the gendered, domestic sphere of the home and the new consumer-oriented society created new physical and social spaces for women in which to gather, to see and be seen, and ultimately to act.

The world of women—white, middle-class women—in the early

twentieth century, then, was one of opposing tensions, particularly for married women and mothers. To fulfill her traditional role as homemaker, a woman was required to physically leave the home for the department store, among other places. When she did so, she entered a commercial space that was in some ways more fully hers socially than her own home, yet she brought money with her to spend that often was not legally hers. Expected to use this money in an efficient and rational way, this composite woman was approached by merchants and retailers as an irrational and impulsive creature. Her very purchasing decisions, furthermore, were made not only with herself in mind, but also her husband and, if a mother, her children.

3

Merchandising, Motherhood,
and Morality: Industry Origins and
Child Welfare, 1917–1929

Over the course of the first three decades of the twentieth century, a particular convergence of social, cultural, political, and economic trajectories took shape, in condensed form, in the commercial persona and historical reality of the "mother as consumer." As we have seen, women *as women* emerged as a central focus and force in consumer culture in interaction with the requisites of an urbanizing, cash economy. These requisites became superimposed on the historical and gendered separation of home from work; hence, a woman's "duty" or "role" became that of purchasing agent. Arising from the domestic sphere and armed with a moral authority, this middle-class woman found a physical and social space—the department store—where she could exercise the power of the purse outside the home, all the while essentially preserving the structure of relations derived within. Women *as mothers*, however, could and did become consumers only if they brought their children with them out of the home and into the stores, literally and figuratively.

In September 1917, a new kind of trade publication began operations in Chicago. The opening editorial of the *Infants' Department* stated that it was "devoted *exclusively* to the line of goods . . . and to the problems that are peculiar to the Infants' Wear Department." George F. Earnshaw (1870–1940) personally financed this modest fifteen-page monthly journal and, initially, distributed it free of charge to buyers, retailers, and manufacturers of children's wear.[1]

The appearance of the *Infants' Department*, which continues today as *Earnshaw's Review* (based in New York City), signaled the advent of the children's wear industry as an industry. The publication provided a forum for disparate actors (manufacturers, retailers, buyers) to come together to constitute an industry in a selfconscious manner. Importantly, it also marked the beginnings of a process that institutionalized the commodity status of childhood and motherhood. This process ultimately reached beyond the initial realms of children's clothing and toys into all forms of goods and media specifically designed for and targeted to children.

Opposite the opening editorial an advertisement offered $100 for the best answers to the question "How can you make this mother your customer?" Pictured is a sketch of a woman (white, middle-class in dress) with an infant on her lap and a small child playing nearby (illustration 1). The children are wearing Vanta Baby Garments, products of George Earnshaw's own knitting company, identifiable by the special feature of twistless tape as fasteners instead of pins.

At its inception, the children's wear industry organized itself in response to particular notions about the "nature" of mothers and the social organization of motherhood. These notions were often ones propagated by the industry itself through the *Infants' Department*, its major public organ.[2] Certainly, the definition and construction of mothers and motherhood were not and could not be the work of a single publication or a single industry. Rather, what is unique in this case are the ways in which Earnshaw and staff writers sought to combine extant beliefs about feminine nature and maternal motivation with the structure and process of a retailing environment.

Key among these beliefs is the idea that a mother instinctively puts her child's needs above all else. Combined with a general climate of fear about children's health during a time of high infant mortality, Earnshaw's publication successfully forged maternal motivation and child health into a viable niche for infants' departments to inhabit. Earnshaw, and the industry as a whole, generally escaped suspicion of exploiting children because the marketplace—in particular, the infants' department—offered the mother a

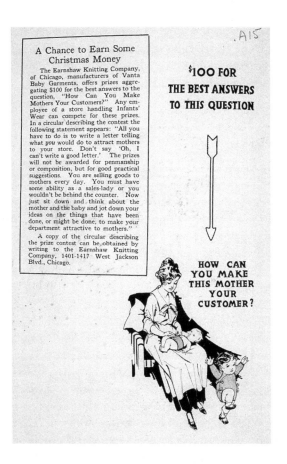

1. Mothers are the featured customers in the première issue of the *Infant's Department*, September 1917, 2.

place to be an active, caring agent and to consume on behalf of her children. The child, initially at least, could remain passive and essentially undefined. Indeed, the more "the child" could be construed as being at risk and therefore in need of coddling and protection, the stronger the moral cover of altruism would avert attention from damaging counterclaims.

FROM MAKING TO PURCHASING
CHILDREN'S CLOTHES

The convergence of several large-scale trends—increased production of children's ready-made garments, a general decrease in the use of domestic help, and married women's increasing participation in the labor force—put middle-class mothers in a position to be favorably disposed toward purchasing ready-made clothing for their children after the First World War.

Increased productivity—the immediate, tangible result of the factory organization of labor—had compounded and transformed the emerging gender-based separation of spheres and division of labor in the nineteenth century; in particular, the mass production of cloth altered women's work in the home. Sewing and stitching have been common activities of women, historically and cross-culturally, with both men and women taking part in weaving. As late as 1820, about 70 percent of the garments made in the United States remained a product of the household. Beginning with government tailors' shops to produce Army clothing in 1812, manufacturers made great efforts to design, cut, and produce standard pattern pieces of cloth for easy assembly into uniforms and eventually into civilian apparel. Over the course of the nineteenth century, ready-made cloth gradually replaced home spinning and home weaving, essentially relieving men of their place in the production of cloth and garments at home.[3]

By the mid-nineteenth century, the first practical sewing machine came into use. This innovation not only sparked a mass market for ready-made clothing, but also "democratized" apparel in the sense that stylistic distinctions of class and station could be minimized or blurred by the effects of mass production—less expensive, identical goods. The first mass-produced complete garments were worn by Union troops during the Civil War. For civilians, it was men's and boys' wear—specifically laboring clothing—which was the first to be mass-produced. Women's wear did not surpass men's in quantities made or amount sold until the first decade of the twentieth century, but by 1910 every article of female clothing could be purchased ready-made.[4]

Children's wear was the last class of everyday garments to come fully under the influence and control of mass production. In the second decade of the century, complete children's garments were only beginning to be made in any quantity in factories, as most children's clothing was made as a sideline to women's apparel. The children's clothing market did not warrant its own section in *Dry Goods Economist*, a long-standing trade weekly, until 1914. Largely a homemade enterprise until the First World War, infants' and children's clothing up to about the age of six for both boys and girls could be pieced together from store-bought cloth using patterns purchased at dry goods stores or taken from women's and mothers' magazines such as *Babyhood*, *Women's Home Companion*, *Harper's*, and *Ladies' Home Journal*. These periodicals reached white, educated middle- and upper-class mothers who were, in urbanizing America, increasingly cut off from their own mothers and from networks and traditions of childrearing and homemaking.[5]

The Bureau of the Census did not include the manufacture of children's clothing as a separate category until as late as 1937.[6] It reported 452 establishments specializing in manufacturing children's outerwear for that year, a number which peaked at 1,983 establishments in 1954 (see figure 1 in Appendix).[7] The *Dry Goods Economist*, reporting that there was only one factory specializing in making children's clothes before 1890, estimated that by 1921 seventy-five such factories existed in New York City alone.[8] Although sparse, these measurements nonetheless indicate that children's garments were being manufactured, and by implication purchased, in increasing numbers.[9]

At this time white, non-laboring-class mothers faced increased time constraints which disposed them toward purchasing more of their children's garments rather than making them at home from patterns. Households were making less use of paid domestic help over the period 1910–1940. Phyllis Palmer estimates that, 6.1 percent of all families used domestic help in 1920, a decrease from 9.3 percent in 1910. This figure rose to 6.8 percent in 1930, most likely because of the economic prosperity of the 1920s, before falling back to 6.0 percent in 1940, no doubt because of the Depression, as the number of domestic servants leveled off while the number of households increased (see table 1 in Appendix).[10]

The inability or unwillingness to use domestic servants placed increased burden on a larger number of women to perform household chores which had been shared previously by children as well as by husbands and paid help. Palmer states: "The years 1920–1945 may be viewed as a transitional period during which middle-class homes changed from being *directed* by a lady-housewife to being *served* by the wife. . . . By the end of the era . . . she was less able to hire another woman to take over many of the physical tasks." Mothers did not likely find significant relief from their children's assistance because children were leaving home for elementary school in increasing numbers from 1910 to 1930. Census Bureau statistics indicate that enrollment for public elementary day school students during this period increased by 22 percent, from 16.9 million in 1910 to 18.9 million in 1920 to 20.6 million students in 1930.[11]

Mothers, in addition, were entering the paid labor force in increasing numbers. Overall female labor force participation rates rose slowly and steadily from 1900 to 1940, from 20 percent in 1900 to 25.8 percent in 1940 (see figure 2 in Appendix). The proportion of the total female work force recorded as married, however, increased nearly threefold over the same period, from 5.6 percent in 1900 to 11.7 percent in 1920 to 15.6 percent in 1940 (see figure 3 in Appendix).[12]

In the period 1910–1930, then, women had less help in the home, either from domestics or children, and increasingly sought to work for wages outside the home which resulted in less time available for making garments, among other traditional domestic activities. In addition, the increase in factory production of children's clothing during this time was matched by steadily increasing household incomes for the emerging urban middle classes, including salaried professionals, managers, and office workers. Middle-class, urban mothers found themselves socially and financially in a position to purchase clothing and other things for their children.[13]

Department stores during these years were hitting their zenith as cultural and commercial institutions.[14] The way to draw customers into the department store for George Earnshaw and other children's wear manufacturers was not merely to "create" demand for particular articles of clothing. Rather, the idea from the outset was to institutionalize children's wear generally, and infants' wear specifically, as a category of goods to be logically, physically, and perhaps even morally separate from other garments.

As a manufacturer of his own line of infants' garments since 1911, Earnshaw was quite aware that mothers were the central figures in household consumption. The *Infants' Department*[15] in the 1917–29 period hit upon and refined a formula—which today is a given in marketing circles—that fused a woman's everyday, practical shopping convenience with an emerging moral ethos to care for and attend to her children above all else. This ethos was made material in a significant and initial way with the advent of a new retail category and a new physical space—infants' and children's departments in department stores. Purchasing children's clothes and other goods took on a heightened urgency and a moral cachet beyond mere consumption during this time, as public concern about infant mortality and child health diminished the friction which tends to arise when children and markets commingle.

Merchandising to the Mother's Perspective
Before the First World War only a handful of department stores and dry goods stores physically separated ready-made infants' and children's clothing and accessories from the rest of their merchandise, although infants' clothes had appeared in the Sears' catalogue as early as 1896. In 1914 the *Dry Goods Economist* did not include infants' or children's departments in its recommendations for store layout. Most often, these goods were stocked by item or category (such as socks or shirts) rather than by age or size. Consequently, they were dispersed throughout various departments of the department store or were sold in small specialty shops. Many mothers, although familiar with department store shopping gener-

ally, were not habituated to purchasing the bulk of their children's garments in specialized infants' departments.[16]

George Earnshaw thus faced several challenges as he pleaded his case on the pages of his newly published trade paper. He needed to convince clothing buyers[17] that it would be worthwhile to devote precious floor and inventory space as well as personnel to a retail category that did not yet exist. The key to justifying a new department lay in demonstrating its sales potential to buyers whose livelihoods depended on anticipating demand and stocking their departments' shelves accordingly. If persuaded, these buyers (most were women) would, in turn, need to justify to their managers the dedication of resources to this new category.

If the mother could be made amenable to a retail space consisting exclusively of children's wear and accessories, Earnshaw argued, then the whole store would benefit from her presence because she acts as the purchasing agent for the family. The importance of the infants' department to the buyer or manager would not be in the mother's small, individual purchases for infants "but in . . . *attracting customers to the store.*" If the mother is repeatedly satisfied with her retail experience, Earnshaw continues, she "acquires the habit of buying everything she wants for the family at your store."[18]

Dispersing children's goods in the customary, haphazard manner, Earnshaw observed, inconvenienced mothers, especially expectant mothers, who had to visit several departments often on different floors in order to outfit a child or to pull together a layette. To bring the woman to the store *as* a mother requires that she find articles she needs for her child conveniently displayed in one area, staffed with knowledgeable salespeople, where she is confident that she can return time and again. An early success story underscores this point.

The buyer-manager of a shoe department in Washington, D.C., reportedly doubled his business by placing children's shoes in a forward position of his store adjacent to where children's hats were displayed. Earnshaw surmises:

> There are many store managers who do not yet realize the importance of grouping all merchandise suitable for infants and young children in one department.
> Any man or woman may be interested in beds, but only moth-

ers are interested in *cribs*. Any man or woman may be interested in shoes, but only mothers are interested in *children's shoes*. Any man or woman may be interested in knit underwear, but only mothers are interested in *baby garments*.

When you put cribs in one department, children's shoes in another and babies' knit underwear in still another you are making what may be a logical *buying* classification of your merchandise, but a very illogical *selling* classification. You are consulting your own convenience but not your customers' convenience. . . .

Once [you] realize that the mother of a family of children is a very busy woman (and a mighty desirable customer) . . . you will make it just as easy as possible for her to buy everything needful for her little ones in *one* department.[19]

Physically grouping goods for the express purpose of selling is the essence of merchandising. What is distinctive about this particular type of merchandising is that the point-of-purchase customer, the mother, and the ultimate end-user of the goods, the child, are not the same person or the same type of person. Classifying clothing and furnishings as "children's" is founded on the assumed *perspective* of mothers who have the financial and social wherewithal to consume on behalf of their dependents.

It was an idea that apparently caught on quickly. By 1921 the *Dry Goods Economist* was singing the praises of children's wear merchandising. As one article noted, L. S. Ayers & Co. of Indianapolis found that "grouping wearing apparel for children adds materially to the sales, that the power of suggestion is a potent factor in making these sales [to mothers], to say nothing of the convenience [to mothers]." By 1928 the *Journal of Retailing* was recommending that department stores make space for an entire separate "children's floor."[20]

The Self-Effacing "Mother": The Foundation of an Industry
Increasing sales in infants' and children's wear meant bringing women into the store not only as women but as mothers. "Mother" at this time, however, lacked definition in any significant way *as* a consumer—a semantic void that the writers for the *Infants' Department* would fill with volumes of rhetorical maneuvers in an effort to give shape to this new commercial persona.

"A Mother's First Purchase in *any* Season is for the Baby," declared an advertisement in the *Infants' Department* for George Earnshaw's own line of Vanta Baby Garments in 1921. Earnshaw, along with staff writers who were buyers, registered nurses, doctors, and mothers, produced editorial and feature copy that creates a profile of the consuming mother—a self-sacrificing being motivated by love and instinct to carry out her duty as purchasing agent for the family. The view that "nothing is too good for baby" in the eyes of a mother had been expressed by the dry goods trade at least since the turn of the century: "In children's garments especially, neither the buyer nor the seller should lose sight of the *fact* that mothers will make great sacrifices to dress their children well."[21] "Selling the mother through the child" had a precedent but does not seem to have become an unashamedly explicit merchandising strategy until children's wear began to sport an identity of its own.

Earnshaw built his vision of a total infants' department on the basis of a belief about the needs and motivations of "mother," which he and others promulgated through anecdotes of merchants' successful practices and through outright exhortation. The entire structure and process of an infants' department revolved around the perspective attributed to its ultimate customer. Segregating children's merchandise was intended to appeal to a mother's convenience; similarly, the variety of stock, the service offered, and the location of the department itself (that is, the fundamental organizational concerns of any retail operation) all ideally should respond to the emotional and practical priorities of the consuming mother.

The first principle of a complete department naturally concerned the variety of stock available. The layette, the first wardrobe for a newborn, was the foundation of a successful department. To avoid confusion that might disconcert "sensitive" (that is, expectant) mothers and that might result in the loss of a sale, one article suggested listing the choices for layettes: "The young mother, starting on her first shopping tour . . . is often quite uncertain as to the articles constituting a layette. . . . Imagine her delight to have . . . a small booklet . . . and to see listed the very articles she needs arranged in groups with the price of individual garments given!"[22] Successful layette merchandising should incorporate a concern for baby's health with suggestive selling, pointing the customer toward higher-end items whenever possible.[23]

The layette became a standard merchandise category during the early '20s and grew in significance with the industry's growth. A mother's choice of layette could reveal her concerns and preoccupations as well as express her aspirations, as illustrated in the following advice to children's wear sellers:

> The main thought [for mothers] in mind in buying a layette, whether simple or elaborate, is the comfort and health of the child. If the essential articles purchased are of good quality the child will be satisfactorily provided for. In fact some of the wealthiest customers prefer the simplest layettes providing the articles are of the best quality.
>
> On the other hand, some mothers take such delight in baby things that they want as complete an outfit as possible, and frequently these are customers of modest means.[24]

Obviously, both are worthy and welcome shopping motivations.

Having no set requirements of what constitutes a complete layette is an ambiguity ripe with selling opportunities. Some stores gave "demonstrations" of the layette, often in conjunction with Baby Weeks which were begun in 1914 by the U.S. Children's Bureau (see below). The preferred approach was to display combinations of items to the unknowing new mother by assembling them, or perhaps to suggest a timetable for their purchase.[25] One writer for *Earnshaw's* surveyed various infants departments and

> looked in vain for assembled layettes. In spite of the fact that Infants' departments are all seeking out the prospective mother; in spite of the fact that she does not know or cannot visualize what she wants . . . the opportunities that the layette offers to help such mothers are continually overlooked.
>
> Personally, I prefer selling the layette in small quantities weekly or semi-monthly . . . . It keeps her coming back to the department constantly for the new items. . . . Help such a mother plan her purchases in advance. Keep her mind occupied in reading the right kind of literature, using for that purpose the Mother's Reference Library.

Here, layette selling ideally would serve the double function of inducting the prospective mother into the world of mass-produced goods for infants and of encouraging her to speculate about the future "needs" of her yet-to-be-born child. These needs would be conveniently met by her local infants' department.

A successful department is a complete department, which is stocked not only with the latest garments but also with accessories like strollers, scales, rattles, small toys, baby books, and, importantly, books about childrearing and child health. The stock, however, would be only the initial draw; it is service—the face-to-face experience of the mother with the saleswoman—which would make or break a department, an industry.

Stock and service go hand in hand, and service covers the location of the department itself, the trade readers were told. Offering service is a tricky business because young mothers are said to be quite sensitive and expectant mothers embarrassed about their condition. This situation is both dangerous and promising because the mother is susceptible, on the one hand, to "all slights" and, on the other, to suggestive selling. The following advice to "the girl behind the counter" illustrates this view: "The undecided customer who needs the most delicate and tactful handling . . . is the prospective mother. Your present sales and future patronage depend on your courtesy and interest. . . . It behooves you then, mademoiselle, to use your head and be as lavish with your sympathetic interest as you know how. . . . Remember that she is abnormally sensitive and that things which wouldn't particularly bother you or me, worry her dreadfully."[26] The mother who is drawn to the infants' department and is satisfied with her experience there would supposedly develop the habit of shopping not only in the infants' department but also in the entire department store for her baby's and family's needs.

Infants' wear buyers were encouraged to use the predominance of women in retail centers, from sales clerks to customers to nurses, as a selling point to their male managers when arguing for a separate department. Feminine collegiality supposedly encouraged an intimate relationship between customer and clerk, especially when conversation centered on the maternal subjects of pregnancy, childbirth, and infant feeding: "[The expectant mother] is extremely susceptible to the right kind of treatment . . . Once she has told her secret to a mother-wise saleswoman who knows how to handle her properly . . . the chances are that she will confine her visits to your store." The trust formed between women would translate ideally into "customer goodwill," a euphemism for a long-term sales relationship.[27]

The criteria for planning the location of a department also took the sensitive mother into account. Earnshaw suggested a "secluded corner" or a separate layette room, so that her "condition" would not be obvious to all, citing a store in Boston the arrangement of which "gives sufficient privacy and a homey feeling." The department should not be near "noisy and irritant" elevators; it should have chairs to rest on and, preferably, should be near restrooms where the mother could take her other children quickly so as not to interrupt the flow of the sale. Indeed, even providing several styles of infant toilet seats in the restroom would draw attention to the "desirability of these devices."[28]

The commercial cosmology propagated to members of the children's wear industry through the *Infants' Department* placed maternal motivation and feminine foibles above and beyond the material and cultural conditions of social class. A woman may act as a purchasing agent for the family because of her position in the division of domestic labor, but *mothers* buy for their children out of instinctive love that transcends the requirements of duty. Mothers are like no other class of trade because they will forego their own happiness to provide for their children, a circumstance favorable to selling better grades of merchandise. "I have never once heard a mother say," a buyer wrote in 1926, "she considered price before quality *or* preferred low price to quality."[29]

The exigencies of motherhood, in this way, promised sales from even the poorer classes. Earnshaw related a story he heard about an Italian woman (apparently of "modest means") seeking a baby carriage. Initially shown several cheap models, she ended by purchasing the most expensive one. The lesson to merchants, Earnshaw exhorts, is transparent: "You cannot judge by the appearance of a customer, by her dress or her hat, the kind of merchandise she will buy. . . . There is only one safe rule to follow in dealing with mothers. Show her the finest you have first and let the mother herself be the judge. . . . A last year's hat may be the sign of a fat roll to be spent on this year's baby."[30] Note the faith in "mother love" to translate into exchange value, particularly higher-priced goods. In this way, a mother's love is expressed through commodities.[31]

It is questionable (and unknowable), however, whether Earnshaw and his staff actually believed that mothers' love for their children is directly proportional to the amount of money spent on them or to the quality of goods purchased; more likely, the *Infants' Department*, as a trade organ, was attempting to persuade merchants and manufacturers that the extent of the infants' market was not bounded strictly by income distribution, or even geography. For instance, Earnshaw admonished the readership for ignoring a large segment of the population that lived in towns of less than 25,000 inhabitants: "Mother love is not confined to women dwelling in cities of over 25,000 population. To her in the tiniest hamlet, as well as to the city woman, her baby is her dearest possession. . . . She is no different from the woman in the city of 1,000,000. She is a mother."[32] The predictable appealed to the "universal" motivations of mothers gains added dimension by placing children at the apex of a mother's possessions.

Under the Moral Cover: Baby Saving and Modern Motherhood
The ideology of maternal consumption articulated by the *Infants' Department* extended from this emotional-instinctive, self-effacing mother to a rational-learned, self-effacing mother who sought knowledge about her child's garments. The "new" mother, trade readers were informed, needs to be educated about the healthful qualities of the garments they purchase and about the proper care of children. Women from "all walks of life" (in other words all social classes) need help and suggestions because "there is no previous training that fits her for the problems of motherhood. It is true her own mother may have reared successfully a large family of children but the methods of a generation ago are not the methods of today."[33] In this way, infants' and children's wear retailing could serve as moral cover, rendering market activity subservient to the greater good of civilizing and modernizing mothers who, in turn, would be better equipped to care for their children.

In the second decade of the twentieth century, infant mortality in the United States was peaking, often hovering between 99 and 100 deaths per thousand live births. Earnshaw started a "save the seventh baby" campaign in 1917, noting that one of seven babies was dying before the age of one, and using stark images that juxtaposed the Grim Reaper and babies (illustration 2). "Of the same number of soldiers," Earnshaw wrote in a reference to overseas

2. A striking illustration from Earnshaw's "Save the Seventh Baby" campaign, alluding to the one baby in seven that was dying before one year of age in the United States in 1916. *Infant's Department*, November 1917, 39.

troops in the First World War, "only 50,000 will die in a year as a result of their exposure to the risks of war."[34]

Earnshaw drew on existing structures and activities, in particular the U.S. Children's Bureau's "Baby Week" campaign, to encourage fledgling infants' and children's departments to offer educational, baby saving lectures, and demonstrations on their premises: "There is no subject on which you can arouse so much interest among mothers as Baby Welfare. The Better Baby movement is spreading throughout the country like wildfire and the department store that is alive to its opportunities will not be slow to realize that by identifying itself with this movement it acquires a prestige in its community that will be reflected in increased sales in all departments."[35] Anecdotes of always "successful" Baby Week programs at department stores all over the country, from Ashland, Kentucky, to Denver to Seattle, remained a staple of the publication's features through the 1930s.

The Children's Bureau (established in 1912) unwittingly helped in building a bridge between children and commerce. It functioned at once as a clearing house for information, a liaison between various women's groups, and an advocate and promoter of children's health and welfare activities. Its existence brought a level of legitimacy and urgency to child health concerns. According to Alicia

Klaus, the bureau, in contrast to politically explicit groups like the National Congress of Mothers, won the trust of middle- and lower-class women as a secular authority with a perceived "non-partisan" attitude toward children's issues.[36]

Particularly through the annual Baby Week, the bureau helped to diffuse child health information as well as to solidify the connection between commercial activity and child welfare. Baby Week embodied the western, initially bourgeois belief in the market as a "civilizing force" to the extent that business became the institutional medium for child welfare activity. The first Baby Week in 1914 was intended as a one-time educational and promotional effort by the bureau to focus attention on and gain support for its mission. Staged in urban dry goods and department stores of the East at first, Baby Week brought the "latest" in medical and scientific information to bear on the care of children. "Perfect baby contests," height-and-weight growth charts, along with physical and mental anthropometric tests, quickly became common during Baby Weeks. As Klaus points out, however, better baby contests had strong racial and eugenic overtones, and Baby Weeks as often resembled patriotic holidays as served child welfare efforts.[37]

Baby contests themselves helped to commodify childhood in that they subjected children to "objective" measurements, making individual children a choice among many "objects."[38] These contests prefigured market research to the extent that they rendered children objects of measurement. The physical measurements taken for baby's health are analogous to the measurements taken of children's "needs" and "wants" a half-century later.[39]

After a limited debut in 1914, National Baby Week in 1916 reportedly was celebrated in some 2,200 of an estimated 14,186 incorporated communities, and in the process brought infant health work to rural America.[40] The *Dry Goods Economist* in 1914 advised that "Getting Baby's Trade" could be done by "making a Direct Appeal to Mothers" and that the "value of special appeal in advertising is nowhere better illustrated than in the Baby Week Sale idea."[41] The article briefly outlined a strategy that the retailer could take advantage of during Baby Week, "a special selling event," by giving prizes for the best babies and by having special merchandising, window trimming, and advertising. The article featured a sample advertisement from the Glass Block Store of Duluth, Minnesota, which suggested having the baby weighed at one of the scales provided and proclaimed "This Week the 2nd Floor is Reigned Over by Her 'Ladyship' and His Lordship, The Baby."

Note that the appeal of this earliest of public advertisements for a Baby Week sale did not suggest underweight babies or infant mortality. To do so perhaps would have implied incompetence on the part of its middle-class clientele of mothers and would have lowered the class standing of the store's appeal. Rather, the advertisement contextualized consumption as an educational opportunity and the store's role as providing a "service" to the mothers in weighing babies and in providing sale merchandise, arguing that these goods were arranged to "make the event informative as well as enjoyable."

By the early 1920s, Baby Week and department and dry goods stores went together as naturally (and as contrivedly) as love and candy on Valentine's Day. These stores coordinated their efforts with local women's groups, hosting talks about infant care on store premises, using the event as the focus of advertising pitches, having "Baby Week" sales and sponsoring demonstrations on such topics as "how to care for a newborn." Slogans such as "Baby's Health—Civic Wealth" and "Utah's Best Crop" testified to the rhetorical status of children as a national or regional "resource." They also spoke to the increasing marketability of children's goods in the context of putatively civic-health benefits.[42] Through Baby Week and its publications, the Children's Bureau became an important first vehicle for the large-scale institutionalization of a children's consumer culture—functioning, as the historian William Leach put it, as an "institutional collaborator."[43]

For George Earnshaw, the challenge was to make every week Baby Week—to routinize childhood sacredness through retail operations and mothers' habits. He propounded a moral and welfare-oriented position in his *Infants' Department* that targeted the health of babies in two ways. First, departments should stock the newest and most "scientifically" up-to-date garments and shoes so as to assist "modern mothers" in their attempt to create the most healthful situation for growing, sensitive bodies. Second, "ethical retailing" meant staffing a store with knowledgeable saleswomen, consulting physicians, providing educational pamphlets by approved sources such as the American Medical Association, and warning consumers about injurious and unhealthful items.[44]

The best way to educate the modern mother in the "methods of today" was to offer, in the infants' department, stock and service oriented toward child welfare. Earnshaw's vision was to institutionalize infants' departments as centers of infant welfare work, alongside "doctors, the schools, the social settlements, the churches and the governmental agencies." He reasoned that "mothers of the country come into contact with the mercantile institutions more often than any other institutions engaged in such work" and thus could be reached more consistently and efficiently than by other agencies.[45]

Earnshaw encouraged buyers and department managers to take advantage of Baby Week campaigns, stating that "successful merchandising has become largely a matter of *educating the consumer*, and in no section of the store is this more necessary than in the Infants' Department."[46] He suggested placing a trained full-time nurse in the department who would become familiar with the merchandise. Her presence would not only educate mothers but also be a great "drawing card":

> If mothers bought for their babies only what was absolutely required, a few yards of diaper cloth, a knitted undergarment or two, and a few dresses would be the limit of their purchases. But the maternal instinct that desires *everything* that will contribute to the comfort and welfare of the baby is enlisted on the side of the merchant who knows how to create desire and inspire confidence, and nothing yet discovered accomplishes these two things so well in the Infants' Department as a trained nurse who can answer intimate questions with the voice of authority, and, merely by bringing to the mother's attention articles she never heard of, arouse in her the desire to possess them for her baby.[47]

Mother education, child welfare, and retailing, in this view, can find a home in infants' departments.

Indeed, department stores, dry goods stores, and infants' departments were for many women the places most favorable for gathering as they exercised their duties as the family's purchasing agent. These public spaces were thus conducive to mother education. An article in May 1918 purported:

The department store is perhaps the greatest single factor in the education of women in this country. . . . It is the one place where the society woman, the business girl, the mother of a comfortable, well-to-do family and the woman of the tenements all meet on an equal plane. . . . Had the suffragettes been able to work through the department stores instead of through women's clubs, churches and lectures . . . the feminine vote would no doubt be universal by now. . . .

When has the mother . . . the time to attend another meeting or church club or society? She must take the time, however, to go shopping; she must buy things for her babies, and there is the department store's opportunity.[48]

The marketplace, in this view, can also serve the moral and political ends of suffrage and other causes. Clearly, for Earnshaw, the more political power women could obtain, the more they could wield economic power, especially if they were of the middling classes who attended clubs and societies.

As Nancy Cott has demonstrated, George Earnshaw was not the first to cite womanhood or motherhood as a bond that transcends class boundaries.[49] What is striking and unique is the manner in which the exigencies of a mother's care for her child are fitted parsimoniously within the vision of a total retailing environment. What is also striking is how womanhood is linked to the assumed equalizing power of the marketplace.

Mother education, for Earnshaw and his publication, was not merely a matter of making goods and services available to potential customers. It worked toward effecting a basic transfer of authority—here, from kin to commerce. For the "young mother" addressed by the *Infants' Department* is one who is dislocated socio-historically, riding a crest of social change which has made her world fundamentally different from her mother's: "But the mother, expectant of her first child, particularly is influenced tremendously by the advice and the warnings of the whisperings of her grandmother, her mother and that old friend who has 'buried ten children' before she was born. This little mother is firmly impressed with and deeply rooted in the old, cast-out methods of years back. . . . No woman will take the advice of a saleswoman against the word of her mother."[50] The article, from 1922, continues to note that dressing babies has changed. When this "little mother" enters an infants' department and receives information which contradicts the advice given by her mother and others, she may question the department's expertise and not her mother's.

Earnshaw and his staff writers acknowledged the tenacity of women's traditional, oral culture in the face of modern goods and services available at retail: "I am always sorry for the conscientious clerk who gets hold of one of these little women . . . If [she] has a mother or a mother-in-law, both have coached her on what she needs for her baby. Possibly their youngest child is twenty years old . . . The next door neighbor . . . has her views, and whenever this woman comes into contact with a mother, she hears something."[51] The answer to this dilemma—how to draw the diminutive young mother out of her traditional realm and into the modern, commercial child-care market—was for individual departments and stores to establish a reputation for serious welfare work and, in so doing, court the confidence of mothers and mothers-to-be.

Trade readers were advised to align themselves on the side of "good sound information on up-to-date methods about babies." The store should offer to send the mother's name to the Children's Bureau so that she could receive literature on baby care by way of a preaddressed card. This card would demonstrate that the store takes an interest in her welfare. It would also get her to sit down and fill it out in the department ("Incidentally, it is impossible to sell a layette to a woman who is standing up.") When the books arrive, the mother will remember the "thoughtful service of the store":

> By this time you have established yourself on the most firm basis— on the universal platform of good fellowship, love, service, or whatever you wish to call it.
>
> Then, when you bring up the matter of merchandise to the mother, all the things which have been told by well-meaning friends and relatives have left her mind, and the clerk will have at least an equal chance.

"Fellowship" and "service" emerge as moves in a commercial confidence game.

No other trade press, or perhaps any other press, of the time so consistently advocated the connection between commerce and children's welfare as did the *Infants' Department*. At times, the moral cover slipped off allowing a view of what lay underneath. Appeals to the readership, however, were always doubled-edged, awkwardly straddling the line between the sacred realm of children's lives and the profane arena of the bottom line, as the following quotes illustrate:

> [Infant welfare] is a sound business venture which pays handsome dividends. It is something more than that, but if we merely look upon the dollars-and-cents issue there it is—a real, tangible thing which can be measured in bankable receivables.[52]
>
> The department stores . . . can do more than any other single agency to save the 300,000 infants who die *needlessly* in the United States every year. And saving babies is more than a good deed—it's good business.[53]
>
> Do you know that while general health is improving . . . infant mortality is not decreasing, and that Death reaps every year a toll of 250,000 babies under the age of one year, your prospective customers?[54]

Long before the success of General Motors was tied to that of the nation, Earnshaw and colleagues found the health and survival of children to be economically beneficial.

The moral cover of mother's interest and child health was not confined to the trade press audience of *Earnshaw's*. Commercial interests incorporated the vocabulary and moral stance of baby saving into their promotions. Across the country throughout the 1920s and 1930s, retailer and manufacturer advertisements for infants' clothes in newspapers, in women's magazines (*Ladies Home Journal, Harper's, Women's Home Companion*), and in the trade press (*Dry Goods Economist*) quickly adopted and aggressively promoted the health and developmental benefits of their garments. *Hygeia* magazine (now *Child Health*), first published in 1924 by the American Medical Association, and *Children, the Magazine for Parents* (1926, now *Parents* magazine) exemplify the new national print media, in which rational, scientifically based child care gained a forum to support the new consumer market for children's goods and child-care advice.

Two regular features that appeared in *Parents* in the 1920s are a case in point. One, "Mother Goes Shopping," was started "to help you in the selection of attractive and practical clothing for your boys and girls."[55] This monthly page displayed various types of clothing, accessories, and toys new to the retail market, complete with fashion commentary about how "fetching" a particular article might look on one's child. It also included the names of some New York retailers who carried the items. The other was a feature by Esther Cundiff of Teachers College, Columbia University, which discussed the healthful and developmental-psychology aspects of dressing children "properly." With articles entitled "Taste Good in Children's Clothing" and "Clothing and Behavior," this feature not only combined a middle-class taste in style with the adjudication of a university professor (as well as being a tease, since the clothing pictured was not for sale ready made but could be made only from patterns purchased through the magazine), it also signaled a view of the child as something other than a health concern.[56]

Beyond clothing specifically, "the mother" stood as a ubiquitous figure, both textually and visually, in consumer advertisements in *Parents* and elsewhere. Overseeing and arbitrating her children's consumption, this mother simultaneously monitored their growth and healthy adjustment to the world. By 1930, however, there was an indication of some dissent within the ranks of the commercial class. A writer for the advertising trade journal *Printer's Ink* scoffed at the overdone "mother appeal," stating that "by and large, the nation's children aren't all living under the constant threat of the Grim Reaper." The writer warned that if this pattern did not abate "mother will have to stop her ears against the din" of advertising, which would be "just too bad for a lot of good, honest products that mother ought to know about for the good of her youngsters."[57]

Earnshaw and his publication accomplished the initial work of institutionalizing the commodity status of children's clothing by providing moral cover for retailers, manufacturers, and advertisers to target with impunity the sacred, domestic sphere of mothers and children. This moral cover wielded scientific knowledge as the rational antidote to maternal traditionalism in the service of child welfare. It was an antidote that could be administered effectively through the medium of the "democratic" marketplace, which offered both a choice of goods and a better life for one's child. Yet it was a traditionalism of sorts, in the form of maternal instinct and self-effacement, that ultimately helped to erect a diffuse but coordinated strategy whereby children and mothers became constructed as fodder for commerce.

With each passing year, however, Earnshaw's insistence that infants' departments build their reputations on baby saving must have sounded more and more like a remnant of a bygone era. The children's wear industry took on a life of its own and steadily carved out a secure place in the commercial infrastructure throughout the 1920s and 1930s. In its first decade, it did so when the rise in real incomes and the extension of consumer credit offered unprecedented purchasing opportunities for a large number of families. By the late 1920s, children's wear was already becoming infused into the merchandising mix of the new low-priced chain stores, like Woolworth's, taking many middle- and working-class dollars from the department stores and virtually leaving behind the issue of child health.[58]

GEORGE EARNSHAW used the *Infants' Department* to position infants' and children's departments at the interstices of women's material and ideal culture. This "culture" was a historically specific configuration of meanings and material things which sat at one intersection between some forms of traditionalism and the pull of modernity. Earnshaw pioneered an industry by building the market at the demand end, that is, the consumer end. In the process, he and staff writers worked toward forging a model of the person—her wants, desires, preoccupations, and foibles—on which a retail structure could be erected.

This consuming subject, the self-effacing and sensitive mother, no doubt is a partial transformation of medical-scientific notions of "the feminine" and is thus constituted in larger regimes of power and knowledge. However, I believe there is also a particular commodity logic at work here. This "logic" is "ideology" in precisely Marx's and Engels's and Williams's sense of the term. That is, the commodity logic found in the pages of the *Infants' Department* is a form of interpolation which inverts social relations by presenting a constructed, historically specific relation as a natural one in the service of creating economic exchange value.[59]

In this case, the members of the merchant class converted the construct of the "eternal feminine," as represented by Woman and

Mother, into a persona essential to the creation of value, both economic and symbolic. This conversion took on added strength and intensity because the putative point and the purpose of the economic activity were to enhance, and even to "save," a child's life. The "natural" relation, the "natural" affinity between mother and child, was exploited and redeployed so that it could be realized only in market terms.

The "mother as consumer," in this context, is the rhetorical and analytic equivalent to Adam Smith's subject, whose inherent propensity is to "truck, barter and exchange." Here it is an explicitly gendered notion of "human nature" borne not only by the division of labor itself but also by the separation of spheres, and tied to childbearing. This mother stands as a cultural site, a node for the intersection of gendered notions of protection and responsibility; she also stands as a gatekeeper at the interface between home and market, between the sacred and profane, who must arbitrate between these spheres.

She must arbitrate because her child cannot do so. The children's wear industry built itself initially on the backs of young and expectant mothers. The industry as an industry began with *infants*, those who were believed ill equipped to express consumer desire. These children, the reader will notice, are given no gender by Earnshaw and his staff writers except where specific items of clothing were concerned. These children have no personality, no self, and not even instinct or impulses at this point. They stand, at this level of discourse, as moral Objects rather than social Subjects. Their innocence and sacredness were overstressed and over-elaborated in the very act of constructing them as beings perpetually at risk.

Mother thus moves to the fore as one who *can* be sold—with all altruistic purpose. The mother is the moral arbiter of children's goods, spaces, and beings; she is the shield against the profanity of self-indulgence, of extrinsic monetary value. As the middle term between market and child, the mother as consumer in a sense purifies economic exchange by imbuing commodities with sentiment. By virtue of her presence in the store, with her children among the goods, and by virtue of her presumed practice of scrutinizing the items she buys for her children, a mother's intervention effectively decommodifies the item, thus the child, and affirms their social bond outside the parameters and rhetoric of exchange.

In effect, the consuming mother can turn commodities into gifts, performing a kind of Frazerian "sympathetic magic" in much the same way that Daniel Miller describes shopping as a ritual of love and sacrifice.[60] Motherhood, beginning in this era, thus becomes expressed and express*able* through consumption—as consumer practice—and thereby commodified, emerging as a value-in-exchange.

4

Pediocularity: From the

Child's Point of View

The "needs" and "desires" of mothers offered department store managers an opportunity to organize their children's merchandise according to age. The construct of the consuming mother together with the rhetoric of baby saving provided a dual shield against the naked calculation of the marketplace and thereby allowed merchants to transgress—or perhaps, transform—a moral boundary. The mother, of course, did not disappear once her children grew out of infancy, nor did the need to clothe them.

It was a logical and consistent step for many merchants and manufacturers to expand into older children's sizes and styles. Children's departments that catered to boys and girls from birth through the high school years emerged in the late 1920s and developed through the early 1940s alongside and in addition to infants' departments in department stores, as well as becoming a staple of the independent store chains such as Sears and Montgomery Ward. These new retail arrangements were to an extent built on the emergent consumption patterns of mothers who were becoming habituated to the organization of the children's wear retail environment. At the same time, an ascendant ethos of consumption is evident in children's wear and elsewhere, one which increasingly recognized "the child" as an individuated, volitional, and socially legitimate commercial actor—that is, as a consumer.

The figure of the child consumer which arises in and extends from the 1930s, I argue, instantiates something beyond the simple material fact that an increasing number and variety of goods, including clothing and accessories, were being made for and available to children. This decade represents a turning point not only in the children's wear industry but, more fundamentally, in childhood. For perhaps the first time in history, the perspective of "the child"—its vantage point on the world—becomes incorporated into market institutions and thereby becomes institutionalized. In varying degrees, merchants, manufacturers, advertisers, store and clothing designers, and researchers began to take, impute, or otherwise garner a child's viewpoint about goods, spaces, and social relations of consumption, favoring it over the mother's.

"Child-centered" does not capture the profundity of this change because that term reinscribes the perspective of parents and adults who are centered on the child. "Permissive parenting," so often associated with Benjamin Spock in the 1950s, also is inadequate in the way that it reinforces a preoccupation with adults' way of seeing and doing. Rather, the shift in question occurs on a more fundamental level—I am tempted to say it is Copernican in structure. I have in mind not just a shift of focus from adult to child, but a change toward privileging the *viewpoint* of the child, making it the basis of authority and action. "Pediocularity"—or, seeing with children's eyes—is an apt neologism for decentering the adult view and centering that of the child.[1]

The perspectival shift I aim to illustrate in this and ensuing chapters has not been singular, unidirectional, or inevitable. It has, however, the character of a historical trajectory. Gestures in this direction can be found, for instance, in Ellen Key's *Century of the Child* (1909), in which she advocated for children's self-determining rights. Ellen Seiter finds a similar emergent belief in the authority of the child in the popular, middle-class directed childrearing literature of the 1920s. Martha Wolfenstein also identifies a new attitude toward childrearing emergent in the '40s, "fun morality," which was based on a new valuation of the child's "impulses" as "benevolent rather than dangerous" and therefore to be nurtured and followed by mothers. The psycho-historian Lloyd deMause posited a "helping mode" of childrearing, arising in the 1950s, whereby the child "knows better than the parent what it needs at each stage of life."[2]

In each of these historical articulations, acknowledging or taking the child's point of view is insinuated not only as a duty but as a moral imperative, because that which emanates from "the child" is assumed to indicate what is right and correct. Pediocularity thus repeats and reinscribes childhood innocence in the ways that it encodes children's "special nature" in their presumed, and presumably unpolluted, gaze. Adults would do well to find their way back to seeing the world as a child, or so a common discourse instructs, but this return to Eden is impossible. The Romantic child of the eighteenth century, Anne Higonnet writes, "shrinks away to an unattainable distance from the adult present." Romantic children (or conceptions thereof) cannot know adults because "they are by definition unconscious of adult desires, including adults' desires for childhood. The Romantic child is desirable precisely to the extent that it does not understand desire."[3] As we will see, the consumer child of the twentieth century, somewhat paradoxically, approaches adults, the adult present, and adult desire *through* consumption, all the while maintaining distinctiveness *as* a child—by keeping a child's perspective.

Consumer markets in and of themselves did not create pediocularity and its attendant impetus to invert authority relations between parent or adult on the one hand and child on the other, but neither are they inconsequential. Markets and market mechanisms are inseparable from the historical process of elevating the child to more inclusive levels of personhood. It is through the medium of the marketplace that children become recognized, treated, and even deferred to as persons by adults on something other than an episodic basis (beyond the confines of the home, playground, or classroom). Early radio and film spoke directly to children, as did comic books and newspaper comics. The candy counter was designed for children's eyes as well. Through consumption, children's "wants," "needs," and "desires"—be they framed as "authentic" and arising from within the child or "manufactured" and created by profit-making industries—gain legitimacy as worthy of large-scale social action, such as the creation of business and industries based on them.[4]

A child's point of view, of course, had been engaged and taken seriously before the large-scale rise of consumer industries. A toy is a toy in large part because it is made with a child's view in mind. Reading materials for children are not useful if they are not in certain ways age-sensitive in both form and content. These products engaged the child's perspective for children's reasons and uses, however. With the coming of the modern consumer society in the early 1900s, seeing through children's eyes unfolds crescively as a way to create value, economic value, such that entire industries are built up around the child's perspective. The rise of educational toys in the 1920s and '30s, as Gary Cross points out, relied on a combination of nineteenth-century child-centered educational philosophy, children's desires for autonomy, and middle-class parents' concerns about imparting skills to their children. It is a formula for fusing the lingering sacral innocence of children with the profane calculability endemic to the workings of the market. The result, over time, has been an ever-proliferating and decidedly children's consumer culture.[5]

The child as choosing subject forms the bedrock of the consumer culture of childhood. This is a construct and a notion which appeals to deeply held beliefs about subjects and subjectivity under market capitalism—the sovereignty of the consumer, individualism, and economic rationality. The trick with and tension around consuming children always returns to their uneasy status as knowing, choosing subjects. Hence, mothers and fathers never completely leave the scene, forever lurking in the food aisles and at the checkout counters. Parents in the 1930s certainly did not, and now certainly have not, abdicated their veto power over children's purchase requests. The switch in perspective from mother (or adult) to child does not obviate mothers or adults; it situates them reactively *in relation to* the "child's perspective," in whatever manner it is configured.[6]

This chapter and chapter 5 focus on essentially the same period, roughly 1915–40. I examine how merchants and market observers assumed, imputed, or otherwise garnered the child's point of view to forge useable models of the consuming child—that is, as a person with self-knowledge, desire, and a growing social right to express that desire. Chapter 4 focuses on three sites for the elaboration of the child consumer: merchants' anecdotes about children's "wants" as encountered on the sales floor of department stores, discussions about "appropriate" girls' clothing styles in both trade and consumer publications, and the rise of the "Toddler" as a clothing size range, merchandising category and named phase of the life course. Chapter 5 deals more directly with the commercial basis for changing size ranges and the development of age-graded retail space for children. Together these chapters illustrate various contexts where positing the child's perspective functions as a basis for commercial innovation. In the process, the knowing, consuming child moves from periphery to center in market dealings.

FRONT AND CENTER: THE CHILD
AS CONSUMER

In the first decades of the twentieth century, proprietors of various commercial establishments had ample opportunity to interact with and come to know children in the role of customers. In urban areas, as David Nasaw discusses, laboring children spent their money in restaurants, nickelodeon theaters, in arcades and pool halls, as they worked in or passed through downtown areas. Except for toys, the candy counter, and perhaps certain magazines and comics, however, most of the goods and services that working or nonworking children purchased during this time were not designed or offered with their exclusive "needs" or "wants" in mind. Consequently, as discussed in chapter 3, there was little children's merchandising (the physical grouping of goods) to speak of until after the First World War, toys and toy departments aside.[7]

Merchants thus had experience with, and models of, children as *customers* rather than as *consumers* in this period—the former indicating a role enacted somewhat regularly at the point of commercial transactions, the latter designating a continuous identity regardless of whether purchases are being made at any given time. Merchants' anecdotes about encounters with children in their stores circulated through the trade press from the second decade of the century onward. In many ways, these stories invoked models or constructs of "the child" which served as a vital currency of business knowledge at a time well before market research on children was regarded as useful and morally palatable.[8]

Store owners recognized early the kind of influence a child can have over the family pocketbook in the homes of the middling classes, which were becoming increasingly centered around nonlaboring, school-attending children.[9] A woman's "duty" as the family purchasing agent increasingly coincided with her role as mother—the "influence" of the ever-present and needy child on the mother was, and continues to be, great. In 1914 the *Dry Goods Economist*, for instance, lauded the first Children's Bureau Baby Week promotion by an appeal that was to become well worn in ensuing years: "Keep the baby's interest in mind, and the baby's immediate family will be interested in your store. And the baby itself will quickly grow into a real customer of the store. Its needs will grow as the baby grows, too. Don't forget that!"[10]

Here "the child" is polysemous. "Baby" is something of a "growth machine," standing for the future not of the nation or of humanity, but of the store. The child represents a growing market, not as a static individual or an abstract type but as an ontogenic and biological being. The very fact of its existence and physical transformation over the life cycle produces a certain form of scarcity and thus certain kinds of needs.

The child also stands for something other than itself—for "the family" and, in particular, for the purchasing power of the family. It provides the strong link in the chain from familial affection to commerce. Nonlaboring children represented an insignificant source of sales as direct customers in the years 1910–30. Nevertheless, the sentimental value and familial affection congealing in middle-class childhood, by the magic of market calculus, could be translated into economic exchange value with relative ease.

In 1915, for instance, *System*, a retail trade magazine, advocated treating "Johnny and his nickel" with respect, because they represent a "buying public which has a far larger purse than Johnny's." The larger public is "all of his grown-up relatives and neighbors." Not only do the candy counter and toy shop have obvious direct appeal to children, the article continues, "but the tie that holds them to older persons—their parents—is the deepest of all affections; and the man who buys things because of some direct or indirect pleasure or benefit which the purchase will cause his children, is legion." When the sale is made "by the concern whose product is altogether or principally sold to grown-ups, then the appeal is indirect; not baldly commercial. It is likely to be just so much more effective on that very account." It is the child's position in the commercial chain which determines that it is important to "know" children and to treat them with the same respect accorded to other customers.[11]

This article also reported on a small-town druggist who ignored the streaks caused by children putting their hands and noses against his glass displays: "Children, as a rule, are very sensitive about the treatment accorded them. . . . Therefore the druggist just mentioned makes it his business to treat every boy and girl who comes into his store with as much care as he would any older person." It is "easier to wipe off marks than to lose business because of scolding the child. . . . But, as a matter of fact, the attitude of mind which makes a merchant or his clerks polite to old and young alike is worthwhile in dollars and cents. It wins the child's friendship and the older person's confidence."[12]

This is common sense. It is rule-of-thumb knowledge about the kinds of beings that children were in 1915 and what their position was in relation to parents and to the family's purse strings. Seeing and treating the child as a person, as a customer, and, importantly, as a person *when* that child is a customer wins the child's good will and, sellers hope, that of their parents, all of which potentially translates into regular sales.

Winning the child over was apparently a paramount concern in the formative years of the children's industry, as the child-customer became an increasingly accepted, if not expected social role. The advertising trade weekly *Printer's Ink* featured an article in 1922 that advocated the use of premiums as essentially mnemonic devices to encourage the child's future patronage: "Children, particularly, are keen on patronizing places where they get a little extra for their money. They urge their parents to take them to the barber shops that have the most imposing hobby horses or that give them a celluloid ball or some other souvenir. When sent to a store, they are inclined to favor the merchant who gives them a lollipop for their patronage. Any remembrance, no matter how slight, will win the favor of the child."[13] As is typical for this period, there is a lack of any age designation, implying, it would seem, that an age range is assumed. The absence of research or intimation of systematic study of the child indicates the extent to which knowledge about what children like, who they are, and what they do is taken from personal observation and anecdotes from retailers.

As folk psychology, this kind of informal knowledge about children served retailers and advertisers well for several decades. One writer in *Printer's Ink Monthly* summarized the dimensions of the child market in 1923: "First, the boy and girl are in themselves markets for certain products: toys, candies, clothing, etc. Second, the child can have a definite if indirect influence on the sale of products for adult use. Third, the child of today becomes the big buyer of tomorrow."[14] The article continues by detailing advertising efforts to capture children's attention, including a Western Electric coloring book, Dutch Boy paint Jingles and colored pictures, and mythological stories created around chocolate characters by the Ideal Cocoa and Chocolate Company.

"Story book" food is said to be an "excellent example" of adapting a product to children's use. "Animal Crackers are really only cookies made in the shape of animals, and Ideal toys are just milk chocolate romanticized." The strategy is direct: "Each idea gets at the parent through the child and at the same time plants the company's advertising in the subconscious mind, so that in later years the adult will find himself or herself influenced unwittingly by advertising done years before." No sentimentality about childhood in this "backstage" publication.[15]

This "storybook strategy"—the attempt to associate products with children's characters and imagery—makes commercial appeal invisible or at least innocuous to parents. Perhaps because this approach is not as forthright and obvious as a direct advertisement, it also effectively circumvents the parent and appeals directly to the child. In order to effect this strategy, however, it is necessary to have studied, or at least intuited, what and how "the child" thinks. In much the same way, comic book and comic strip characters (which turned into radio characters and, later, television characters) also tend to circumvent parental scrutiny and reaffirm a child's world filled with play and fantasy.[16]

Throughout the 1920s and 1930s, advertisers and merchants came to the realization that grabbing the child's attention through story books or characters and other items of children's culture helped pull the parents into the store. By 1930 an advertiser was asking the readers in *Printer's Ink Monthly*, "Has enough attention been given to the appeal to children, the buyers of a few years hence; or is this a far-fetched idea?" He was making a case for the importance of trademarks and brand name or company recognition. Echoing what many "modern psychologists" contend, the author pointed out that "the majority of permanent impressions which influence our actions and desires are received before the age of six."

Children's unique perspective has clear implications for package design. With a hunch that children favor "abstract"' over "concrete" design, the author conducted "some case studies" with a four-year-old child (clearly his daughter). He found that she could identify not only children's products by the images on the packaging but also adult products in a similar manner. "Is it not the same with us adults? What packages stick out most clearly as we think back to childhood days?" he inquired. Here, not only is the child's experience held up as worthy of examination in its own right, but the child's memory that every adult can supposedly access must also be consulted for its truth-revealing quality.[17]

The learning curve for advertisers and merchants was apparently steep. Another writer for *Printer's Ink* asserted in 1931 that "manufacturers are awakening to the realization that even youngsters of two and three are a market whose tastes can be cultivated profitably."[18] If advertisers can get children to recognize and pay attention to their products, then these items may become part of one's "lasting impressions." Advertisers and marketers began to realize that turning children from intermittent customers who episodically make purchases into more or less continuous consumers required seeing the world through their eyes.

Commercially appealing to the child quickly became less something to hide and more something to pursue. In 1932 *Printer's Ink Monthly* made the case for specially designed packages for children, stating, "Nearly everything that appeals to children appeals to grownups. But the reverse is not always true. Children are rarely interested in a product designed for adults."[19] Again we see a generalization about children without age specifications, apparently based on rule-of-thumb knowledge. The writer advocated asking children about their perceptions and designing packages to appeal to them. Children's views and choices were beginning to be invoked as indications of a legitimate, authoritative, desiring self. Note how designing for adults is counter-indicative of a children's culture.

One *Printer's Ink* article from 1933 lists an array of media and promotions—display cases, radio serials, premiums, miniature models, clubs, games, special packages, story books, and essay contests—as effective means to reach children directly.[20] In the 1930s clubs, contests, and collectibles proved especially appealing for children who could send away in the mail for "membership kits" and the like. Advertisers and marketers were quick to pick up on the trend and soon flooded the market. These promotional efforts increased sales as well as the visibility of the company's name or brand. A welcome addition, perhaps a sign of hope, premiums, clubs, and contests became a central aspect of many promotions to children throughout the 1930s, supported by radio shows and an emerging set of popular culture heroes to "worship." Additionally, promoters hoped that these efforts would lead to loyal consumers when the children grew into adulthood.[21]

If children were appropriate targets for premium marketing, they were still off limits for direct market study.[22] They could only be understood through anecdotal accounts and through analogy from psychological science. An article in *Printer's Ink Monthly* in 1933, written by a psychology professor from Northwestern University, discusses the results of national advertising studies "among 10,000 women and other consumers." These "other consumers" were not children, however.[23] It is difficult to manufacture and advertise for a "child's world" if that world remains only vaguely understood.

These rules of thumb and anecdotes would not remain for long at the level of informal knowledge. The first moment or phase in disciplining the knowledge about children's consumption practices involved the direct application of child psychology to children's market behavior. The most prominent practitioner in this area in the 1930s was E. Evalyn Grumbine, assistant publisher and advertising director of *Child Life* magazine. Grumbine had written a number of articles summarizing and extending academic research on such topics as children's color preferences.[24]

In 1938 Grumbine published *Reaching Juvenile Markets: How to*

Advertise, Sell and Merchandise through Boys and Girls, in which she offered the following age divisions of the children's market:

GROUP I	infancy through three years
GROUP II	four through six years
GROUP III	seven through nine years
GROUP IV	ten through twelve years (girls)
	ten through thirteen years (boys)
GROUP V	thirteen through fifteen years (girls)
	fourteen through seventeen years (boys)
GROUP VI	sixteen and beyond (girls)
	eighteen and beyond (boys)[25]

Gender differentiation begins around puberty and incorporates the tendency for the earlier physical and perhaps social maturation of girls.

She makes no claims about the desire or potential of capturing children in the first group. Children in GROUP II exhibit "imagination with a broader scope" and can be capitalized on with products utilizing fairy tales and fantastical characters to capture the child's attention. Self-assertion and self-confidence "are strong" and "purpose, enthusiasm and persistence develop" for the seven- to nine-year-olds of GROUP III. These tendencies were successfully exploited by Cracker Jack, with toys placed in every box of its product, which children could then collect and trade.[26]

In GROUP IV, the ten- to twelve- or thirteen-year-old range for boys, Grumbine cites the campaign by the Hecko-H-O Company (maker of cereal oats) to link the child radio star and cowboy Bobby Benson to its product. Through a series of media promotions, boys were encouraged to become members of the H-bar-O Rangers Club by sending in a boxtop from the cereal. In return, they would receive a membership certificate, ranger's button, and picture of the star and his horse, among other things. A reported ninety thousand children became members of the club in the first three months of the campaign. The reasons for success are transparent for Grumbine. Boys and girls in Groups III and IV have a "high spirit of adventure," and "the influence of those of their own age group is stronger than the influence of adults, hence they pick heroes of their own age."[27]

In addition to reading hero worship and a penchant for collecting things into the nature of children, the development toward personal autonomy—another "inherent" characteristic—helps make commercial efforts morally palatable. Movement toward autonomy can be nurtured and profited from by many manufacturers if they (1) understand that children do not want to be treated like children (also recall the example above of "Johnny and his nickel"), (2) appeal directly to children through appropriate media (without alienating mothers), and (3) offer child-scaled goods and services (watches, telegrams, and toasters that allow children to make toast for the "whole family"), all of which purportedly help make children feel connected to the "real world" while associating particular products with those positive feelings. Along these lines, *Child Life* magazine sponsored building a "modern home" for children with child-scaled furniture and fixtures, put together with the cooperation of 108 manufacturers.[28]

For Grumbine, children's autonomy is rich with the potential for exchange value: "An important factor in the growth and development of the juvenile market is the trend toward stimulating greater self-expression in children themselves. Progressive mothers and educators not only allow children to make their own decisions during the early years of childhood, but urge them to choose their own clothes and work out plans for their own rooms."[29] Freedom of expression, the apex of freedoms in a liberal democratic society, is coupled with perhaps the noblest form of selfless action—that of enhancing the child's ability to make choices. Goods, products, commodities serve as the age-transcendent media for engaging in this expression of self.

To "know" the child is to know the age of the child, and to know the age of the child in this sense is to comprehend the appropriate timing and cadence for "self-expression," not to coerce a singular vocabulary: "Instead of being exploited, children can benefit materially from their experiences by taking part in the various activities promoted by the national advertisers, if those responsible for creating campaigns will work from a sound basis of knowledge of the child—his growth and development during childhood. Advertisers can thus contribute something of value to children during their formative years; at the same time they will secure better results from their advertising to boys and girls and spread much good will among parents and educators."[30] In this way, markets are made to serve children; exploitation is avoided by consulting objective, disinterested knowledge about the nature of childhood in order to intuit and make use of a child's view on the world.

From about 1915 onward, merchants realized that treating children as individuals with identifiable desires and concerns of their own could increase business. Once the child's perspective was acknowledged, it was but a small step toward studying it and creating products, displays, and advertising techniques to appeal to it. It is a somewhat larger step to legitimize this perspective, especially when it takes the form of desire for consumer goods which call bodily attention to the child, like clothing. In the case of children's fashions, legitimation of the child's view and desire came in the form of "training" children in good taste.

BEAUTY, SIMPLICITY, AND FUNCTIONALITY: A PUBLIC VIEW

Early in the century the ability of a child to change styles and exercise discretion over purchases was reserved for older girls. As early as 1902 a writer for *Dry Goods Economist* relates that "children's styles are more or less staple and are not subject to the changes and whims of fashion as are the styles of women . . . But when the young girl reaches the age of 15 she begins to have opinions of her own in regard to fashion . . . and if the buyer wishes his department to find the same degree of favor in the eyes of the coming generation that it has so long held in the parents' estimation, it behooves him to exercise utmost discretion and discernment in his selection of models."[31] The child in this excerpt is in her teens. Lacking a market for ready-made clothing for younger children at this time, it is doubtful that merchants had much opportunity to observe younger children on the retail floor and to formulate a model of the "child customer."

By 1912 the consumer press began to discuss the educational, social, and psychological benefits of children's garments. A writer for *Home Progress* equated the "greater freedom" granted to children and a "growing desire" on their part to determine their own wardrobe, claiming that "even in the very young, happiness or unhappiness is caused through certain costumes which they wear."

The author advises parents to "give the children a chance to choose whenever it is possible, and study the 'why' of their choice."[32]

This is an early expression of a view that was to become prevalent in the late '20s and take hold in the '30s: the child "knows" better than the parent about his or her well-being or self-being. This "knowledge" may not be expressed as reflective, purposeful thinking but as "internal" or "instinctive." It is an early indication of what deMause called the "helping mode" of childrearing,[33] in which "virtue" is seen as natural and coming from within the child. In this instance, the parent is to observe and study the child to discover the child's preferences.

The belief that a true form of knowledge is immanent in the child fit uneasily with the traditional concern about children becoming inappropriately (and perhaps pathologically) selfconscious about their appearance. One important source of selfconsciousness is being dressed inappropriately for an occasion. Adequate dress alleviated the problem. An article in *Children's Royal*, a short-lived trade journal directed to upper-class courtiers (1919–23), offers the view that it is the child, rather than the adult, who is the focus of the clothing and occasion: "This donning a party frock for a party and a play frock for play resulted in a total lack of self-consciousness of clothes."[34]

The writer asserts that boys, who find dressing a bore, do not have the same inherent vanity as girls. The way to combat the self-conscious vanity of girlhood is to emphasize harmony between the child, the occasion, and her clothing. Dressmakers, the readers were told, now emphasize the social hygiene, not the handicap of clothes. The article ends with the admonition, "Don't suppress a child's spirit."[35] This position was to become standard advice by the late '20s.

Vanity and ostentation, both "dangerous" consequences of overfocusing on self and appearance, have a decidedly feminine location. From an article in *Dry Goods Economist* from 1920: "That woman rules in the world of fashion—a long-accepted adage—is now being challenged to-day. Thus one concludes as she watches prim little Miss Dorothy wandering about in the big store selecting her wardrobe. Mother apparently comes along just to pay the bills . . . Miss Dorothy goes to parties, just like mother. She knows what she likes, and mother lets her select what pleases her most, and so Miss Dorothy becomes Queen in her world of fashion." Presenting some of the newest items available on the market in "dainty little dresses" and "smartly tailored head wear," the article is centrally about securing the child's trade. The manager of a children's department relates that "grouping in this one spot everything for children from 2 to 6, from little vests to shoes, aids materially in making shopping easier for mother, as well as increasing sales through suggestion."[36] Here is the inkling of a suggestion to merchandise for the two- to six-year-old. In this case, the appeal is a dual one—spatial organization for mother's convenience, like that beginning to be implemented in infants' departments at the time, in addition to merchandise appealing to the young child whose point of view is thought to have a measurable influence on her mother's actions.[37]

Ostentation—albeit good for business in the form of "influence" sales—not only makes a child self-conscious, but also draws attention away from the child as a person and toward her or his accoutrements, away from inner value and toward extrinsic markers of value. One woman in the *Ladies Home Journal* advised in 1913 that "boys look best in tans, browns, grays and blues, and the beauty of the little garments should be in fit and finish rather than in any ornamentation." "How a child looks" came to preoccupy many writers in popular journals throughout the 1920s. Articles such as "Your Child's Right to Beauty," "Dressing the Well-Dressed Children," and "Good Looks: Let Your Child Have Her Chance to Be Beautiful" in women's magazines of the time point to the increasing social and sartorial visibility of children in the public world of the urban, white middle classes.[38]

Whether it is the child or the mother who chooses suitable clothing for her children, the thrust of the discourse guides her to acknowledge and act on the child's point of view. In this view, the social world of observers (peers, classmates, and so on) becomes central to the child's conception of self and self-presentation. To recognize the "social hygiene" of dress for children is at the same time to recognize the potential harm that the social world can inflict. "Over-" or "inappropriately" dressed children may not look well and therefore not feel well, especially if they are made conscious of their dress.

The effect of clothing on the child came to occupy a substantial amount of copy in both the trade and the consumer press. All writers assented to the notion that "simplicity" is the key to "the child's" happiness; no one took the idea of simplicity literally and called for a uniform for children or an end to children's fashions. Rather, the cumulative effect of much of this "talk" was to elaborate and extend the relationship between a child's well-being and her or his clothing, helping to integrate childhood into a sartorial-commercial world of shared display and concern about appearance.

Esther Cundiff, of the Teachers College of Columbia University, provided a voice of expertise and authority on this issue. She wrote numerous advice articles for *Parents* magazine, often in the form of fashion spreads which presented the styles that were available from the magazine's pattern service:

> Good taste in children's clothing has not had enough attention from the average mother . . . It is not only important in the everyday life of the child, but is also desirable to develop it for manhood and womanhood, and training along this line should begin early.
>
> The young person, who was a child yesterday, is suddenly resentful of what she considers "babyish" clothes.[39] She insists on the latest style in sport models and expresses a deep-seated desire for a black satin dress. In the meantime, her brother develops an amazing taste in sport hose, brilliant neckties and baggy knickers. He voices the opinion that a raccoon coat is essential to his manhood.

Here, in 1927, we see an early fissure opening between the taste and knowledge of the parent and those of the child—one that would become emblematic of youth culture in ensuing decades. The mother is potentially at fault for not paying attention to the child's "everyday life." Style enters the picture not for its own sake, but as an expression of a child's emerging sense of "taste," and thus as an emerging selfhood, which must be trained.[40]

If "good taste" benefits the child in the future, then training the child in these "principles" is a duty. Stylistic clothing for older children enables a child to fit into a larger social sphere of her or his own. "Social health" is realized as a kind of invisibility of dress, a gesture toward "fitting in" or "belonging." It is a virtue that avoided "showing off" at a time when "flaming youth" and flappers were being flouted in the general press.

"The child," here as elsewhere, is most often a girl. The training of the child in "taste" or in the ways of style was somewhat of a mantra in industry and consumer publications alike during the late '20s and '30s. Any steps made along these lines were always framed carefully so as to avoid the implication that the writer was advocating a vain, self-conscious "Little Miss Dorothy."

One writer in *Parents*, for instance, sees "educating girls from age six to sixteen in the art of dress" (note the age range) as preparation for the exercise of choice. Clothing, she says, is supposed to contribute to one's *self*-satisfaction, and not to the satisfaction of one's neighbors. Hence, she argues, the power of self-expression comes only through the power of choice and, in this case, the choice of dress. "One can't begin too early to give a girl confidence in her own judgment so that she may make decisions that satisfy her when she is grown."[41]

Clothing, especially for females, is central to one's identity: "There is no time in a woman's life when she does not like clothes."[42] But controversy inevitably will ensue between mother and daughter if the mother persists in imposing her will: "Much of the controversy between mothers and daughters is over the matter of clothes, and most of it is the result of the mother's feeling that she has the right to dress her child. The result of such a policy is that at the first possible moment, namely when she can lay hands on some money, the daughter runs out and buys in a spirit of abandon. When the packages come home the trouble begins."[43] The solution, again, is located within the child. The approach is one of active self-restraint on the part of the mother who should purchase clothes that appeal to and sensorially satisfy the child. Mother can only guide the child along her own lines of taste, revealing at strategic times the criteria for appropriateness: "If there is any class distinction in clothes it is not between the woman who wears expensive clothes and the one who wears inexpensive ones, but between the woman who wears the right thing at the right time and the one who wears the wrong thing. Let the children, when buying, have in mind what the thing is for. If the costume is for a party let them be as fancy as they like. Gradually the seed will grow into a clearly defined policy."[44] Thus, a feeling of quality can be nurtured in the child.

In a similar vein, the same writer continues, taste can be inculcated by mothers who should allow the child to experiment with color. Most children are said to have a good color sense but very few have a feel for line, she argues. The eye for beauty is an educated one: "Very scant skirts are offensive to us not probably because they are immodest but because they are ugly, because the tight short skirt is inartistic. A full-length mirror offers the best means of educating taste in line. Don't be afraid that it will make your daughters vain. I know of no better preventative against vanity than the habit of consulting a mirror."

The proscriptions for dress should be read, in part, as an expression of middle-class anxiety in the face of a changing economy of taste, in Pierre Bourdieu's sense. Big discount stores like Montgomery Ward, Sears, and others in the mid- to late '20s began to impinge on the department store's domain by offering many goods, including clothing, at prices lower than what could be had at the major urban establishments. Concomitantly and consequently, stylistic class distinction in children's and adults' clothes became less pronounced, prompting department stores to voice concerns about consumers "trading down"—or purchasing what they considered lower-quality merchandise. The discourse on taste in children's clothing, evident in these quotes, at once invokes a sense of children's personhood as well as a backhand recognition of the equation of class standing with right and wrong taste. Taste, for the writer quoted above, is apparently a product of education and not of bloodline; hence the concern for transmitting it properly to the next generation. Cultural capital in this way can be nurtured through female comportment and display.[45]

These parental advisories from the late '20s situate clothing and clothing choice directly in a developmental sequence, corresponding to the acquisition of self-confidence, inner virtue, and judgment, rather than only age-appropriateness. Discernment is the issue. The mother returns not only as the arbiter of consumption, but at times as a potential obstacle to consumption to the extent that she intervenes and acts as an instructor in the art of self-expression. The intervention, this time, occurs along the lines of taste and beauty for the older child, rather than the lines of health for the infant.

No writer in the '20s and '30s is yet prepared to give all decisions over to the child; some things need to be taught. Power, in the relationship between parent and child, often surfaces in these re-monstrations. The child may be seen and acted toward as a person, and given the status of a person, but this status is not yet complete. From an article in *Babyhood* in 1930: "If [a child of five] is forced to wear clothes that are different from those worn by other children around him, he is more likely than not to become shy and self-conscious—or else sullen and perverse, according to his nature. If he is over-dressed, he may become self-centered—developing an exaggerated sense of his own importance, which is a most deplorable trait in youngsters. If he is carelessly or conspicuously dressed, he may be subjected to the criticism of others—always a devastating experience for a child."[46] The complexity of "making" full persons is revealed here. As a subject with feelings, the child is "forced" and "subjected." Appearance must match some inner truth with the social truth of the child's peer world.[47] It is never too early to teach children quality, and early lessons inform future behavior: "the child made to realize from the very start that simplicity, modesty and good quality in dress are the distinguishing marks of the lady and gentleman, is not likely to be attracted by glittering ornaments and 'loud' patterns later in life." Again, the class concerns of the writer translate into proscriptions which, paradoxically, "natural-ize" taste as a function of "education." Simplicity and modesty stand for a restrained, bourgeois sense of comportment.[48]

These same concerns expressed to the public translate into busi-ness opportunities when presented to the trade audience. In 1932 a writer in *Earnshaw's* invoked similar reasoning as she explained to the trade audience that "modern youngsters" are definitely "style conscious," a situation which can be nurtured to the benefit of all: "Barber shops which, formerly, refused to accept children as cash customers, now derive a large revenue from finger-waving the 'babies.' Best & Co. advertise a 'Tots'' manicure as a means of developing pride in fastidious finger tips. 'Foolishness!' 'Artificial-ity!' you say. So, what? To teach a child daintiness through the enticing medium of a grown-up manicure is no crime."[49] The di-dactic intent again serves as moral cover, protecting childhood with the shield of social training against both vanity and bald commercial intent.

Children evidently could wear "fashion" and be fashionable so long as the social attention paid to style did not hide their intrinsic worth as learning, emerging persons. In accepting the inevitability of the stylistic change in children's garments, these writers still deemed it important to maintain some lines of demarcation between childhood and adulthood in this manner. Giving over to children the "right" to choose their own clothing was tempered by the argument that making choices was an "educational" process. In this way, the rhetoric both maintained the distinction between market and child and united the two in the form of "choice" and "individuality," highly regarded values of democratic, consumer capitalism.

THE RISE OF THE "TODDLER" AS SUBJECT AND MERCHANDISING CATEGORY

The "toddler" is by far the most elaborately nuanced commercial persona to have arisen in the 1930s to demarcate a phase of childhood. It offers a concentrated illustration of the indispensability of a knowing, consuming subject to serve as the focus for and embodiment of commercial appeals. The advent of "toddler" also marks a turning point in children's consumer culture, and in culture in general, in the way that commercial interests and concerns coalesce and interact to essentially institutionalize a new category of person and new phase of the life course. It is no longer useful, after the toddler, to think of a commodity as an "object outside us," as Marx famously remarked, for commodification becomes increasingly inseparable from the very journey through the early life course.[50]

The term "toddler" appears to have been in use only since the late eighteenth century, according to the *Oxford English Dictionary* (compact edition). It refers simply to "one who toddles, especially a child."[51] Currently, it is both a scheduled period of childrearing and a clothing size. It starts at about the age of one, when children begin to walk unsteadily, or "toddle," and ends around three, when toilet training is assumed to be complete.

As a clothing size, it is indicated by the letter "T" after a numbered size on clothing tags, to avoid confusion with similarly numbered sizes for the "children's" range. That is, a 3T is a size three in the toddler range rather than a size three in the "children's" range of 3 to 6. Toddlers' clothing currently comes in sizes ranging from 1T to 6T to accommodate varied body sizes.[52]

The difference between a toddler's garment and a children's garment of the same numbered size is its style and fit, that is how the child *looks* rather than the physical size of the garment. Toddlers still wear diapers and garments must be made full enough to accommodate them. Also, the stance of the child is different from that of older children or adults, because toddlers sway back and walk flat-footed in an effort to balance. Consequently, their stomach protrudes. Children's wear designers closely adhere to these developmental constraints.[53]

Sometime around 1930, the term "toddler" began to be used with great frequency as a size range and as a merchandising category, and soon after, as an age-stage designation. Before the 1930s, "toddler" seemed to refer only to the children themselves, especially those aged around two, three, and four years. For instance, an article entitled "Summer Vogue for Toddlers" in the consumer magazine *Babyhood* (June 1924) displays fashion sketches of models but gives no age range.

The market potential for toddlers as a size-style range, however, was not addressed until the mid-'30s. A writer for *Earnshaw's*, after touring a manufacturing house that specialized in toddler dresses, speculated about the promise for this range in 1934: "And if it requires so many dresses to take care of these one-two-threes, what about all the other garments worn by these same ages? Then, too, there are the little boys, with all their needs to be supplied. These little boys and girls grow up into two-to-sixers, and on and on."[54] A size-style range, just barely visible in the '30s, had already aroused speculation about merchandising and stock turnover as the children grew into the next size-style range. This writer offers the emergent formula for what was to become the hallmark of children's wear merchandising: as each size range becomes associated with a general style or look for that age, the next-older range offers the possibility of new distinctions on which new value may be added.

In 1936 the "toddler," as a commercial persona or construct, began to take shape. A long-time industry observer explains some of the characteristics of toddlers in terms that resonate with merchants catering to a small but commercially viable middle class: "Toddler dresses are made up in crisp batiste, in organdy and dimity, in swiss or shimmering broadcloth, in dainty pastels and adorable prints. For the Toddler boy, they are more tailored, naturally, yet keeping a touch of the baby, which satisfies both mother and father. . . . . All these are designed and cut to fit the busy little folks who are just beginning to realize their importance in the scheme of things. Little boys, little girls each have their definite niche in the world of style and merchandise today. . . . Infants' or baby clothes won't do. Clothes for these Toddlers are made with the proper fit and feel which do so much for a child's appearance and poise of mind. Even a small child likes to feel properly dressed." Toddlers require their own type of undergarments, also: "Proper under- clothing for these toddler styles is also quite necessary. Undies must follow the curves of the body and allow freedom of move- ment. They must be designed for ease and convenience in training to sanitary habits. Yet they must not interfere with the style and lines of the outer garments. The sagging panties and bulgy bloom- ers of yesteryear are gone from sight." The article concludes by urging retailers and buyers to "study this interesting episode" and to include and feature toddlers' in their infants' department, ap- parently as a subdepartment of the infants' department.[55]

The harsh economic conditions of the mid-'30s severely con- strained the amount and scope of a customer base that would have the financial wherewithal and cultural capital to regard their chil- dren in such decidedly ostentatious terms. A toddler dressed in the prescribed manner clearly signals that the family was not being fed with government assistance. The imputation of agency, desire, and selfconsciousness to the child both helped to assuage the con- cerns of merchants and manufacturers and situated demand in something other than a bourgeois preoccupation with conspicuous display.

In this view, the toddler is an emerging person whose "likes" and feelings count as much as those of anyone. Boy toddlers and girl toddlers are different from each other, of course. The girls manifest femininity in "dainty pastels and adorable prints" and boys' garments are more "tailored," more mannish for their "poise of mind." The special designation "toddler" is important not only for the parents; the toddler herself or himself is now a person available for scrutiny by others whose feelings, needs, poise of mind, and choice are being discovered and invoked as legitimate authority. These toddlers are concerned with how they look and are more than aware of the distinction between "proper" and "improper" dress.

To the extent that the discourse of this trade article represents a moment in the commercial construction of "toddlerhood," it also stands for the first step in transforming the sacred child of sentimental domesticity. It is a movement away from internal value and toward external markers of value. Note how toddlers' complete worth is not confined to some value thought intrinsic to the child; children are valued partially for appearance, for how they display style and line outwardly to some observer. This narrative must invoke the child's own perspective. To do otherwise would be to profane the sanctity of the priceless child who is beyond all imposed value. The rhetorical move of placing desire and a degree of autonomy *within* the child effectively embeds the concern with appearance in the realm of agency and volition. "The child" is thus several steps removed from dependency only a year or two beyond infancy.

A year and a half later, a trade writer called catering to toddlers the "third stepping stone" in building an infants' department.[56] She explained to the trade audience that "the child at this age is leaving babyhood and each day becoming more of a personality. His clothes, too, must begin to have personality. Each little figure and individual type must be considered."[57] Manufacturers, the trade audience was told, now make clothes for one-, two-, and three-year-olds with more "charm appeal," an appeal that sells.

Repeating the dichotomy of "charming frock" and "manly suit" for toddler wear, the author lists eighteen items of dress requisite for the toddler classification.[58] She calls for toddlers to be "housed and treated as a separate division and given in charge of a saleswoman who has the understanding and interest of this group at heart."[59] This type of saleswoman "becomes interested in the *personalities* of these small toddlers themselves, and plays up to them, as well as to their parents and relatives."[60] Again, direct appeals to profitability are made by imputing personhood to the child. As a "personality," the child requires an "individual" style. Not yet autonomous but nevertheless a person, the toddler can be exploited through his or her parents and relatives, who now supposedly can feel free to turn the youngster into a (carefully mediated) clothes horse.

"Toddlers" as a category is made possible by "the toddler," a social person who evolves from the crawling dependency of a basically asexual and sartorially colorless infancy in the 1920s into a persona and fixture in the size-style commercial pantheon of children's clothing in the 1930s and beyond. The toddler gains its identity in contradistinction to the infant by its ability to stand and walk. This event demarcates a biological, social, and psychical transition in the life cycle, denoting the first stage of a willful individual capable of movement, choice, and direction. In the 1930s this "upright child" unfolds as a boundary condition for a market designation. The toddler was now both morally ready and socially able to take her or his rightful place in the emergent commercial order of things. Differentiated from the complete dependency and hypermoral arena of infants, a toddler is also a vehicle more amenable than an infant for the expression of style, taste, and gender. These expressions are concomitantly taken as expressions of "personality," of personhood, and are graphically depicted as such in various advertisements using the images of toddlers which have extended into the present.[61]

Two basic developments grounded the discovery of and belief in "toddlerhood" and in the attendant personality of the toddler. One is the rise of a new morality in middle-class childrearing, beginning in the 1920s. The other is the emergent visibility of young, popular culture icons, like Shirley Temple, in the 1930s.

The "New" Childrearing and Shirley Temple
The new childrearing was formed selectively from academic psychology (and perhaps helped along by the popularity of Margaret Mead's work). Beginning in the 1920s, parents—mothers especially—were bombarded with numerous often contradictory messages about children's needs on the pages of women's magazines and in the new *Parents* magazine (established in 1926). Advice from experts like the psychologist J. B. Watson often merged with advertising appeals advocating the purchase of particular products. Both made use of a similar language of development and both offered essentially the same solutions to childrearing problems.[62]

This "new" morality has been characterized by Martha Wolfenstein as "fun morality" in that fun, once thought "suspect, if not taboo, has tended to become obligatory."[63] For Wolfenstein, who examined the advice literature of the Children's Bureau from 1914 to 1945, the basis of the new fun morality is a change in the valuation of the child's impulses. Briefly, the impulses—such as crying, thumb sucking, feeding, and masturbation—were negatively appraised in the literature of 1914 as things to be controlled or eliminated. By 1945 the impulses "appear as benevolent rather than dangerous."[64] They become positively valued as indications of what is good and right for the individual child; nature is to be individuated and nurtured. The consequence, Wolfenstein notes, is that it has become a mother's duty to nurture the play impulse, thus making "fun" an imperative which is not always achievable. One scholar, writing in 1950, determined from surveying child training methods as found in childrearing magazines from 1890 to 1948 that "personality development," as opposed to physical training or moral development, emerges in the 1930s as the prime focus of childrearing advice.[65]

This positive valuation of the child's impulses, combined with the medicalization of mothering discussed in chapters 2 and 3, forms the basis of the new middle-class childrearing. As Ellen Seiter notes: "Experts advised mothers to care not only for the body and its [baby's] health but for the mind and its rate of development. They increased the demand for nurturing behavior in constant supply. The new child psychology was a child-centered model. Implicitly in its proscriptions was a disavowal of maternal authority and an upgrading of *the child's own desires* as rational and goal directed."[66] The efforts of Earnshaw and his publication in the period 1917–29, as we have seen, sought to disavow maternal authority in favor of the authority of the sales clerk, the physician, and store-bought products. On the horizon, in the 1930s, "the child"—here in the form of the toddler—stood as a new figure poised to undercut the traditionally superordinate position of mothers and parents.

Since its inception, *Parents* magazine has been a leader in promoting and disseminating parenting advice based on modern psychological and medical models of child care. According to one scholar, *Parents* was established by a businessman, George Hecht, who saw a market in intelligent mothers and fathers in need of a popular publication on the rearing of children.[67] Closely aligned with Teachers College and the founder of the Child Study Association, Sidonie Gruenberg, *Parents* regularly offered "study guides" with which parents could facilitate home discussion groups about the issues featured that month (such as discipline and children's allowances). Directed to the educated classes, *Parents* was an important vehicle for these new views, especially in its ability to advocate developmental child psychology to a national, albeit middle-class, audience.

According to Seiter, the publication helped to "popularize the idea that childhood is divided into discrete observable stages" and encouraged mothers "to see weekly and monthly changes in their children's development." Child psychology came to understand childhood as a patterned, predictable sequence of stages, notably in the works of Freud, Hall, Gesell, Piaget, and Erikson. Under the intensifying gaze of psychology and medicine, the commercial persona of the toddler emerged not only as a merchandising category but also as an embodied, individuated, and natural "personality." The surveillance of childhood made possible by discrete measurements also made for market distinctions; the construction of toddler personality gave that market a face. During a period when, as Jackson Lears put it, "the autonomous self . . . was being rendered unreal" by the growth of an interdependent market, those same market relations helped signify and bring to the fore an autonomous child-self in the person of Shirley Temple.[68]

Americans in the 1920s witnessed the rise of several juvenile actors on the silver screen. Douglas Fairbanks Jr. and Jackie Coogan led the way, not only with numerous screen appearances but in being featured frequently in advertisements for boys' clothes. With the advent of the "talkies" in the 1930s, child stars like Jane Withers, Gloria Jean, Virginia Weidler, Judy Garland, and Mickey Rooney appeared on the scene.[69] All had their own lines of clothing or endorsed clothing for children.[70]

A cultural and merchandising space was defined for these actors by the early success of Shirley Temple, both as an actress and as a product endorser. Temple gave "toddlerhood" a boost with her on-screen persona as a befrocked, precocious, curly-haired young girl who exuded a definite personality. She also became a commercial persona as she hawked her own lines of clothing. From her feature film and licensing debut in 1934 until the early '40s, the Shirley Temple name and image added materially to sales of dresses, socks, coats and snow suits, hats, hair bands, and raincoats. An advertisement in *Earnshaw's* by Kramer Bros. in 1936 urged the trade to "Cash in on Shirley's Tremendous Popularity" with its line of Shirley Temple Socks, which meet "No Sales Resistance." Besides the expected paid advertisements, *Earnshaw's* also printed unpaid listings of "Shirley Temple Resources."

Temple was five years old when she made her feature film debut. Her stage dresses were designed with a toddler "look," and her retail line of dresses maintained a toddler line throughout the 1930s, even though she was not a toddler herself. One children's fashion observer explains the success of Shirley Temple frocks by their simplicity: "They follow one pattern almost invariably: a skirt (about the size of a postage stamp) that falls in soft pleats from a round collar of a contrasting material or appliqué; no belt—Shirley wisely favors the pinafore fashion which shows off a small round tummy to best advantage; and, for trimming, a bow of baby ribbon or an appliquéd nursery figure. Even her party frocks use no trimming except touches of hand embroidery and edgings of narrow lace."[71] Note how the "round belly," a physical attribute of the toddler age, is described as a deliberately displayed marker of status—as if this feature added to the positive valuation and authenticity of the actress and her appearance.[72] Note also how the author discusses Temple's "look" as a consequence of her own deliberation, rather than that of her handlers.

As a commercial persona, it may be said that Temple "performed" toddlerhood well past the toddler age and was looked on as a toddler even as she moved through middle childhood. The production of trademarked Shirley Temple dresses for the toddler range by Nannette Manufacturing Company of New York City included numerous styles and variations on the basic silhouette and continued into the early '40s. Temple's birthday became an annual occasion for special promotions. In addition, the Rosenau Bros. Manufacturing Co. of New York offered Shirley Temple designs in Big and Little Sister styles, sizes 3 to 6½ and 7 to 12 years.[73]

Aware of the potential impact of a child's on-screen appearance, each of the big Hollywood studios (Twentieth Century–Fox, MGM, Universal, and Paramount) hired big-name designers for the children's wardrobes by the late '30s; among the best-known were Vera West of Universal and Edith Head of Paramount studios. They crafted clothing with an eye toward the apparel market in addition to the movie-going market, although direct tie-ins from film to manufacturer did not exist at this time.[74]

The accessibility of Shirley Temple and others as child stars provided visibility for style in the developing fashion system for children. Social theorists from Georg Simmel to Herbert Blumer to Fred Davis have stressed the necessity of conspicuous display in order for fashion to develop and a fashion system to thrive. In the midst of the Depression, children and parents alike found that they could emulate screen stars, at least their clothing. Robert and Helen Lynd observed Shirley Temple permanent waves on third-grade girls. The Shirley Temple doll, by many accounts, was a "must have" for young girls in the 1930s.[75]

Both the "new" childrearing and the increased visibility of the child star, especially Shirley Temple, informed and gave impetus to the rise and elaboration of the toddler size-style range, particularly for girls. The new mode of childrearing uniformly recognized the young child as possessing personal desires and healthy impulses. This view enables a construction of the toddler as a person, or a person in progress, who is therefore "less" sacred—less sacred than the crawling, hyperdependent infant. The toddler-as-person is that much more *able*, developmentally, morally, and *subjectively* to desire material goods, make choices, and "feel properly dressed."

Once trade members and parents alike accepted that the toddler is no longer an infant although not yet a "full" person, then the way was paved to identify and take seriously the particular commercial "needs" of the toddler. These can be met, some would say, only by special merchandise. If the toddler is gaining or manifesting a "personality," then Shirley Temple, and other actors, stood as publicly shared models for how that personality could be expressed by white, middle-class girls.

Note how observers discuss Temple, and toddlers generally, from an aesthetic point of view as, for example, in descriptions of the visual "line" of the clothing and the charming dresses. The toddler girl, especially, becomes one who is seen, viewed by others, and no doubt evaluated by onlookers. She is also assumed to be separately aware of her appearance and, as such, she stands as a model of agency. "The child" becomes an object for display and scrutiny and, at the same time, a subject to be engaged, at once a type and an individual.

MORAL TENSIONS accompanied the emerging model of the child-person-consumer in the '20s and '30s. The growing ethos that it is the child's view which is to be indulged most assuredly sat well with industry members who were facing shrinking markets after the crash of 1929, even as parents, pedagogues, and market observers sought to give direction to children's clothing choices. Fears expressed about overly selfconscious and vain children also sat uneasily with the increasing stylization of children's clothes and with the reinscription of the feminine "duty" to care for one's looks onto the young girl. The retail floor, where children were concerned, became something of a classroom in which to train the child's taste as well as a hedge against the temptation of parents to "trade down" by purchasing increasingly available, similarly styled lower-priced clothing.

In this context, the "toddler" designation was not merely one of size or age range; it instantiated a version of the child consumer. Given content and personality by Shirley Temple and other, subsequent commercial personae, the toddler arrived on the scene already a consumer—a choosing, desiring subject—without having to purchase a thing. Toddlers could want and chose, in effect, because they were constituted as pre-given consumer subjects. Temple so effortlessly represented and performed toddlerhood in large part because of her femaleness, that is, because of her cultural location as one who surveys herself ever cognizant of the gaze of others.[76]

As Ariès's work intimates, how children *appear* visually and bodily is paramount to their placement in socio-historical space. Worries about children's clothing consumption are worries about children's personal, gendered display—about how one renders the self socially and publicly to others. In particular, merchants and observers during this time made a significant commercial investment in femininity, making the young female body an intersection of taste, individual choice, and markets. The young girl's body in a different way also served as a significant cultural site for the realization of exchange value—its growth and maturation made for new social distinctions on which markets were built. The next chapter examines how the new size-style ranges enfolded physical growth, social development, and the child's perspective into merchandising strategy in the 1930s.

Reconfiguring Girlhood:

Age Grading, Size Ranges, and

Aspirational Merchandising

in the 1930s

The adult practice of seeing with children's eyes gradually found its way into the children's wear marketplace by the 1930s, as working conceptions of the child consumer increasingly drew on the "child's perspective" for insight and legitimacy. Merchants and market observers assumed, imputed, or otherwise contrived the child's point of view to forge usable models of the consuming child—as a person with self-knowledge, desire, and an accruing social right to express that desire. Extracting and elaborating general characteristics of the consuming child assisted in transforming the child's identity from that of an isolated, intermittent customer toward that of a consumer in a continuous and abstract sense. Understood *as* a consumer, "the child" thus could be individualized as someone with desires and, at the same time, universalized as a category of social being who remains in need of training, direction, and some measure of protection.

In the 1930s, pediocularity played an additional role in the commodification of childhood, beyond recognizing the child consumer as a person in and through the marketplace. More fundamentally, perhaps, the child's perspective—mainly a girl's perspective—was made manifest in the very age stages and structure of childhood.

Beginning in the 1920s and solidifying in the 1930s, American girl-hood and to a lesser extent American boyhood underwent a trans-formation, from a grossly defined stage of the early life course to one in which various named age-size clothing designations made for finely grained distinctions within a trajectory of childhood. The new designations of childhood also took material and spatial form in new retail clothing departments designed for children of various ages. In the 1930s in particular, entire "floors for children" were built to clothe children from infancy through the high school years. These departments and subdepartments quickly divided and sub-divided along gender lines and along an emerging age-stage para-digm of growth, maturation, and, as I intend to show, personhood.

The severe economic conditions of the 1930s limited the exter-nal, retail sales growth of the industry. Between 1929 and 1939, according to the Census of Business, retail sales for "infants' and children's stores" decreased over 55 percent in receipts, from just under $30 million in 1929 to $13.4 million in 1939.[1] These condi-tions, however, did not inhibit as drastically the industry's internal expansion, (that is, the growth of its infrastructure) and perhaps even encouraged it. The industry turned its attention toward re-making the stages of girlhood at a time when mass production made a multiplicity of expressions in dress available for middle-class girls and their parents. One result was a proliferation of new size ranges and new forms of retailing which were extended only partially to boys' wear. The new size ranges and forms of retailing represent, in material form, the interlacing of life course distinc-tions with merchandising strategy.

In this chapter, I examine the rise of several new size ranges, particularly for girls, and the accompanying spatial merchandising in retail spaces which concretized and linked the commercial and social divisions of childhood. In addition to the toddler category discussed in chapter 4, two other size ranges arising in the decade, "Children's" and "Girls'," represent additional ways that the inter-nal trajectory of childhood, and girlhood more specifically, trans-formed in interaction with market considerations. I also detail how the iconography and physical makeup of retail spaces for chil-dren's clothing became explicitly designed to appeal to the child as the decisive customer. To lay the groundwork for these discussions, it is necessary to first examine several historical factors, including age grading and schooling as well as clothing expenditures, size categories, and size ranges before the late '20s.

ON THE MORAL IMPERATIVES OF AGE GRADING
IN THE MODERN ERA

When George Earnshaw championed the creation of a separate department with special merchandise for infants in the period 1917–29, he was riding a crest of change in age grading and age stratification which had already spread through much of American urban culture. Before the twentieth century in the United States, intense age norms and the scheduling of life activities based on age were uncommon and relatively unsystematized. No doubt, the distribution of rights, statuses, activities, and responsibilities according to age is a general and universal characteristic of all human societies, as is the recognition of the gross life stages of childhood, adulthood, and old age. However, in the West, especially with the extension of capitalist modes of production, clock time as well as the timing of the life course takes on finely graded forms.[2]

Historians tend to concur that the kind of age stratification apparent in the late twentieth century did not exist in the same forms or with the same intensity before the mid-1800s. Joseph Kett notes that the age ranges of family members were wider in 1790 than today and that then, unlike now, it was common to have ten- or even fifteen-year age spans between siblings. In some colleges in colonial New England, attendees' ages could range from eight to twenty-five. Howard Chudacoff supports this view by showing that "peer marriages" (between partners within two years' age of each other) increased in frequency from 1864 to 1925, contending that America was becoming a "peer group society."[3]

Birthdays, a visible marker of age awareness, were not widely celebrated before the 1890s. The preserve mainly of the well to do, day-of-birth celebrations were as much a display of child etiquette for adults as a party for children until the late nineteenth century. Standardized birthday messages in the form of cards or postcards were, at first, revamped Christmas cards. Only later, in the second decade of the twentieth century, were they produced exclusively for birthdays. Certainly, more efficient record keeping in urban areas allowed the celebration of one's exact birth date to be feasible. Yet it wasn't until the 1900 federal census that age statistics were kept and used with any degree of purpose.[4]

The most significant factor contributing to increased age stratification that historians point to, in addition to urbanization and industrialization, is compulsory schooling. Graded common schools developed first in New England during the 1840s and, as the student population increased, larger buildings to separate grades were needed to replace one-room schoolhouses. Reformers like Horace Mann and John Philbrick, who were interested in establishing a common school system, set out to systemize the education process by dividing students on the basis of age and grade. This categorization differed from the much older European system, also discussed by Ariès, in which advancement was premised on the completion of a task rather than on one's chronological age, if known.[5]

By the 1870s, age-graded schooling was standard, though by no means universal, in the United States. Its structure initially reinforced the old categorizations offered by textbooks, used for at least a century prior, which were loosely graded according to the relationship between age and reading ability. This curriculum allowed students to move on to another level or reader once he (or, increasingly, she) mastered the previous level. Eventually, in the 1880s, textbooks began to be produced specifically for the graded system, helping to fix chronological age closely with school grade.[6]

Once established, an assumed or proposed trajectory of development can function as an argument in favor of its own transcendent reality. For instance, one effect of the emergent age-based systemization of knowledge and ability was to make intellectual precocity suspect, thereby placing, through institutional means, limits on how much children could achieve "beyond" their years. Precocity came to be regarded as a "disease," or a threat to the social order, in nineteenth-century America. Childrearing literature linked intellectual precocity in children with the other, more substantiated "dangers" of sexual and mental hygiene.[7]

Age stratification through graded schools was part of a larger process of "normalization" in the public sphere. It included the advent of statistical conceptions of normality and the invention of the normal personality and of normal sexuality. The graded system, according to Chudacoff, "locked a significant proportion of

American children into age-determined groupings and engendered in adults the assumption that these groupings were intrinsic to the educational experience." The belief in a "proper" or "normal" movement through the school system became the rule by the 1940s, such that schools began the practice of "social promotion" (promoting students to the next grade regardless of achievement) to avoid having non-achieving students branded as failures.[8]

The premise implicit in the "normal" growth and development of a child is that movement through the stages of the early life course constitutes a moral as well as a biological imperative. "Moral" here stands for a synchronization of activities and behavior and, I would say, goods or materials with a determined "appropriate" stage or sequence. The partitioning of childhood also occurred at the level of the commodity, as toys, and later media, were developed and merchandised increasingly with particular ages and stages in mind.[9] In children's wear, the problem of fitting children with the correct size and, importantly, the appropriate style of clothing in the early decades of mass production and merchandising instantiated emergent tensions between commodity culture, gender, and children's personhood.

SIZE AND SIZE RANGE

Children, unlike adults, have clothing available to them in size ranges, rather than only in discrete sizes, as was true throughout the 1900s. Size and size ranges are never a matter only of the physical fit of clothing. Clothing style—in the general sense of the cut and silhouette of a garment—offers an indication of the gross age or maturity of the wearer, in addition to displaying social statuses and identities like gender, ethnicity, race, and social class.[10] Age incongruities in sartorial display, such as children "dressing up" like adults or adults dressing "like children," highlight age-appropriate boundaries identified usually only when they are crossed.[11] "Size" and "size range" always involve considerations of style which, in turn, indicate some configuration of social identity; a size range is, in a sense, always a size-style range.

Specific to class and historical context, as well as confounded with gender display, age-appropriateness in children's clothing differs in important ways from the age-related considerations endemic to children's toys and reading materials. Unlike reading or playing with toys, clothing literally covers the child, serving as a visible environment of the body. Clothing is something seen by observers differently from how it is viewed by oneself on oneself; it is a form of continuous display in ways that toys or reading material is not. Clothing, in this way, relates to the presentation of self—the public display of the child—in and through contexts more encompassing than either reading or playing.

Technically, size range delineates an age span, divided according to gender, giving to children's clothing an intended stylistic or functional coherence. For example, the size range now called "infants'" designates the total length (24 to 26½ inches) that is typical of three- to six-month-old children.[12] It also implies that certain features like the weight of fabric, the length of garment, the looseness of fit, and perhaps the inclusion of certain materials (like wool or cotton) will be present. The discourse on the toddler (chapter 4) offers an angle on the sartorial bridge between age and style.

Size range also includes issues of gender display. Concerns about how transparently clothing indicates the sex of a child have intensified since the 1920s. According to Paoletti and Kregloh,[13] such things as the girl-pink, boy-blue coding for infants became solidified only after the Second World War in the United States. Indeed, as they point out, the *Infants' Department* recommended pink as the color most suitable for *boys* in 1918. In any event, color serves as an instantly recognizable marker of gender for a particular age-size range where others might fail.[14]

Apparel manufacturers faced serious problems with sizing once the technology for ready-made clothing made mass production viable, particularly in the 1920s and 1930s. The variations of the human form, the requirements of fit, and the morphological differences of sex complicated attempts to construct an "ideal body" against which all deviations could be measured. Sizing differs for men's and older boys' clothing as opposed to women's and girls' clothing. For males, industry practice became standardized by taking and using actual measurements of waist, inseam, chest, sleeve, and back; sizing for females offers more variation within a particular size and much of the cut of women's clothing assumes difficult-to-achieve body proportions.[15]

As more kinds of children's clothing were made in factories

during the first two decades of the century, these garments became differentiated along age-sex lines. Data from a survey of family expenditures by the Bureau of Labor Statistics in 1918–19 provide some insight into the kinds of clothing purchased by families for various age groups and probably the kinds of clothing available for purchase. The survey, interestingly, gathered data on a number of age ranges: under 4, 4 to 8, 8 to 12, 12 to 15, and 15 through 18 for both sexes. Thirty-five to fifty items for each age-sex group were listed as having been purchased by at least some families in the survey. Some items were infrequently purchased, such as raincoats, wristwatches, handkerchiefs, and felt hats, each purchased by less than 5 percent of families.[16]

As expected, shoes are among the most heavily purchased items for boys and girls in all age groups, because of the difficulty of home manufacture. Similar conditions explain the uniformly high rankings for stockings among girls and socks among boys (both hovering in the 90 percent to 95 percent range of families purchasing these items). Garters stand out as a highly ranked item for all ages of both boys and girls (around 75 percent of families purchasing) at a time when stretch fabrics and elastics had yet to be used in hosiery, either home-made or mass-produced. Other items of relatively frequent purchase included girls' nightdresses, cotton union suits, and rompers for children under 4, which fell into the 40 to 50 percent range.

Beyond similarities across age and gender groupings, there are substantial changes accompanying age. The most general of these differences is simply the increase in the number of items purchased by families as children age. As children get older, more and more of their items of dress are bought by parents (or, possibly, by themselves). Gender differences become evident as children age, with a higher proportion of a family's budget, regardless of income, being spent on a girl's wardrobe, which outpaced a boy's wardrobe in kind and number as the children reached the 15 to 18 category. Certain items seem to be associated with only one age group; dresses for boys under 4 and rompers for boys and girls under 4 completely drop out at older ages. Waists and blouses were hardly purchased at all for girls under 8 (4.6 percent) but frequently for those over 12 (40.7 percent). Also, underwaists steadily decrease in frequency as the boy ages, and disappear as a girls' item after the age of 8.[17]

These measurements give no indication of the scope of the children's wear market in 1918–19.[18] They do, however, offer a snapshot of the general availability and consumption of children's wear when the industry first began to organize itself.[19] In the ensuing decades, age-specific clothing would become a matter of style as much as one of content, indicating and solidifying a graded, gendered stepladder through childhood. Tensions of age, size, style, and gender in children's clothing began to emerge as children's wear increasingly came under the auspices of mass manufacturing during the 1920s and 1930s. The sizes and the coordination between size and style remained in flux through the 1930s and are not entirely resolved today. The relationship between age and physical size has proven variable and confusing.[20]

From about 1910 onward, but especially in the 1930s, the divisions and trajectory internal to middle-class childhood underwent a transformation from a grossly differentiated to a more graded series in which stages of the life course were nuanced by changes in appearance and clothing. These "new" stages of childhood gain their impetus primarily through an effort to closely match size and appearance to girls' physical growth and social maturation.

NEW SIZE-STYLE RANGES OF
THE '20S AND '30S

The variability of some early size ranges for both boys and girls helps to reveal the progression of their changes over the course of both childhood and history. Around the turn of the century, when there may have been as few as a half-dozen manufacturers exclusively devoted to making children's garments, standardized size ranges in children's clothes were virtually nonexistent. A gross categorization was operative in women's magazines such as *Ladies Home Journal*, *Harper's Bazar*, and *Women's Home Companion*: birth to 18 months; 18 months to 6 years; 6 years to 14 years. As far as I have been able to discern, there were no proper "names" to these age ranges, except for the youngest, referred to as "infants'" or "babies'." With minor variations, this tripartite division of childhood and children's sizes held fairly stable until after the industry began to organize itself in the 1920s, when sizes and ages were coordinated and given names.

In 1923 the *Infants' Department* changed its name to the *Infants' and Children's Department*, laying claim to another age group and market. At this time, the designation "children," for clothing purposes, applied to girls between infancy and about 15, while for boys, it extended only to around about 7 or 8. After about the age of 7, boys' wear, then as now, followed much of the styling, proportion, and manufacturing process of men's wear. Currently boys' wear goes to a size seven and, according to a textbook on children's wear design, by about the age of four a boys' "trousers are cut, more or less, like men's."[21]

Sartorial childhood becomes divided and subdivided according to age, gender, and style components as some order is brought to sizing and size ranges. As "the child" ages, her or his clothing becomes differentiated in terms of choices presumed to belong to different genders and ages. Both fashion and style become increasingly important markers of personhood as they move to the forefront of considerations of "appropriate" wear, especially for girls.

Three-to-Sixers Are "Children"
The toddler had a personality, or at least a right to one. As a social type, "the toddler" arose in contradistinction to the infant. As a size range, it carved out the ages of 1 to 3, leaving the first year of life to "infants'" and "babies'." Up from toddlerhood, in terms of size, is the 3 to 6 or 7 range, now known as "Children's." One textbook on children's wear design from 1989 repeats the wisdom of an earlier age, characterizing children of this age range as "still charmingly unselfconscious, but old enough to be fashionable. . . . [The average five-year-old] is beginning to assume adult proportions and the legs grow rapidly; his trunk develops more slowly; and the size of his head changes very little. There is yet no indication of a waistline, and the baby stance is still strong."[22] For both boys and girls (girls' sizes run to 6X, boys' to 7), each children's size for preschoolers aims to match the child's chronological age.

The contradictory view expressed above by contemporary designers (unselfconsciousness yet fashionable), as we have seen, can be found in similar form in the proscriptions offered by many observers in the '20s and '30s. Flora Krauch, a writer for *Earnshaw's*, described the older child this way in 1937: "By four years many children have opinions of their own, and at six we find them displaying decided likes and dislikes. As children mingle with others at play, at nursery school, kindergarten, and Sunday school, they observe the clothes worn by their companions, and thus form impressions. Saleswomen hear many a story of the child coming home begging for something that has appealed to it because some other child was wearing it."[23] Already enmeshed in a social world of peers, "the child" here seems eager to emulate others. No thought, of course, is given to the possibility that it is the parents who are engaging in the game of conspicuous display through their children. Invoking the child's perspective invokes the child's desire and can exonerate parents and marketeers from suspicion.

In 1937 industry boosters were quick to accept unquestioningly the reported peer consciousness of these children as they move into various public worlds before formal schooling. In this version of "the child," its preference structure solidifies as the child gets older. Gender markings were also thought to increase in importance for the three- to six-year-old girl who is "demanding more style" in dresses, lingerie, separate skirts, and blouses. It is customary, the writer notes, to run higher-priced lines in this group, implying that style considerations can outweigh those of price. The merchant is reminded that "style is important" and advised to "have comfortable chairs so that the child may rest while mother goes through the preliminaries. And, by all means, mirrors low enough to attract."[24] A selfconscious child is good for business, even if she is a worry for educators and some mothers. If she is concerned about her looks, then more merchandise can be moved more frequently.

The 3-to-6 age, size, and style range is not conspicuously marked with a specialized name like "Toddlers." It represents a further subdivision of the earlier infants' range, which has covered anywhere from six months to six years. "Children's," as an age-size category, represents a time after toddlerhood and before the onset of formal schooling. There is reason to believe that the upper limit to this range had already been accepted as an appropriate boundary before the advent of the children's wear industry. Children under the age of six were often limited in their household chores and responsibilities in rural life of the 1700s and 1800s. Also, a "2 to 6" range was in use in clothing pattern books as early as the turn of the century, and there is no reason to believe that it originated then. In 1936 an upper limit to infancy was formalized when the U.S. Supreme Court, when deciding on import duties for various types of clothing, ruled that it ended at the age of six.[25]

Girls'
Until the late 1920s, it was common to encounter boys' and girls' clothing (either ready-made or as a pattern) offered in two-year intervals, like 2–4–6 or 6–8–10, as shown in a clothing feature spread in *Parents* magazine in October 1927. No toddlers' range depicted quite yet. Size ranges for both boys and girls at this time seem to depend partly on the whim of the manufacturer and the style of garment. In this *Parents* magazine spread, a set of shirt and shorts is available for the ages of 4, 6, and 8 years, whereas a girls' kimono dress covers 2 to 8. A bloomer dress is suggested for 2 through 10 and is matched with a boys' two-piece suit, which has the more limited range of 2 to 6 years. These two garments make a "brother-sister" set, a product which became quite popular in the toddler range in the '30s and remained so until the 1960s. In both instances, gender asymmetry is evident in that the girls' outfit is intended for a wider age range than the boys.' For older children it appears that girls' outfits could start from 6 or 8 and usually end at 14 or 15 as shown in another sketch, whereas a girls' pleated dress is made for 6, 8, 10, 12, and 14 years.

These intervals and varied size ranges are typical of the time and illustrate a comparative lack of distinction among, in particular, girls between the ages of 6 and 14 or 15. Between these ages, a girl grows in manifold ways: increased length in torso and limbs and increased curvature of hips, waist, and rear end, as well as breast development. These features are basically ignored by the style of her clothes at this time. It is as if a girls' emerging adulthood/womanhood is masked.

Size ranges for girls older than six remained in flux from the 1920s until the late '30s. For girls reaching middle childhood, their bodies became both a problem for design and an opportunity for profit. By 1923 industry members and observers had already begun to express uncertainty about the content and categories of early girlhood. A regular writer for *Earnshaw's* opines that the period from five and a half years of age to about eight is a difficult one for girls. The concern with this age range, a range neglected by both buyer and manufacturer, is again more about style than about fit. The "larger six-year-old who grows out of infants' early" is sent to the department for older children where "it is found that the size six in such departments is entirely too old in style and out of proportion. That comes because the manufacturer, instead of grading up from the infants' size, grades down from the larger sizes and the more mature styles. The child of six, therefore, jumps at once from babyhood to girlhood without an intermediate stage. But why should a child of six wear a direct copy of the garments worn by her fourteen-year-old sister only cut to the smaller size?"[26] The mother, supposedly discouraged by this void in the age-size spectrum, turns to the "dressmaker and home sewing circle" and away from retail departments. The writer calls for a department for 6- to 16-year-old girls, physically located adjacent to the infants' department, with a separate buyer who could cater to the changing needs of girls in that range. No similar concern was expressed for boys.

The concerns expressed above are recurrent. A young girl of six, it is assumed, should not look like a fourteen-year-old nor like a young child. A void existed that apparently did not exist before in the commercial-sartorial chronology of girlhood; its appearance, I believe, is evidence of the elongation of the period of childhood dependency widely thought to have accompanied industrialization and compulsory schooling.[27] The remedy proposed, unsurprisingly, was to create a retail department to fill the void. A separate buyer, attuned to the requirements of "the growing girl," would express her wishes to manufacturers, jobbers, and department store managers, and effect a change by demonstrating sales in this category.

One marker of age in a girl's dress was (and, to some extent, still is) indicated by the length of the hemline. An article in *Babyhood* expresses the current wisdom on the subject: "Designers usually concede that—considering children of average size—girls under the age of ten should wear their skirts above the knee."[28] A sign of an older girl is that her dress would get longer as she approached high school age, presumably because her legs become objects of sexual interest to be displayed with modesty.

The issue here was not to eliminate or somehow change the size range itself but to change the styles available at retail within the range. The effect of this sort of thinking about girlhood, however, actually involved a change in size ranges beginning in the 1930s. A writer for *Earnshaw's* noted in 1935 that "the most significant change in the Girls' Department in the past couple of years has been the greater separation of size ranges into seven to ten and twelve to sixteen."[29]

Illustrations 3 and 4 show some of the variations in style and age and size for girls for 1933 and 1936. In illustration 3 notice the lack of differences between "older" and "younger" sister. The hemlines are nearly the same, and all that distinguishes the older sister, in the 7-to-10 range, is a sash around her waist. The wide collar keeps the older sister looking more like her younger sister. For Iserson Imports (illustration 4), the difference in the length of the hemline between a 2 to 6 and a 7 to 12 is clear. The cut on the older sister's dress seems to vary slightly, hinting at the developing form of an adolescent as well as distinguishing hemlines. The differences in these clothing age indicators mark the beginning of a differentiated Girls' category in the mid- to late '30s.

The tension in this category is, at base, one of sexuality and sexual display. Young girls just out of the children's range were said to be wearing clothing "too old" in style. Concerns about girls' dress and physical appearance were paramount in the changing childhoods of the '20s and '30s, if the Lynds' Middletown studies are any indication. They encountered decided anxiety among parents about dress and sexuality among girls of high school age and younger youth in both of their studies covering these decades. Mixed-sex paired dates were on the rise, girls' "immodesty" in dress was seen by some as "aggressive," and, by the time of the second study in the 1930s, this attitude toward female self display was being noted by adults in younger and younger grade school girls.[30]

The industry's response was to create an intermediate category, 7 to 10 or 12, through the efforts of buyers and manufacturers alike. It differentiates girls who no longer exhibit the "babyish" postures

3. Age differences for girls were not always clearly designated by clothing design or cut. In this trade advertisement, older sister and younger sister are virtually identical stylistically. Note the similarity in their hemlines. *Earnshaw's*, January 1933, 87.

4. Iserson Imports makes the distinction between older girls and younger ones apparent with a different hemline for each. *Earnshaw's*, February 1936, 8.

of children six and under, but who are preadolescent in both morphology and social characteristics.

The opportunity for merchandising through a finer-grained grouping of goods was not lost on industry members. The merchandiser and buyer for the Associated Dry Goods Corporation, and a regular writer for *Earnshaw's*, expresses the situation in this way in 1934: "The limit of age in the Infants' Department is six so that the mother is the deciding factor in a sale. (Though we say this with reservations having observed tiny customers expressing their preferences with considerable emphasis.) There is little question, however, when a girl goes into the Girls' Department that she is the one whose choice is final, that is, completes the sale." The writer continues, stating that the major problem is size assortments.

The writer also offers something of a typology of children who should be fitted: "little girls just out of the Infants' department who take straight line or babyish styles"; stout girls; tall, lean athletic girls; the "tailored type"; and the "feminine type." The Girls' Department must be prepared to fit all these types: "Fortunately the trend in the wholesale market within the past few years has been toward specialization of size and type, so that we can more easily find the seven to ten or twelve merchandise, the so-called chubby, and the teen type[31] . . . the ten or twelve to sixteen range, each styled and patterned with these various girls in mind."[32] Note that the imprecision of the categories continues, even for one whose livelihood depends on such knowledge.

For this writer, girls have become divided by sizes as well as by types. A "type," in this context, refers to a subcategory of person identified in terms of an intersection of physical maturity (size and shape) and a fairly consistent preference structure for a particular style or mode of self-presentation. These caricatures are not based on age or size exclusively but gesture toward a class-based set of distinctions in which body shape and clothing style implicate markets or market segments.

The delay of social maturity brought on by compulsory schooling and late entry into the job market, compounded by the availability of many styles in an era of mass production, seems to have first produced a void in the age trajectory internal to girlhood. This void then becomes a market for dress styles between the six-year-old girl and the blossoming girl of the early teen years. The 7 to 11 or 12 range split off from the older range from the former girls' 6 to 14 or 15. Only much later, in the 1950s, did another subdivision, the "subteen" or "preteen" girl, arise (see chapter 6).

A MICRO-ECOLOGY OF
CHILDREN'S DEPARTMENTS

The inevitability of development, and of a gendered, sequential development, carries with it the promise of new markets. These dynamics, however, could have made for a sustained market and industry only if they made practical sense by being grounded somehow in the day-to-day experiences of mothers and children. These experiences are the mundane activities of minding children, going to school, associating with peers, and shopping. The growth of an industry does not occur only in the realm of ideas; in this case, it occurred on the sales floor where merchants and mothers and children met face to face, handled the garments, and involved themselves in various orders of negotiation about their purchase. My concern is with how the commercial spaces, and the interactions therein, changed in relation to the growth of a "child world" of ready-made clothing.

By about 1910, Leach points out, there were "special" spaces set aside for children in department stores. Most of them were play areas where mothers, while shopping, could leave their children to be supervised by adults. "Checking" one's children was part of the "service" that department stores offered for decades. These areas offered more than a space in which children could play. They became commercial spaces, often located next to toy departments. Some provided services like children's haircuts while mother was shopping.[33] An article in *System* in 1915 describes one store's arrangements:

> In addition [to the large playroom], the store has several small rooms in various parts of the building devoted to the use of children. One of the larger of these rooms opens off from the children's clothing department. Nursery pictures hang on the white-tile walls, and there are toys for the youngsters to play with. . . . A door leads to a little toilet room that is fitted out with special child-size accessories.

Another room nearby is devoted to babies, and a nurse watches out for the youngsters while their mothers shop in the department. Parents . . . find these rooms particularly convenient, and an added "reason why" for shopping at the store which provides them.[34]

Not just spaces, these were *places* for children that were scaled to a child's proportions and decorated with images and iconography of childhood. They were provided primarily by department stores and by some hotels as well.

The intent and appeal are clear and familiar: if one caters to the child, the mother's appreciation and business will follow. This is the same thinking that guided the early infants' departments: promote child health as an added incentive to visit and shop. It is a dual appeal which can also be seen today in many advertisements for toys, cereal, and the like. Where the educational, health, or developmental appeal of any child's product is, so can be found the influence of "the mother" or mother-surrogates like the state or advocacy groups.

Mother appeal has remained constant in some form from the 1920s until today. The change in approach in the 1930s involves the transformation of the retail arena into a place built according to the presumed views, anxieties, and concerns of the child. As early as the 1910–20 period, but increasingly over the '20s and '30s, children's wear retailers sought to offer service, goods, and store atmosphere that appealed directly to the children.

One merchandiser of boys' clothing reported to the *Dry Good Economist* in 1920 that he increased sales by making the department attractive to the boys:

Immediately upon taking the department, I determined to make the children who came to it feel at home and to this end laid my plans in such a way that I would build up an atmosphere that would have particular appeal.

In the department proper, I established a number of small swings and put in other contrivances that children delight in. I further made arrangements for the older boys. With the purchase of $10 or more I gave a subscription to the *American Boy*. I bought by lucky purchase several thousand Boy Scout knives at far below the Boy Scout list price and I sold these to every registered customer of the store at actual cost.[35]

This merchant urges others to "study the boys' ways" and to be "sincere with the youngsters, to really like them and to show that you like them without any ostentation."

The grouping of clothing by age categories brought with it problems not previously encountered. Retailers began to realize that children did not like being treated "as children" and would not be favorably disposed toward their store and merchandise unless appeased with "equal" treatment. A writer for *Dry Goods Economist* discusses the gendered aspects of personhood and salesmanship in a story where a "salesgirl" talked down to a boy by using baby talk ("Put your hannies into the coat sleeve."). The writer explains that neither mother nor boy was pleased with the treatment. "Just as mothers and fathers want their little girl babies to be sweet and dainty so they want their little boy babies to be sturdy and manly— 'real boys.' Little boys with curls and velvet kilts with large lace collars have gone out of date." Boys' and girls' clothing sections should be segregated as early as possible, the writer continues, and no later than the age of two. For when a boy is "treated like a little man," the infants' department will find it profitable.[36]

Gender and subordination are directly linked, as in the allusion above to the effeminacy of Little Lord Fauntleroy collars and curls.[37] They specify the kind of interpersonal relationship that a salesperson should develop with each sex: "Salespeople for the baby boys' section should be chosen with regard to a slightly different angle than that needed by those who serve the baby girls. What was said already about the dignity and the desire for privacy for children is true, of course, for both boys and girls. But little boys particularly appreciate matter-of-factness in a salesgirl."

Because it has greater variations in style than boys' wear, it is girls' wear which carries sales and the possibility of future sales. The finer distinctions and gradations within girlhood extended and elaborated these kinds of value. Sales clerks and retailers echoed the virtues of this differential treatment for boys and girls as early as 1919. *"Take her seriously and sincerely. . . .* Don't patronize or talk down to her. Don't call her 'my dear' or 'girlie' or 'honey' or any similar expression. Don't override her evident preference in order to sell her mother. If possible in such a case take a tactful middle course."[38] The buyer and merchandise manager for the children's department of L. S. Ayers & Co., Indianapolis, related to the

Dry Goods Economist in 1921: "We treat the children as much like grown-ups as possible. . . . And we find that it pays. It takes a special type of saleswoman to please little girl shoppers, and to hold boys at all, as the latter are invariably bored to death with the whole process of shopping."[39]

The child as customer, as we have seen time and again, is the child as person. To treat her any other way threatens "customer goodwill." The focus on the child's comfort and wants was to extend far beyond the confines of brief and intermittent encounters with saleswomen. This attitude toward seeing and treating the child as a person, as a person-customer, became encoded in the physical layout of retail departments, as merchandising itself in these departments gradually took into account the position, perspective, attitude, and emergent culture of children and youth. Ultimately, it is the child's perspective—rather than that of the mother—that becomes institutionalized by being incorporated into the physical structure of children's departments and floors.

As the idea of infants' departments caught on in the early 1920s, retailers began to organize their other "juvenile" clothing along an age sequence. Many mothers and mothers-to-be also had children who were not infants, and shopping for them all in one general area made sense commercially and practically. Throughout the '20s, *Earnshaw's* reported on the openings of infants' departments and the expansion of these departments into older children's clothing. In many instances, entire floors of the store came to be occupied by juvenile apparel and merchandise. A typical arrangement of the retail space allocation of juvenile clothing until the late '20s basically followed the size ranges of the time: infant's departments to age six, then one large department for girls to the high school years (6 to 14, 15, or 16), and one department for boys, who often shopped in or near the men's departments.

New ideas for departments were often devised by observant merchants who spied the activities of children and parents. For instance, *Earnshaw's* reported on a "Twixt-and-Tween" section which was started at the Charles Trankla & Co. store in Grand Rapids, Michigan. This section was "devoted to the needs of the girls of twelve to sixteen, the twixt and tween age." Noticing a lack of business from girls of this age, the buyer decided to physically separate this section from infants' and children's. She reasoned that this type of girl was an "independent and willful creature [who] felt herself too grown up to buy her clothes in the Infants' or Children's department."[40]

The buyer situated this "section" so that girls could shop without having the embarrassment of passing through the other departments stocked with younger children's clothes. She located it "immediately in the path of the young lady as she steps from the elevator. Here is displayed merchandise carefully selected for this . . . young lady so she must no longer report to the baby section when selecting her wardrobe."[41] The mother's convenience is catered to as well since she can shop for different ages of children in "one neighborhood," with the infants' and children's department located in back of the "twixt-and-tween" section.

In this way, the separation of age-graded sections takes into consideration the differences between age groups as much as the similarities within them. It is a pattern which becomes a model for the design of juvenile clothing departments in the 1930s and beyond.

For instance, in 1939 the Saks Fifth Avenue store in New York City and a Kerns store in Michigan each built entire new floors for juvenile wear which were planned precisely with an idea of age-space progression in mind. The intended customer, however, was different for each location. From an article by one of the designer-builders of these floors, we learn that "children detest complication. They love and understand only those things which are direct and plainly marked. Thus not only a correct relation of departments is required but a simple, clearly defined one. As to location, it is certain that it is more convenient for the mother to make purchases for all her children on the same floor. Older children, however, are often reluctant to shop on a floor where 'all those babies' are shopping."[42] With mother and child both in mind, the floors were constructed to place all juvenile wear on one floor, and to put the older children's clothing up front at the entrance. Note the progression of the customer as show in illustration 5, a map of the Saks store. After disembarking from the elevators at the bottom of the map, one enters the store either through the girls' or boys' section, beginning with older children's styles and descending in age until reaching the layettes and nursery furniture in the back.

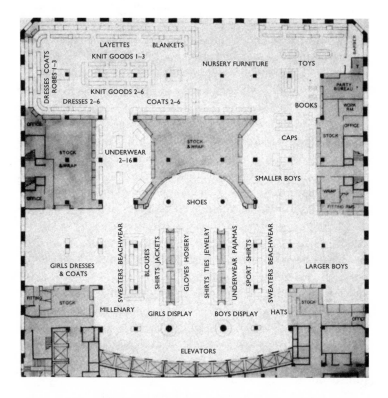

5. Floor plan of Saks Fifth Avenue in Manhattan shows how younger children must pass through the older children's areas to reach their own. *Bulletin of the National Retail Dry Goods Association*, October 1939, 72.

This arrangement, the designers thought, could work in promoting the store. It also promoted the idea and practice of progressive, age-graded desire and consumption: "The younger children on the other hand are delighted to see the older children shopping as they go through these departments, for all children want to be older than they are. The little boy and little girl seeing the big boys and big girls buying will long for the day when he too can come to these departments and buy." The child as a customer, then, is to be developed through age emulation and a longing to be older. "The child" acquires desire by observing an unmistakable and fine-grained age progression, objectified for her or his eyes, and through which he or she can eagerly pass.

The longing to be like older children—to be "independent" and more of a "person"—is exploited by designers by being grounded in the child's phenomenal experience of the retail environment: "It will be to this particular store that he will want to go because he will have subconsciously developed the idea that here is really the only place where big boys and girls buy their clothes. In this way a valuable shopping habit is created. With the older children's departments located at the entrance end, the other departments follow in logical age sequence with the infants' department at the far end of the girls side of the floor." Note how the imputation of children's perspective, agency, and emergent autonomy is deftly turned into exchange value.

This space is an aspirational space, designed to invoke a longing which could only be met through consumption. The sequence allows stores to feature the "more desirable" age-style clothing while hiding the "less desirable" in the back. The clothes are defined as more and less "desirable," of course, from the standpoint of the child. Note that this sequence and the reasoning behind it are opposite from those of the "anchor store" in a shopping mall, which draws the customer past the "lesser stores." It is a formula, however, which continues today in clothing, toy, and other retail spaces where kids of different ages might come into contact.

The Saks store in New York shows that the upper-class mother is its primary customer by decorating in Early American style with murals by French artists. At Kerns, where the management considers the middle-class child the main customer, the stock is exposed on low-hanging fixtures where "children can see and reach the clothes," rather than being placed behind counters. Also, "counters and display tables have been made a convenient height for the children."[43]

At Kerns, child-height mirrors and low fixtures for the child's own selection were complemented with color schemes thought desirable by children: "Most children's floors are painted in what the adult believes to be children's colors; that is, pastel shades, yet tests have proven that children prefer brilliant primary colors. For the younger children's departments at Kerns we have used brilliant yellows and reds, in the older departments less brilliant yellows and greens. In Saks we have used pastel shades to appeal to the parent, with spots of primary color for the children." The experts here position themselves on the side of the child, as knowing more about what the child "prefers" than the child's own mother, and thus design for the child's perspective, thereby adjudicating it, making it material. The mother is appeased at Saks with pastels but it is the child whose patronage is sought.

The generic pattern and reasoning in these examples became standardized in the 1930s and grew in prominence over subsequent decades. Different age categories of young people's clothing have concatenated into a variety of permutations. New divisions arose within standard ones. For instance, the infants' department, which often included clothing to the age of six, began to be divided into three and sometimes four sections. Some stores, like the Broadway Department Store in Los Angeles, had a Layette Room for newborns, then a room for infant accessories like furniture, walkers, and carriages. Next, a bedding section was followed by a "toddler" and then a "two-to-six" section.[44]

Expansion into different ranges was uneven, as one might expect, throughout the '30s and into the '40s. Some stores followed a similar organization, including toys and accessories as part of the merchandising mix; some expanded into "junior" sizes for the girls.[45] Wanamaker's of Philadelphia opened a "juvenile floor" with ten individual shops in the middle of the Depression, using a graduated color scheme "from palest yellow in the Infants' Salon to deep buff in the University Shop." A large and strong store like the Bon Marché of Seattle, however, did not expand its juvenile sections until the end of the Depression.[46]

Complementing the visual and spatial components of these

stores were many varieties of iconography. Some stores included hobby horses for boys, child characters like Peter Pan painted on the walls, clowns, animals, and all varieties of images thought pleasurable to children. The manager of a children's wear department in Oakland, California, set up her floor so that "ducks, squirrels, rabbits, bears and monkeys proudly stand guard at either end of the [clothing] racks."[47]

Others offered child-centered services, including playrooms and a child's barbershop. In 1932 the Brooklyn shop of Frederick Loeser & Co. was having trouble drawing customers to its children's department in the rear of the store. Mr. Loeser decided to install a child's barbershop at the entrance to attract attention and to offer a free "finger wave" (a popular hairdo) with every haircut. In addition, the store offered a "party shop," complete with hostess, coloring books, and "easily visible merchandise." The intent was to "[divert and hold the] attention of children who might become tired and restless to the extent of discouraging their mothers from completing their shopping plans." Increased sales reportedly followed these innovations.[48]

As the floors and departments became increasingly child centered, they were given trendy and suggestive names to indicate the age range of the clothing with a touch of flair and uniqueness. Schuneman's of Minneapolis had the "Hi-School Shop" (10 to 16) and the "Gradster's Shop" (7 to 14). Wanamaker's floor included the "Early Americans" shop for toddlers, the "Juniette Shop" for girls 12 to 16, and the "Go-With-Er Shop" of girls' accessories. These tactics extended the idea of playrooms, which were meant to hold children until their mother returned from shopping, to shopping areas for children. The trend, emergent in the 1930s, was not to segregate children into a separate room, but to create a children's space that moved them from periphery to center, from dependency to autonomy, from object to subject.

THE COMMODITY status of both child consumers and childhood as a site for consumption gained a significant degree of institutionalization from the mid-1920s through the 1930s. Children's views—their wants and desires, their presumed aspirations to be treated as "older" than their age—acquired increasing cachet in the children's wear industry, to such an extent that the very size-style ranges of the clothing and the structure of selling spaces responded, in multiple ways, to constructs of "the child." In the flux of the changing social order of personal display for young girls and the rearranging of age-stage transitions, merchants, manufacturers, and market observers forged morally palatable solutions by working toward synchronizing age with gender and style considerations. Movement through the micro-stages of childhood, like movement through the store, involved something of a choreography of these personal elements, all the while reasserting and reaffirming the child's perspective and choice.

Merchants made pediocularity material. Child development and age grading provided a vocabulary that helped tie consumption to "natural" growth. Industry boosters, merchants, and manufacturers extended the morality implicit in human "development," in the working toward personhood, outward onto the world of goods. In so doing, they helped to interpolate the process of becoming a person into a commercial calculus whereby product choice, personal autonomy, and self-expression could be seen as coextensive.

By no means exhaustive, universal, or complete by the end of the 1930s, this posture toward the children's market and its institutionalization set the fundamental parameters and dimensions of a children's consumer culture which would unfold in subsequent decades. This culture rests on emplotting children's aspirations to be less dependent—to be older—onto spaces and designs which give children a sense of propriety or ownership over "their" goods. A successful approach to the children's market, emergent in the '30s, addresses children *as* children with appropriate goods and spaces, while speaking to them as nonsubordinates, as persons.

In the ensuing decades, new iterations of childhood and youth arise and transform in tandem with new merchandising and marketing, further blurring the demarcations between stages of life and the goods which putatively give them expression. The growth of the teen and preteen in the context of the postwar baby boom, the topic of the next chapter, extends and elaborates the connections between commerce and childhood.

6

Baby Booms and Market Booms:

Teen and Subteen Girls in the

Postwar Marketplace

BABY (MARKET) BOOM

A month before the bombing of Pearl Harbor in December 1941, an article in the national advertising trade journal *Printer's Ink Monthly* predicted a "boom in the baby market" for 1942. Citing Census Bureau figures on the increase in the number of marriages in 1939 and 1940 and noting the crowded conditions in maternity hospitals,[1] the author observed that there would "probably be at least 100,000 more births in 1941 than in 1940, and this should give baby product manufacturers about 2,450,000 under-a-year prospects for their output. Add this to 1940's 2,350,000 births—and we have 4,800,000 babies under two years old in the United States—a record number."[2]

The extent of this market, the author explained, was vast. Citing dollar amounts spent on advertising in 1940 by manufacturers of baby food, bottle warmers, bottle guards, cod liver oil, "special" cereals for children, "special" baby shoes, diapers, and small children's clothing, the author made a familiar argument: that "any originator of a health-protecting product or device for baby or a labor-saving item for mother has a good chance of selling it to the American public."[3] This article anticipates by about three years the demographic phenomenon now known as the Baby Boom.

Conventionally, the boundaries delimiting the Baby Boom are 1945 to 1964, during which time there were over four million births per year. The magnitude and duration of the high birth rate reversed a downward trend evident during the Depression. Between 1929 and 1944, according to Levy, the number of children aged 14 and under declined by 1.5 million. Between 1945 and 1960, that number increased by about 20 million.[4] Some of these were the result of postponed births but most were the children of younger couples.

The article in *Printer's Ink Monthly* also identified the monetary significance of this phenomenon in its title, "Boom in the Baby Market." According to the *Oxford English Dictionary*, the word "boom" came into use in the 1850s in the United States as a "particular application of the word 'bomb.'" An explosion gives off a "boom" which resounds beyond its origins. The acoustical variant has allowed for the metaphorical extension of the term, most often into the field of economics and business. The noun "boom" refers to: (1) "A start of commercial activity" going off "with a 'boom'... a sudden bound of activity in any business or speculation"; (2) "The effective launching of anything with éclat upon the market." As a verb, "boom" means to "burst into sudden activity or briskness; to make rapid (commercial) progress; to advance vigorously."[5]

From the outset, this demographic phenomenon—an increase in the birth of babies—was framed as a business opportunity. Children and babies, regardless of any specific tastes and preferences, represented prospective consumers whose effective demand for products would unfold in the near future. Sheer numbers of children would ensure a certain level of this increased demand. In retrospect, this initial "boom in the baby market" was only a prelude to two decades of previously unseen population and economic growth.[6] Babies and business were virtually equated.[7]

Earnshaw's was now under the editorial direction of its long-time staff member Walter Hudson, who took over after the death of George Earnshaw in 1940. Hudson also tracked the birth rate for trade use. In January 1942, at the outset of American involvement in the Second World War, Hudson encouraged optimism:

This healthy birth rate plus the fact that there will be more money to spend for baby clothes should mean a very successful year for you. Think of anything if you can that will be affected less by priorities than baby clothes! We don't believe there is anything.

The national income was up 17% in 1941 over 1940. In 1942 it should be at least as high or even higher. Admittedly taxes will be steeper. Automobiles, vacations, household appliances, etc., will go by the board. Not so with baby clothes.[8]

Note the marked departure from the rhetoric of the *Earnshaw's* founder and namesake. It is the "health" of the birth *rate*, rather than that of the children, which is of concern.[9] Yet Hudson's application of the fundamental working assumption of the mother's (or family's) devotion and sacrifice to prioritize the baby's "needs" continues.[10] His lack of concern about hiding or tempering his commercial designs on childhood is indicative of a general shift in posture in favor of the business side of childhood in the postwar era.

Those involved in children's wear were among the first to recognize and act on the market potential of an increased birth rate well before it became a historical demographic phenomenon. Whereas the market for children's books, bicycles, and other things an older child might use would not be realized for several years after birth, children's wear merchants and manufacturers were in a position to "sell the child" (and mother) even before birth. And the children's wear industry was poised for the boom. At its disposal was an infrastructure of buyers, merchandise managers, manufacturers, designers, and publications that had developed during the struggle with weak demand in the '30s. Integrated into this infrastructure were age-graded merchandising, several concatenated age-style ranges, a consumerist conception of "the mother," and a construction of "the child" as an ever-demanding and knowing customer. These elements, put together, provided the industry with the right tools at the appropriate time to accommodate and exploit the dimensions of the coming demographic explosion.

The quantitative growth of the child population also led to the geographic expansion of the industry. Several regional markets opened from the '30s through the '60s. The Los Angeles Apparel Mart in 1936, the Miami Apparel Mart in 1944 and the Dallas Mart in 1964[11] joined the New York market and the Merchandise Mart in

Chicago as regional centers. Also, smaller markets in Denver, San Francisco, and Seattle opened their doors in the 1960s. More trade shows also testified to increased market activity. For instance, there were twenty-seven trade shows listed in *Earnshaw's* for the spring 1952 season; for spring 1959, that number doubled.[12]

A variety of changes in children's wear accompanied these changes in volume after the war.[13] Departmental and industry segmentation, which began in the '30s, accelerated through the '40s and '50s. The pattern of one retailer, Strawbridge & Clothier of Philadelphia, exemplifies the general trend: in 1937 the store spatially divided teens' (see below) from girls' merchandise and gave each an individual buyer; in 1948 it separated toddlers' from children's wear, giving each its own buyer; in 1951 the same was done for teen and subteen merchandise (see below). The Woodward & Lothrop department stores, based in Washington, separated merchandise and added buyers in exactly the same manner and in the same years as Strawbridge & Clothier.[14]

Giving a merchandise classification its own buyer indicates that management is committed to that classification and takes its profit potential quite seriously. A buyer's job is to scour the manufacturing landscape in the attempt to judge which new style trends will work for her department's patrons. She must buy the right kinds of items, in the right amounts, and in the right sizes to decrease overstock.

During this time there was renewed interest in infants and young children because of their growing numbers. This interest became evident in changing consumption practices. The purchase of children's clothing as gifts arose as a significant category of retail sales. One survey of buyers by *Earnshaw's* in 1959 estimated that 51 percent of infant and toddler playwear was sold as gifts, primarily for birthdays and Christmas. Even so, the consensus of those surveyed was that gift purchases were not nearly as strong as a "few years ago." Earlier, in 1957, an article in the trade magazine *Stores* reported that 75 percent of all infants' wear sales were for gifts.[15]

A change in gift-giving practices was noted by the merchandise manager for Strawbridge & Clothier in 1957. Commenting on the multiplication of clothing assortments for children, he observed that the practice of buying a complete layette before birth was being replaced with gifts given at baby showers for the mother-to-be.[16] This practice had consequences for merchandising as well as for sales because merchants understood that "better merchandise is usually purchased by grandparents, more popularly priced items by those giving regular or shower gifts." The manager explained that most of the waking hours of "toddlers and two to sixers are spent in utility clothing, such as corduroy or denim overalls, slacks, play suits, etc." Boys' and girls' suits therefore are for "dress-up" and thus exact a higher price at the counter.[17]

Children's wear in the 1950s filled a niche from which it would never retreat; it had become a standard, staple item worthy of increasing expenditures by parents and other relatives. With a high birth rate to support it, the traditional rate of "markon" or "markup" of children's wear was set in the range of 33 to 39 percent for most non-discount merchants.[18] The infants' department and other juvenile divisions had began "pulling their weight," and thus were noticed by department store managers mindful of profit margins, turnover, and inventory.

In 1956, for example, one industry "expert" reported that while the infants' departments had contributed only 10 percent of department stores' volume since 1954, its contribution to profits increased 67 percent over the same period. With a birth rate that had increased 47 percent since 1945, the author concluded that "Baby business is *Big Business*" and that: "Mothers, cousins, uncles, aunts and friends are spending an average of $150 for the initial purchases for each new baby. This is a startling amount when compared with the average department store charge account of about $100 per person. Remember, we speak now of initial purchases only, not total expenditures per year for infants wear, which is about three times the initial purchase."[19]

Figures like these attracted so much attention to infants' and children's wear that grocery stores began selling juvenile clothing, a trend which apparently worried traditional retailers.[20] These figures also were not lost on specialty stores, discounters, and chain stores (also called "family stores"), which profited as well from the boom.[21] Independent dry goods and department stores, however, continued to lose ground in the 1950s, declining by 60 percent from their high point in 1929.[22]

The industry quickly expanded in response to the annual influx of four million new children as the number of infants' and children's stores expanded nearly tenfold from 1939 to 1948, according to the Census of Retail. Less marked, but steady growth continued for 1954 and 1958 until the number of stores fell in 1963. After 1948, as the birth rate remained high, family stores[23] gained steadily in the 1950s until 1963, when there were 22,927 stores, about doubling in number from 1954. When the Baby Boom ended after 1963, the number of infants' and children's retailers went into a decline, as did sales figures for these retail categories, whereas family stores continued to grow (see figure 4 and table 2 in Appendix).

With each successive year in the demographic boom, a new layer of children added to a developing ordering of age-styles, forming a finely differentiated moral sphere of consumption and personal display. Family stores and "children's floors," now standard arrangements for many department and chain stores in the prosperous 1950s, brought together the entire range of childhood into a single setting for mutual comparison.[24] The leading commercial-cultural figures in these settings during this time were teenage girls and the subteen girl.

TEENAGERS AND PEER ARBITRATION

The recognition of the "teenager" was not expressed commercially to any significant degree until the '30s and did not become a size range until the '40s. For the apparel industry, "teens" referred only to girls' clothing. Boys' clothing beyond the age range of about eight to ten was often relegated to men's wear; teen boys' wear thus was rarely discussed in trade magazines like *Earnshaw's* and *Stores*.[25] "Teen" went out of use as an age-size designation in the 1950s, in favor of "adult" size ranges such as "misses" and "juniors." At the same time a new size category, the "subteen" or "preteen," came into use, which provided a stepping stone to young womanhood.

The teenager is an outgrowth of "adolescence," first invented and named by G. Stanley Hall as a life stage, from about age thirteen to seventeen, that is beyond childhood but precedes the adoption of adult responsibilities. Adolescence is a transitional period characterized by an attachment to peers, a search for personal identity, and a rebellion against adults. A twentieth-century phenomenon, adolescence arose at a time when minors were being excluded from the work force. Troen argues that adolescence became institutionalized in the period 1900–20 as educators and employers began to recognize that unschooled teenage youth were becoming an economic liability to society and business. Grace Palladino contends that the economic pressures of the Depression finally pushed adolescents out of the work force and into high school in record numbers, helping to create and solidify them as a recognized, and self-recognized, age group.[26]

Thus school, especially high school, may be thought of as the institutional "home" of adolescence as it provides for peer contact and the daily opportunity to gauge oneself vis-à-vis others. The enforced age segregation of high schools has engendered, among other things, a youth culture of adolescence. Talcott Parsons argues that high school, as opposed to elementary school, tends to expose the student to a wider range of social statuses and to cross-sex relationships which often continue outside the school in the form of dating. The result is a prestige-stratification system of informal groups which is often independent of one's curricular achievements. Attaining prestige in high school, according to Parsons, "is itself a form of valued achievement."[27]

Adolescence became popularly recognized as a developmental period of rebellion in the 1930s. The goal of achieving prestige privileges the peer group and "other-directedness" over the values of adults and parents.[28] *Parents* magazine, initially devoted to parents of younger children in the 1920s, began coverage of older ones with a piece titled, "The Adolescent and His Clothes" in April 1931. The title is curious because the article expounds almost entirely on the dress of girls, which parents, the author writes, tend to see as a "moral issue, rather than what it is—a matter of mere custom." The author advises taking a generational perspective on the girls' dress: "The lowness and sheerness of present-day frocks shock us because 'in our day' only 'fast' girls wore such attire. . . . A considerate parent will not attempt to make his daughter conform to the standards of his youth. Nothing will make your child rebel so hotly as the remark, 'they didn't do it that way when I was young.' "[29] Sexuality, again, organizes the discourse around girls' dress, this time in a bit more explicit way than with the Girls' size range.

The article also suggests that children be "trained" early on the issue of clothing costs. Adolescent rebellion was not yet a threat to be countered by parental action but a known and expected reaction to be planned for and to be solved within the adolescent's view of the world. Her tastes are taken seriously and are to be indulged so long as they are within the parents' means.

The "teen girl," as an age-size-style range and as a commercial persona, apparently originated from, among other things, efforts by girls of high school age to achieve stylistic affinity with young adult women and distinguish themselves from younger girls. Recall that the Girls' category arose in part because of parental concerns that a young girl should not wear the same style and cut of dress as a fourteen-year-old. Teenage girls, who at that time were also concerned about looking too much like "little sister," set their sight on fashions for college-aged women—what was then the Junior category. In the social world of high school in the mid-'30s, dating and school dances telescoped the importance of girls' self-presentation at a time when they were being overtly discouraged from attempting to enter the professional workplace. Palladino notes how advice givers in magazines reinforced the centrality of beauty and popularity for a girl while warning against going "too far" on a date. Looking "older" was an achievement for some girls which, in time, led the way to a youth culture.[30]

Merchants' anecdotes from the 1930s, and recollection in subsequent decades, tell of high school girls "sneaking" over to the Junior section to find clothing with "sophistication." A dress in the Junior category would be cut for a young women's full figure, which some of the more physically mature high school girls could wear without much difficulty. An article in 1946 in *Business Week* offers some evidence of this process. It profiled an upstart manufacturer, Teentimers of New York City, and gave insight into the origins of the teen age-size category. The company began in 1942 first as a Junior (woman's) size manufacturer. It was discovered then that "about 25% of its output was sold in special teen-age corners by enterprising children's wear buyers who wanted to keep purchases of this between-age group safely tucked away in their own departments."[31] Responding to local demand, buyers merchandised and sold women's styled clothing to high school girls, thus helping to create a new category, a new persona, and, in some ways, a new category of person—the teenager.

There are other clear references to teen merchandising in *Earn-shaw's* and *Stores* as early as 1936, including a short survey of "successful teen girl buyers," implying that the category was not entirely new. That same year, the coat group of the United Infants' and Children's Wear Association agreed to eliminate the manufacture of matching hats to coats in the 10-to-16 range. This practice allowed the manufacturer to eliminate "loss leaders" in coats and, at the same time, sell juvenile millinery for teen girls. Girls' wear buyers reported plans to "open separate millinery sections similar to the 'hat bars' which have done so well in the junior miss field. A real opportunity to merchandise 'teen millinery is open to those stores who go out after separate headwear business."[32]

Separate spaces echo the merchandising strategy brought to bear on younger size ranges. The conditions for a viable teen market, however, were not completely analogous to those for creating an infants', toddlers', children's, or girls' market. Girls of high school age presumably had already passed through the age-graded stages of childhood and become "full persons" in both the developmental and the commercial senses. As a cultural phenomenon "teenagers" were new and foreign to many of those in the industry in the late '30s and early '40s. Merchants thus did not have a well-worn teen persona to draw on as they did for other categories.

In 1937, however, there was recognition of an "adolescent girls' psychology." For instance, Jordan Marsh, Boston, reported the results of an informal survey, taken by its "Family Information Center," of twelve- to sixteen-year-old girls who were asked to score themselves on their own attractiveness: "Anyone familiar with the adolescent girls' psychology knows how large 'personal attractiveness' looms up in her mind—and how grateful she is for tactful, constructive suggestions. We venture to say that this score card has built up a host of youthful loyal followers for the 'teen department here, although the atmosphere of the Family Information Center is kept definitely non-commercial."[33] "Suggestions" would be given by saleswomen who staffed the center, intimating that the girls lacked "constructive" beauty advice from their peers. This belief would be short-lived.

An audience of peers was cultivated by new national media for teen girls. The article in *Business Week* mentioned earlier also traced some of the origins of teen publishing to the late '30s. A publisher named Edward McSweeney, on advice from the advertising manager of the department store chain Best & Co., launched *Mademoiselle*, directed at a younger women's market. "And while *Mademoiselle* split up exploitation of the women's market only as between matrons and nonmatrons, it did show that specialization by age groups was possible and profitable."[34] Helen Valentine, promotion editor of the magazine, became the first editor of *Seventeen* magazine, perhaps the most successful young girls' magazine, which began in 1944 and remains in operation today. In 1942 *Parents* magazine published a short-lived publication, *Calling All Girls*. By 1945 *Miss America* and *Junior Bazaar* rounded out the field. These magazines provided not just beauty advice but social advice and role models confluent with a middle-class version of the "responsible" teen, who although a bit more socially gregarious and adventurous than her parents was nonetheless safe and non-threatening.[35]

By far the most prominent aspect of the new teen departments was the way in which the stores institutionalized and appropriated the clique structure of white, middle-class teen girl peer society into their merchandising strategy. Stores and departments sponsored "fashion boards" or "teen councils" composed of local, "popular" high school girls.[36] Teentimers, Inc., had chartered clubs for its 750 franchised departments, which staged local, peer-judged fashion contests.[37] Retailers also made efforts to court the "most popular" girls from the high schools to serve on fashion boards and model clothes in an attempt to draw "followers." These cliques worked closely with owners, buyers, and merchandise managers both as the fashion leaders of their generation and as "translators" of youth culture for merchants.[38]

The "Younger Crowd Shop" at Powers department store of Minneapolis offers an early example of both in 1942. The department, at the top of the escalator, was considered "ideal" because "the younger crowd can enter it without having to go near the baby department and as it is next-door to the college shop these youngsters in this age group feel very much grown up."[39] As with younger children's departments, separation from younger groups and proximity to older ones was a key component.

The persona of the teen girl offered by buyers and merchants was that of someone who is fashion-conscious, knows what she wants, and isn't shy about expressing her opinion: "This style conscious younger group . . . is more or less a puzzle to the older generation, but is also giving this new group more freedom in the selection of its apparel. If the girl does not like the hat, dress, coat or undies she is frank to say so and will not wear any costume unless she approves." Members of the fashion board at Powers, consisting of nine girls, met with the manager frequently to discuss current styles and trends, a practice which was said to be the basis of the department's success. The girls were also given a proprietary stake in the department by taking turns at being hostess on Saturdays, when the department registered girls for a mailing list. From this list, a back-to-school fashion show drew an estimated thirteen hundred girls.

The manager's ability to involve the girls did not, however, undermine her knowledge of "correct" attire. "While they tell her what they want . . . [the manager] is an expert in putting over her idea of what is really smart for the hi-school girl." Publicly, however, the clothing is labeled with a tag showing the board's "approval" of the style so as to foster a sense of fashion leadership.[40]

In 1942 the manager may have been a source of advice, but as "the teenager" grew into cultural and commercial prominence, other reports indicate that she ascended to the position of an informed, albeit malleable, decision maker. One buyer of teen wear in 1947 describes her department's efforts to involve the high schools: "Realizing that teen agers are perhaps the most fashion conscious and fashion-vulnerable of any age group, we place great faith in our fashion shows. Twice each year in autumn and spring, we visit each high school and junior high school in our city [Roanoke, Virginia] and county with a fashion show held at an assembly for the entire school."[41] Here, the fashion board comprised "representatives" from each high school, who chose the fashion show models from their respective schools.

The schools, "from principals on down," gave "excellent cooperation" to these shows. They were complemented by a store-sponsored "High School Day" where seniors were allowed to staff the store once a year. The schools cooperated by excusing these students from classes. High School Day was topped off with another fashion show to which "all high school students" were invited and for which all local newspaper promotions were "prepared by the art students at the local high schools."

Events such as these, repeated in a variety of ways throughout the country,[42] reinforced the conception of girls/women as objects of adornment, to be seen and valued for their physical appearance. Teen girls enter womanhood as persons capable of appraising their appearance and clothing. Teen fashion shows became widespread in a time when the ultra-feminine "New Look" of Christian Dior (circa 1947), and its fitted waists and tops, contrasted drastically with women's previous appearance in factories and in military clothes. Although designed with elements of masculinity, the New Look reinscribed the legitimacy of the male gaze upon women and provided a context in which the teen girl and teen market came of age.[43]

The teen girl market flourished because girls were treated as persons in their own right. This enfranchisement carried with it a sense of reliance on their collective judgment and a proprietary claim on the materials and spaces in the retail world. Time and again, retailers reported in *Earnshaw's* that the key to the success of their teen departments was its visual, spatial, and stylistic distinctiveness from younger children's areas. A representative from Derby Sportswear in 1951 encourages buyers to maintain their focus on the teen girl: "There are many ways to attract the teen. She is gregarious. She likes to mingle with a group, to go and do what the other girls do. She loves to design and model. She is conscious of the impression she makes on boys. A store should be the outlet for these emotions. A teen department should be separated from children's and properly planned to provide a special section for her."[44] The Teen Shop of Lansburgh & Co., Washington, was separated from the girls' department by elevators and by a distinctive architecture and color scheme: "This drop ceiling semidivision serves a double function: it clearly distinguishes the Teen Shop for the approaching customer, and it gives a cozy 'this-is-our-shop' feeling which sets off the teener as distinct from the *Girls' Shop*, a psychological advantage which teen buyers recognize."[45] For industry boosters, the centrality of the teen department was key to the customer's psychological identity as "a teen." A retail outlet was also to serve as a setting where identities could be rehearsed for a receptive audience.

By all accounts, movement into the teen department was a rite of passage for the young white girl of the middle class, especially in the early 1950s. The teen buyer for Bonwit Teller of Philadelphia explains to the *Earnshaw's* audience: "This is the first time that our young lady is breaking away from the little-girl clothes she has been used to. . . . If the teen department is merely a continuation of the same kind of clothing, she will go to another department or shop where smart merchandise is carried. Teen-agers today are very fashion-conscious; they read the fashion magazines and know what is being shown for their big sisters—and they want to do the same things."[46]

The social movement to styles for older girls was to be accompanied by an interactional ascension to adult-like personhood, where the clerks would avoid talking down to the girls. "We talk with them, they're part of the family to us." One store manager in San Francisco went a step further: "Probably one of the important features of our sales training program is the fact that we instruct our clerks to serve their customers as individuals—not as children. Our teenagers are . . . exactingly clothes-conscious."[47] Another buyer stated: "You have to court their friendship. . . . You cannot assume you are going to inherit their patronage from their parents. They don't appreciate that attitude. All of a sudden the teen-ager is aware that she is an individual, and one with grown-up sagacity concerning clothes."[48]

Patience is said to be the key to helping the teen customer sensitive about how she looks. But the mother always looms problematically in the background: "Often a mother will bring up all her daughter's bad points before the embarrassed young lady . . . All it takes is time and patience to fit her properly . . . and if time and really personalized service is offered, we can fit any youngster."[49] Unlike in the infants' and children's departments, the mother is less an ally and more of an obstacle to manage or overcome. If necessary, the store sides with the teen, attempting to demonstrate an "understanding attitude" to the mother. The sales clerk here offers a model for how the mother might more effectively treat a teen.[50]

With a sense of a growing distance between the teens' world and the adult world, many merchants expressed a preference for young sales clerks and a youthful atmosphere. At Falk's Teen Shop in Boise, Idaho, the strategy in 1950 was to sell youth with youth: "The store management feels that younger people can better understand and work with Teen-Age clientele. It is an acknowledged fact that if older people offer suggestions, they are 'old fogies' who could not possibly know what was right."[51] The same store built a teen "gift bar" to direct older adults to an assortment of merchandise known to be desired by teen girls, on the assumption that choosing an appropriate gift might be beyond the abilities of adults. The Cincy Hi Shop sought out not only young clerks in 1953, but selected those who *appear* and *act* "youthful." "We try to get salespeople who dress young, look smart, and talk the teen agers' language, and thus avoid the teacher type of a relationship between clerks and customers."[52] Here a leveling of the age-power relationship was thought essential to sales.

A growing consensus was quickly emerging about the increasing maturity of the teen girl. At the Cincy Hi Shop, the manager in 1954 reported having trouble keeping girls in the teen departments because they continually moved toward the women's department looking at junior sizes. "To combat this, we try to make Cincy Hi shop as sophisticated as possible." A buyer for a store in the District of Columbia confirmed this: "Our teens want junior styling and junior fit. We've found that typical teen sizes only fit the subteen. We tried a special selection of carefully styled, well made teen dresses, but our teen customers breeze right past them for the junior styling."[53] The buyer went on to explain that about 95 percent of the sales were made without the teen's mother present. When mothers are present, "the teens tell the mothers what is style and what they want." Indeed, teens rejected the term "teen," preferring instead "young junior" or other designations.[54]

The problem of what a "teen" is in this context and what her clothes were was not yet solved three years later. In an article for *Stores* in 1957, the merchandise manager for Strawbridge and Clothier of Philadelphia lamented the lack of a "true teen size." Few manufacturers, he complained, cut a true teen size. Instead, the teen was opting for Junior styling. The store which does not offer at least some "true teen" resources lacks the "fashion authority" needed to merchandise not only to the teen, but also to the up-and-coming "preteen" (or subteen, as discussed below).[55]

In addition to specialized clothes, specially trained sales clerks, and distinct rooms, many teen departments were equipped with jukeboxes or had popular music piped in. Coca-Cola was mentioned often by buyers and managers as a feature for winning and maintaining teens' interest. The upscale Broadway-Hollywood Shop in Los Angeles went one step further as early as 1944 by promoting a Saturday fashion show called a "Coke Sesh." The weekly program allowed all the girls to model recent styles for each other and their peer clientele.[56]

When the phenomenon of the teenager began in the mid-'30s, the target population was a relatively small group of high school–aged girls from middle-class families who were not especially limited by economic conditions. By 1959, however, *Life* magazine was calling teenagers a "$10 Billion Power."[57] The "generation gap" that widened between teens and parents through the '50s and '60s did so most obviously through the medium of consumption: clothing, music, fast food, film. The "gap" was also bridged, however, at least within the sphere of commercial enterprise, by taste and style mediators. Sales clerks, buyers, and merchandise managers, themselves no longer teens, acted as a liaison between the teen world, the market, and at times motherhood.[58] In some cases, the teen girl was a style critic and fashion peer to her mother. The reputation for style savvy on the part of teen girls was behind an article in *Parents* magazine, "What Teen-agers Think of Their Mothers' Looks," in which teen girls were asked to rate and advise their own mothers on appearance.[59]

"The teen" was in constant need of definition by marketeers and the public media. Teens' wants, desires, and spending money had to be rediscovered each season in order to manufacture, merchandise, and market for the appropriate consumers.[60] Near the surface in all public and trade discussion was the sexual life of these "fun worshippers," as one article in *Newsweek* called teenagers in 1961. People like the market researcher Eugene Gilbert made a living by figuring out and translating teenagers' wants and desires into the kind of information that business could use.[61]

Retail operations recognized the social structure of teen peer society. They encouraged peer arbitration of style in events like fashion shows and reinforced the teen aversion to elder/parental authority through an emphasis on the youthfulness of their sales clerks. In so doing, local stores and departments provided space, materials, and personnel for the creation of this particular version of female, peer society. They provided the lead in the commodification of this phase of gendered childhood.

The persona of the "teen girl" helped to demarcate and give shape to the upper reaches of a commercial-sartorial hierarchy of age progression. The public visibility of these white, middle-class teenagers served as something of a stylistic and social goal for many girls occupying the age group immediately below them, who also aspired to independence and personhood through consumption and personal display.

"Teenager-hood" as a goal gave rise to the "subteen" or "preteen" girl, essentially completing a configuration of graded age-size-style ranges for girls of the white middle class by 1960. The preteen came into prominence in the mid- to late '50s at a time when 76 percent of the 24,000 public secondary schools had junior high schools for students 12 to 15 years old.[62] The existence of junior high schools effectively made passage in and out of them a marked event and an opportunity for age distinction. Just as teen girls sought "adult" junior styling in their clothing in the 1940s and '50s, a younger category of girls encroached on and appropriated the styles of their "older sisters" in the 1950s and 1960s.

The emergence of the subteen (now "preteen" or "Tween") age-size-style range differs from the pattern evident in the teen and earlier girls' and children's ranges. Not until the late '40s was the subteen range, which varied from 10 or 11 to 12 or 13 years old, discussed in the trade press. One source attributes the category to dress manufacturers who turned out "toned down" (or less sophisticated) versions of teen dresses for girls a few years their junior. One dress manufacturer traced the origin of the subteen category to as early as the 1930s, when, as he explained to *Earnshaw's* in 1961, he won over dress manufacturers and buyers with a new size category. Apparently, he had read a study of how 300,000 girls in the 7–14 range could not be properly fitted. Noting that many girls were jumping to junior (teenage) sizes, he convinced manufacturers and buyers to try a new, intermediate range. Regardless of origin, subteen styles, unlike the other merchandising categories, were slow to catch on and tended to be grouped with younger girls' clothing in promotions and merchandising rather than with the older ones.[63]

Eclipsed by the numerical prominence of babies and by the cultural prominence of teens in the early '50s, it was not until about 1955 that "the subteen" began to be elaborated as a distinct commercial persona in the clothing industry. One merchandise manager asked in January of that year, "What Is the Retailer Doing for the Sub-teen?" Recognizing that there are "over four million Sub-Teens this year and more coming in the next ten years," the writer chastised retailers and buyers for ignoring this potential market.[64] Once retailers accepted the category, the writer offered essentially the same strategy for institutionalizing subteens that had been successfully employed in developing children's, girls', and teens' sections and departments.

Once one was convinced of the need for a separate subteen department, the only question was its social and spatial placement. The writer continued: "To expand the Sub-Teen department, we may have to move *it* or other departments off of the children's floor. . . . The question then arises, where does the *Sub-Teen Department* belong? On the children's floor or on the Teen Age . . . floor?"[65] The retail answer to the lack of elaboration of a preteen commercial persona in the mid-'50s was just on the horizon.

As millions of girls began passing through the 10 or 11 to 13 age range each year, retailers, managers, and buyers took notice. A buyer for Lyttons, Chicago, wrote about the future market potential of the subteen who, if satisfied, could be "kept" (as a customer) in her teen years and beyond. To make a loyal customer of this girl, her needs must be known: "The sub-teen girl is an entity unto herself. She has quite different problems in dress than her teen-age sister, or her younger sister who can wear the 7–14 styles. . . . She definitely has a more grown-up feeling than two or three years ago, when blue jeans . . . reigned supreme."[66] Accordingly, subteen merchandise was not to be advertised with that for 7–14 girls, and sales personnel should treat the subteen girl "as a young lady with a brain, not as someone we barely tolerate during adolescence, or as a forgotten member of society." Still a "child," the subteen girl required education in the principle "that to be a lady she must not only act like one, she must dress accordingly." The notion that the subteen girl is eager to pass from the tomboy stage and make her way toward conventional attire is important in the development of this category, for it also relied on the notion that by appearing to be older, one was more "sophisticated"—more feminine.[67]

The subteen classification continued to meet with a lack of enthusiasm in the '50s. One reason given is that the physical attributes of girls aged 10 or 11 to 13 are quite varied. Some are tall and lanky (or "gawky"), others short. Some have breast development while others do not. It is a sizing nightmare for the manufacturer and a potential fitting disaster for the retailer. With frequent changes in styles, it is also difficult to stock and merchandise for this category when, in a year or so, many of the girls will want to move on to "older" sizes.[68]

Another reported difficulty was that girls were said to want to pass over this brief and diminutive category and move right into teen-styled clothing—they didn't want to be "sub" or "pre" anything. Teens, on the other hand, by the mid-'50s were expressing discontent with the term "teen," preferring instead to shop at the "Deb Shop," "Jr. Assembly Shop," or "Jr. Prom Shop."[69] The process of "distinction," as elaborated by Bourdieu—in this case age, rather than class distinction—persistently drove retailers and manufacturers to innovate both "older" clothing styles and "older" identities. In the world of the high school and junior high, independence and maturity—or at least their public, bodily markers—functioned as a form of cultural capital.[70]

The promise of a steady population of subteen girls growing out of the Baby Boom helped make "subteens" a standard retail category in the late '50s. The physical construction of the departments, the logic of their placement in relation to other departments, and the advice given to sales personnel reveal an isomorphism with teen departments based upon an analogous construction of "the customer." This customer, like the teenager, is peer conscious, age conscious, and fashion conscious. Some retailers and manufacturers sponsored fashion shows for this age group (the "schoolgirl" group in trade parlance) as early as 1947.

A merchandise manager from Carson's, Chicago, in 1959 explained the subteen girl to the trade audience:

> She spends as much as she can possibly beg, borrow or steal from her dazed parents. She loves to shop. All we need to do is expose

this *Newteen* to the things she likes, and she is on our team—selling herself, her mother, and her pals. . . .

Our customer needs a feeling of security, of close friendships with contemporaries. She idolizes the age group just above her and does not want to be confused with "those infants," who is anyone just a year younger or a grade behind her. This makes her want a Subteen department, a corner of her own.[71]

The strategy and hope is that the exigencies of the subteen's social world will serve as the impetus for the acceptance and success of this category. (Note the attempt to coin a new category, the "newteen.")

However much the actual or imputed desires of the subteen girl focused on being "older," her immaturity was something to be acknowledged and accommodated. One retailer not only created a separate department, but also an alcove with a bar and two stools "to be used for subteen giggling as well as trying on clothes."[72] The disparity between the sought-after "sophistication" of the subteen girl and her chronological and social age was not lost on retailers: "The salesperson should always remember their insecurity, shyness, their desire to be glamorous and independent of the rules; their urge to all look alike. The Fashion Board members told me that they like 'The helpful kind of saleslady.' . . . One (complete with pink lipstick) said 'Someone older than we are knows more about clothes.' "[73] Not quite as knowing as the older girls who were their "teen idols," subteens needed approval of their peers confirmed by sales help. Playing upon this lack of confidence, some retailers offered "charm classes" to entice the girls and their mothers into the store.[74]

As the market position of the subteen increased, there was some confusion among retailers who came in contact with them. One buyer suggests luring the subteen into the department with her own lingo. Four years later, retailers were advised not to use the subteen's slang because "it is very profoundly theirs and these girls sometimes consider this 'patronizing.' "[75]

Resentment at having to please preteens was also voiced by retailers. In an *Earnshaw's* editorial, we learn that some specialty shop owners "claim [subteen merchandising] is not profitable, they dislike catering to 'brats' and resent hearing them say 'It stinks,' no matter what is shown them. These retailers say they don't want to be psychiatrists in addition to merchants, and the aggravation of trying to please subteens isn't worth the gain."[76] Attempting to defend the relevance of department stores at a time when strip malls were beginning to spring up in postwar suburbs, the editorial stated that specialty shops do not find the subteen business profitable because pre-teenagers like to shop in the "adult environment" of department stores, which gives them a more "grown up" feeling. The subteen—like the parade of commercial personae over the previous two decades—can be shaped to fit a variety of beliefs.

The sales results from subteen business were apparently worth the hassle of pleasing these girls. *American Girl*, originally a Girl Scouts magazine, conducted a survey of 2.1 million girls of this age range, a range which had expanded to include 10- to 14-year-olds by the late '50s. The results, published in *Earnshaw's*, indicate that $450 million was spent by and on subteen girls for the 1959 Christmas season alone. Of that, $5 million went to cosmetics. Respondents reported receiving $138.5 million worth of merchandise as gifts and $7.152 million in gift cash. Sales figures like these certainly caught retailers' eyes.[77]

These figures also encouraged *Earnshaw's* to begin a monthly special section called "Sub-Teen World" beginning with the September 1960 issue. The continuing ambiguity of this social-style-market category is set forth in the opening for "Sub-Teen World": "The Subteen Girl. Who is she? She's a girl who walks into your store and boldly asks for an 'ultra-sophisticated' dress . . . and blushes when her date compliments her. She's a girl who defiantly specifies her taste in clothes when she walks into your stores . . . and walks into a party with bated breath awaiting approval. Half girl and half woman, she's one of a total of 8,500,000 sub-teen girls in this country today."[78] A year later, this woman/girl tension evoked a predictable question: "Are Subteen Dresses Becoming Too Sophisticated?" The writer noted that manufacturers of sub-teen dresses, who were anxious to keep her in their lines "past her time," had started producing dresses more suited to a teen girl's figure and disposition.[79]

For a brief time, the industry debated a new "g" size to fill a gap between subteen and teen styles. It never took hold, possibly because too much money and energy had been devoted to building subteen departments for buyers to start again on a new category and a new educational campaign. The "preteen dilemma" of how to keep girls of the 10–14 range (note the widening of the range) from "jumping" to the "young junior" department became chronic and, in many ways, is unresolved today.[80]

The express desires of middle-class teens and preteens to look and act "grown up" and the retailer's and buyer's ability to indulge these desires combined to produce some age ambiguity in the physical appearance of the girls. Accessories in the form of jewelry and purses for the junior high school market and the widespread use of lipstick and other cosmetics seemed to push the preteen into the "young woman" euphemism often applied to her. The "Little Lady" line of Helen Pessel began merchandising cosmetics for girls aged 6 to 14 in 1946; it was joined by the children's toiletry company Tinkerbell in 1952.[81]

Foundation manufacturers, like Munsingwear and Teenform, began producing brassieres for young teens in the late 1940s, along with girdles. Marketing the concept of the "beginning bra" for preteens in the early 1950s brought new styles and new problems. Among these were problems of fit and sizing and the adaptation of the undergarment to more "sophisticated" strapless dresses for preteens.[82]

By the early '60s, preteens and the preteen market were pushing up against teens in terms of age-style distinction. Age slippage became apparent. A typical example is an article in *Parents* in 1962 about "teen dress" that focuses on the *preteen* range of twelve- and thirteen-year-old girls. The blurring between chronological maturity, social maturity, and the stylistic expression of maturity of these girls became a subject for public moral concern at this time.[83]

Life magazine profiled this age group in 1962 in an article titled "Boys and Girls: Too Old Too Soon: America's Subteens Rushing Toward Trouble." It sometimes mocks the desires of the featured young girls (suburban, white, and middle class) to look and act like adults. The implications of the preteen girl's ambiguous social identity were left unclear. In this article and others accompanying it, the efforts of girls to groom themselves to appear "older" were depicted visually in the frame of humorous juxtaposition as benign attempts to mimic adults—with the cuteness of a kitten falling out of a tree. However, when the sexual consequences of grooming were considered, the visual confluence of preteens' actions with those of adults presented a striking and no doubt morally gripping picture to the American readership.[84]

The cause or blame for this sexual precocity is placed neither on the girls themselves nor on the industries organized to transform their life stage into exchange value. The *visual* blame in the article is placed most squarely on mothers who are shown to be indifferent to the children's preoccupations and actions or who otherwise permit the use of lipstick and "early pairing off," among other things.[85] The *textual* blame is placed on "parents," some of whom "once suffered from unpopularity [and] are nowadays very concerned that their offspring be well-adjusted and popular."[86] One mother of a featured preteen explains her position vis-à-vis her daughter's peer world: "I think to some extent we parents are swept along with them. . . . And directing all facets of a child's development seems overwhelming—especially when there are so many influences to make them sophisticated earlier. The makeup—I understand that in some good grooming courses at school they teach them to do this. Lipstick too early—they start at 10. You can't stop your child; everybody does it. I think the harm you do by making them different is worse than just going along." The defensive posture, the acknowledgement of peer influence, the relation of physical appearance and commodities to generational tension— all these are emblematic of the changing boundaries within and between various "youth cultures" and an "adult sphere."

AGE STAGE AND gender differentiation continued serving the market demand for novelty after 1940. The "teen girl" emerged out of the age-size-style reorganization of the 1930s into a full-blown commercial persona, a moniker, and an embodiment of a new youth culture. Not only did teen girls acquire their own clothing and selling spaces, they became peer arbiters of their own style and, in some cases, gained proprietary status over their own retail environment. Fueled by the boom in babies and inspired by teen girlhood as a desirable identity, the subteen category and girls themselves found room to present and manifest another shade of consumer personhood in the 1950s.

Concluding Remarks

Markets have not invaded childhood—either now or over the last century. They provide, rather, indispensable and unavoidable means by which class specific, historically situated childhoods are made material and tangible. The story of the rise of the child consumer presented in the preceding chapters offers empirical, conceptual, and theoretical support to the idea that markets are indispensable to the making of social persons in the ongoing consumer culture of childhood and, indeed, in consumer culture at large. These are persons who in turn use markets to remake themselves, as we have seen most clearly with teen and preteen girls in the '40s and '50s.

My contention throughout has been that to understand consumption as a keystone of personal identity in modern and postmodern times, as many scholars convincingly argue, one must not look primarily at adult practice for evidence of a consuming self. One must investigate those cultural sites where consuming selves arise, transform, and grow to the point of co-creating other consuming selves. For social selves are neither ontologically or historically static, nor do they arise in isolation. "Children's" consuming selves never emerge exclusively through the efforts of children themselves, nor do they remain the exclusive "property" of chil-

ever changing

dren as industries, parents, teachers, and media interact to mold and influence the growth of children. Children's consumer culture is thus an ongoing historical accommodation of adult interests and children's selves, of sentimental and monetary values.[1]

Consumer culture and consumer capitalism, as we now know them, are impossibilities absent the continual integration and reintegration of childhood with the commodity form. We do not suddenly become consumers as young adults or teenagers. It is not useful, as I hope this book has demonstrated, to think of children—of persons generally—along the lines posed by neoclassical economic thought as initially independent, encapsulated beings who confront an equally clearly identifiable "market sphere" and who thereby make discreet choices within it or become merely socialized into it. Consumption has become a necessary and indispensable context—though not sufficient in itself—in which the person or self develops because commerce produces most of the material world with which a child comes into contact, including her or his possessions. It is around consumption and display—in the interaction with the material world—that personhood and agency tend to crystallize. Where one is, so the other shall be found.

The rise of the child consumer is part of a larger movement toward enfranchising children as full persons in Western culture that is evident in, for example, recent court cases which have given children in the United States a limited ability to "divorce" their parents. The movement is also international in scope, culminating in 1989 in the United Nations Convention on the Rights of Children. In a series of fifty-four Articles of Resolution, the convention outlined children's rights in matters such as "free expression of opinion," "the protection of privacy," and "freedom of association."[2] According to Hart, these stated rights differ from an earlier UN declaration on children in 1959 in that they emphasize self-determining rights in addition to protective ones. He concludes that the 1989 convention "is a strong indicator of the increased, formal, societal emphasis being given to participation and autonomy . . . for children." The attempt to foster consumer autonomy and commercial participation for children, as we have seen, preceded these formal statements by several generations.[3]

Beyond the discourse on rights, there is some evidence that the desired qualities in children expressed by parents have changed since the 1930s to favor "independence" and "thinking for oneself" over those of "obedience" and "loyalty." These are qualities not only favored of children in middle-class homes but, as we have seen, also nurtured in and by the consumer marketplace over time. Adding to the view that children are now intricately bound to consumption are studies showing that "materialism," or the desire for material goods, is fast becoming a dominant value among American youth.[4]

The consumer personhood of contemporary children continues to exist in dynamic relation to the position and to the "appropriate" actions of mothers. Increasing maternal employment, single-parent (mother) households, and dual-wage-earner families have left a large number of children on their own after school. Many of these children have taken on added household responsibilities, including cooking for themselves and doing some of the family shopping, as opposed to only personal shopping. Marketers have been quick to spy these trends and to create products designed to appeal to the child-family shopper and to the overworked and time-strapped mother.[5]

Increased sales in, for instance, ready-made meals, frozen dinners, and pizza and in dining out have all been attributed by food industry observers to the increased presence of mothers in the workplace. Women's increased presence in the work force has rarely been compensated with home assistance from their spouse, when present. Employed mothers today report that they do not have the time or the energy to monitor their children's consumption and media practices and hence "yield" to their children's requests more frequently than their parents did for them. Caught in the contradiction between the ideology of intensive mothering and the desire and need to engage in paid work, mothers often express and alleviate guilt with purchases for their children.[6] For marketers, working mothers' time constraints and their desire to keep the peace in the household represent a selling opportunity.[7]

Children's insistent requests for goods, especially in public, can make for embarrassing moments. In marketing research circles, these persistent requests have come to be known as the "nag factor." Children report to market researchers some fairly elaborate strategies for begging and nagging parents into submission. Nagging one's parents to purchase something probably dates at least as far back as the candy counter and early toy stores. It is a child's way to exert influence by expressing preferences from a position of relative powerlessness. What is distinct about children's nagging in recent decades is that it has become part of advised marketing strategy, something encouraged and counted on by children's marketeers, as children's influence on household purchases continues to extend beyond cereal and soft drinks into big ticket purchases such as vacations, cars, and major household items.[8] Trained professionals, like the social worker Cynthia Whitman, write guides for parents on how to say "no" to their children.[9] *-□ resist giving in'*

It appears that personal independence and consumer autonomy for children are becoming one and the same. Consumption by older children in many families emerges as a necessity or as part of the family's allocation of labor. In recent decades, the increasing absence or increasingly limited availability of working mothers to supervise their children's consumption has helped make all but the youngest children potentially "autonomous" consumers. One author interviewed over three hundred "parents, teachers, pediatricians, educators, children's clothing designers and manufacturers" to put together a parent's guide to "kids, clothes and independence." Calling children's clothes one of the "great underground issues of parenting," she writes: "clothes actually are a pivotal childhood issue. Preceded only by food, clothing is the child's earliest opportunity to exercise personal autonomy and then to experience the results."[10] Autonomy can be realized in all aspects of children's dress, from the morning dress routine to sleepwear and from school clothes to fashion.

Another author equates the discovery of "baby's own style" with "personality": "Your baby's distinctive personality will slowly unfold like the petals of a flower. As mothers, it is our job to *allow* the unique style of each of our children to blossom freely." Mother's "job," much as it was in the '20s and '30s, is to enhance or at least not impede a "natural" progression toward individuality. This individuality arises through offering the child choices from the earliest possible age: "One fun and easy exercise is to give your child color choices. Using colored paper . . . let your child pick out favorite colors. . . . I did this with my daughter when she was fifteen months old. Invariably, she gravitated toward her vivid, warm, Spring colors. . . . Children instinctively know what they like, and color is important to them from the very beginning." Resorting to "instinct" to explain the apparent expression of preference by pre-linguistic children, the author paradoxically negates the presumption that the child has a "choice." The search for individuality begins within the child (*her* colors), as if preexistent and natural.[11]

What may be called "laissez-faire mothering" represents the complementary position to the agentive child consumer. The overwhelming thrust of children's marketing favors the active child over the passive mother. When confronted with charges of "exploiting" children for material gain, the children's industry invariably responds by invoking the "sophistication" of children and their ability to understand commercial intent, a position that held sway when children's television was deregulated during the Reagan years. The market (or the media message), so goes the argument, is not a danger to anyone who can comprehend it. It is an argument which lost some of its thrust at century's end in the wake of a number of school shootings, in particular the incident at Columbine High School in Colorado in 1999, where video game violence figured prominently in public discourse about the "causes" of the rampages. Unsurprisingly, the parents of the perpetrators—and mothers by strong implication—were criticized for not monitoring their children's consumption and media use.[12]

A discourse of vulnerable children needing protection has arisen strongly in recent years as a counterbalance to the images of the agentive child consumer proffered by marketing appeals, and perhaps as a reaction against the rampant commodification of childhood witnessed in the 1990s. Children, particularly boys and particularly those of grade school age and younger, are now also being defined as susceptible to video violence, whether in games or film, by politically active mothers and sympathetic politicians. In a similar vein, a report by the Federal Trade Commission in 2000 accused the film industry of enticing younger children with edited previews of movies that they should not be allowed to see because of their rating.[13]

The battle here is over the very *model* of the child as a social actor. When children are understood as impressionable, incomplete beings, it is incumbent on mothers and others to act as their arbiters and agents. The extent to which children are understood to be either autonomous in, or exploited by, media-commercial culture varies, it seems, according to the extent to which observers either express unwavering disdain for the corporate world or embrace the view of the agentive child. Those who see corporate culture as the nemesis of childhood also tend to see the child in innocent, or at least sentimental, terms, as one who is vulnerable and in need of protection; those who understand children as active in the creation of their world tend to downplay concerns about corporate exploitation.

The view of the child as a willful, knowledgeable, and desiring agent who is making her or his own decisions and exercising self-expression through the medium of the commodity form is, of course, favored by those who work in and profit from children's industries. One cannot "sell the child" without a child that is salable.

THE COMMERCIAL mentality undergirding the rising children's consumer industries has effectively delimited "the child" as an analytical isolate by defining children as individuated, naturalized consumers. At the same time, the material and ideal culture supporting commodified childhood works toward extracting "the child" from many traditional constraints which adhere to age-based subordination. In the process, children's consumer culture, Joe Kincheloe argues, has become based on an "affective opposition to the adult world." To be sure, the subversion of adult, specifically parental, authority constitutes the modus operandi of much of kids' and youth culture since the Second World War.[14]

A detailed examination, however, of the discourses surrounding the advent of new size-styles ranges, mainly for girls, and of age-graded retail spaces for children adds dimension to this understanding of children's oppositional stance. As we have seen, threats to autonomy arise not just from adult and parental power, but also from the possibility of children being associated with those younger than themselves. Children's consumer culture has been built upon a graduated sequence of differences, each step associated with materials and symbols thought appropriate for children to distinguish themselves from those who represent subordinate identities. The most immediate distinctions made by children are those they make among themselves. Aspirational consumption and spaces, in this way, take the child's perspective and invoke it as legitimate authority, as an appropriate basis to enact commerce vis-à-vis childhood.

The model of the agentive, desirous child consumer is not the creation of the children's wear industry alone. It is rather the product of an intricate convergence of, and interaction among, diverse historical and cultural factors like schooling, age grading, and women's participation in the work force. The children's wear industry did not independently invent the age stages and gender designations found in children's clothing, nor did it simply copy extant stages and designations. Rather, the emergent infrastructure and trajectory of the industry through the 1960s offered a template for the treatment of the child as a customer. This template is a social persona which helped coordinate the tensions between children's wants and parents' concerns, regulate the cadence and movement between ever finer distinctions of age-gender grades, and, ultimately, institutionalize the child's perspective as a basis for marketing practice. In a sense, the industry did its part in forging a kind of structural agency for children in that it provided sets of constraints from which choosing subjects could arise who would appear to have chosen as if unconstrained. Children's wear, as both a commodity and an industry, participated in the transformation of childhood in a collective attempt to express it and sell it.

This book does not presume closure of any kind—historical, theoretical, or in terms of content. The voices of children are absent, except as they were captured by merchants and researchers, but not because they are unworthy of contemplation and inclusion. Their absence or minimal presence regarding consumption serves to reinforce the thesis that their consumer personhood has been emergent and slow to be recognized by academic (nonmarketing) researchers until recently. The place of consumption in the lives and worlds of racial and ethnic minorities is now only beginning to be addressed, in particular in the work of Elizabeth Chin. Class-specific experiences and articulations of consumption throughout these years also are not addressed—the middle-class focus of the industry and of popular publications perform a kind of erasure of these worlds which, I believe, can be "unerased."[15]

Acknowledging, accepting, and understanding these limitations should not detract from the central purpose of this book; namely, to offer a general problematic and invite engagement with it in new and unforeseen ways rather than only to present an isolated problem to be "solved" once and for all. In other words, I hope to have offered generative insights rather than intransitive statements. These limitations also should in no way detract from the fundamental assertion that one cannot understand children and childhood, at least since the beginning of the twentieth century, without examining the world of consumer goods and consumer social relations. Analyses and reports of the emerging global market for children's goods bear out the necessary and intricate connection between children's personhood and children's consumption in a manner similar to that described throughout this book.[16]

In the historical commodification of childhood, the child has retained a duality theorized by Ariès and articulated by Zelizer. "The child" registers both the innocence of guileless motivation and the culpability of desire—as something to be coddled yet policed through moral scrutiny. It enters the profaneness of everyday commercial relations while retaining that sense of sacredness which accompanies the belief in a preexistent, authentic self.

Children's personhood, consumer or otherwise, today confronts all as a kind of Durkheimian social fact: regardless of one's feelings about children's consumption or their social insubordination (or superordination, for that matter), we must all position ourselves in relation to the putatively and potentially agentive child. To fail to do so is to commit something of a moral transgression.

This case history of the children's wear industry offers a way to apprehend some of the processes by which contemporary childhood and consumer culture have become interwoven, asking whether one can any longer exist without the other.

Appendix

Figures and Tables

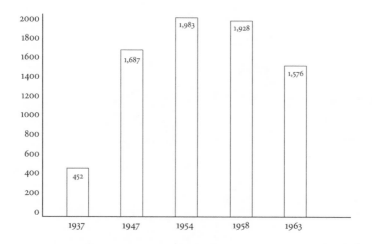

FIGURE 1. Number of Children's Outerwear Manufacturers, 1937–1963. SOURCE: *U.S. Census of Manufacture*, 1937, 1947, 1954, 1958, 1963.

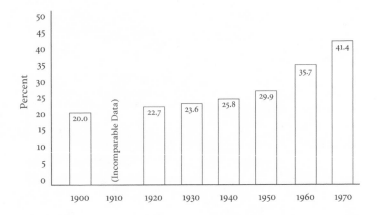

FIGURE 2. Labor Force Participation Rate for All Women, 1900–1970. Rates are for all women 14 years and older before 1947 and 16 years and older after 1947. SOURCE: *Historical Statistics of the United States, Colonial Times to the Present* (Washington: Government Printing Office, 1975), part 1, series D 29-41, p. 132.

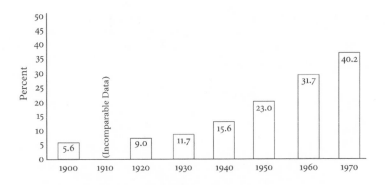

FIGURE 3. Labor Force Participation Rate for Married Women, 1900–1970. Rates are for married women 15 and over, 1890–1930; 14 and over, 1940–1966; 16 and over thereafter. SOURCE: *Historical Statistics of the United States, Colonial Times to the Present* (Washington: Government Printing Office, 1975), part 1, series D 49-60, p. 133.

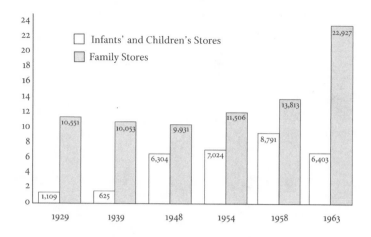

FIGURE 4. Number of Retail Establishments for Infants' and Children's Wear and Family Stores (in Thousands), 1929–1963. SOURCE: *U.S. Census of Retail*, 1929, 1939, 1948, 1954, 1958, 1963.

TABLE 1. Number of Domestic Servants (in Thousands) and Percentage of Families with Domestic Servants, 1900–1940

	1900	1910	1920	1930	1940
Number of servants, including laundry, trained nurses, cooks, other	1,509	1,867	1,484	2,205	2,098
Number of families	15,964	20,053	24,201	29,905	34,949
Percentage of families with servants	9.5	9.3	6.1	7.4	6.0

SOURCE: Phyllis Palmer, *Domesticity and Dirt* (Philadelphia: Temple University Press, 1989), 167 n. 22.

TABLE 2. Retail Sales (in Thousands, 1984 Dollars) for Infants' and Children's Wear Stores and Family Stores, 1929–1972

	Infants' and Children's Stores	Family Stores
1929	$ 174,378	$ 3,221,875
1939	96,676	3,089,921
1948	961,554	7,217,331
1954	1,341,837	n/a
1958	1,489,182	8,138,161
1963	1,139,850	8,819,686
1972	913,962	11,780,079

n/a = Not Available
SOURCE: U.S. Census of Retail, 1929, 1939, 1948, 1954, 1958, 1963, 1972.

Notes

CHAPTER 1 *Introduction*

1. On the emergence and cultural import of cross-merchandising, see Englehardt 1986; for monetary estimates see McNeal 1992; McNeal 1999.

2. Cook 1995; Seiter 1993; Cross 1997, 84–86.

3. Qvortrup 1990; Qvortrup 1987; Qvortrup 1993. On childhood sharing subordinate status with women, Oakley 1993; on children as a minority category, Oldman 1994.

4. On children's participation in the creation of space, Holloway and Valentine 2000; on the use of media, Sara McNamee 1998; Buckingham 2000; Seiter 1999. On children as social actors, James, Jenks and Prout 1998; James 1998. For the ethnographic approach, see Fine 1987; Thorne, 1993; Connally and Ennew 1996; Corsaro 1997; McNamee 1998; Adler and Adler 1998; and Strandell 2002.

5. On structural approach see Leach 1993a; Leach 1993b; Kline 1993; Steinberg and Kincheloe 1997; Giroux 2000. On children's agency and empowerment, see Seiter 1993; Seiter 1999; MacNamee 1998; and Buckingham 2000. The quotation is from Seiter 1993, 9–10.

6. See, in particular, Zelizer 1985; Zelizer 1994; Parry and Bloch 1989; Slater 1997; Slater and Tonkiss 2000; Comaroff and Comaroff 1997; Carrier 1997; and Frank 2000.

7. Kopytoff 1986.

8. Zelizer 1985.

9. Zelizer 1985, 11; see 73–96 for defenses of the useless child in the early twentieth century.

10. Zelizer 1985, 11; Kopytoff 73–77.

11. Cook 1995; Kline 1993, 143–73; Leach 1993a; Leach 1993b, 85–90 and 328–30; Forty 1986, 67–72; Cross 1997, 50–120.

12. Durkheim 1915, quotations on 53–55; on ritual interdictions, 339–47.

13. My use of the sacred with regard to consumption differs from that discussed by Russell Belk, Melanie Wallendorf and John F. Sherry Jr. (1989), who concentrate on the transformation of secular things into sacred objects, whereas my focus is on children as sacred beings and childhood as a sacralized cultural site. See Langer 2002 for a similar understanding of the sacred and profane in children's consumer culture.

14. Douglas 1966, quotation on 2. On lost childhood, Elkind 1981; Postman 1982; Winn 1985. See Lynott and Lougue 1993 for a critique of the "myth of the hurried child"; see Buckingham 2000 for a critique of the beliefs about ravages of technology on children.

15. On developmentalism see Rawlins 2002; deMause 1974 on the helping mode; and Seiter 1993. On scientific motherhood see Apple 1987 and also Schlossman 1988.

16. Zelizer 1985, 211; but see Zelizer 2002 for subsequent caveats. On advice to mothers see Ehrenreich and English 1978; Apple 1987. On mothers and women as consumers in the 1920s, see Leach 1984; Benson 1986; Seiter 1993; Cook 1995.

17. Althusser 1971.

18. Cross 82–100; on the UN Convention see Hart 1991; see also Cohen and Naimark 1991; Wilcox and Naimark 1991.

19. This tendency finds expression in the common parlance "children's own"—children's own space, own culture, etc.—as if children were unconnected to adult culture and structures; see Stephens 1995.

20. Modell 1989, 12–16; Chudacoff 1989.

21. See articles in Valentine and Holloway 2000; see Valentine 1996a; Valentine 1996b; Valentine 1999. See also Adler and Adler 1998 and James 1982 for other instances of children's transgressive behavior.

22. Rose 1984; Spigel 1998; see also Hendershot 1998.

23. Cook 2002a; see also essays in Cook 2002b.

24. Cook 2002a; on children's dress style see Flusser 1992, Kaiser and Chandler 1991. On advertising see Cook 1999; see also Alexander 1994.

25. For the contemporary portrayals of children see Cook 1999; Higonnet 1998; Kincaid 1998; on child pornography, see Giroux 2000. For a

view of the Calvin Klein incident from the advertising trade, see *Advertising Age*, 4 September 1995, and 11 September 1995.

26. Strandell 2002; Kenny 2002.

27. See References for the various journals and magazines examined.

28. See Leach 1993a, 10–11, on cultural brokers.

29. Roland Marchand's history of the early advertising industry in the United States, *Advertising the American Dream* (1985), is the exemplar of this approach. Not to be slighted are Jackson Lear's history of advertising and consumer culture, *Fables of Abundance* (1996), and William Leach's inventive use of archival and trade material in *Land of Desire* (1993b).

30. Becker 1982.

31. See Mauss 1979 for a discussion of the relation between person and persona in the Western tradition.

32. See Dennis 2002 and Kline and dePeuter 2002 for examplary analyses of what I call commercial personae; also see Cook 2000a for the emergence of children as the object of market research.

33. Kline 1993; Seiter 1993; Cross 1997.

34. Wilson 1985, 2–3.

35. See Rubenstein 2000, 1–8, for a discussion of the relationship between children's dress and the cultural interpretations of children's maturity or age-related social status.

36. Key 1909.

CHAPTER 2 *A Brief History of Childhood and Motherhood*

1. Ariès 1962, 33–34, on miniature adulthood; 54–62 on distinctive morphology and clothing.

2. Ariès 1962: 62–99 on games and fairy tales, 119–21 on specialized literature, 241–68 on scholastic practices and age segregation.

3. Wilson 1980 on the centrality of Ariès's "invention" proposition; Vann 1982 on "presentism." See Pollock 1983; Wilson 1980; Calvert 1992, 10–11, for other challenges to Aries's historiography. DeMause 1974, quotation on 5; Beales 1987, quotation on 106.

4. Ariès 1962, quotations on 34–36.

5. Ariès 1962, quotations on 35–38.

6. Stone 1977, 57–58.

7. Shorter 1975, 191–204; deMause 1974, 3.

8. Pollock 1983, 68–90 for critiques; see 262–71 for conceptions of childhood in the sixteenth century and special laws regarding children.

9. Pollock 1983; Higonnet 1998, 26; Ariès 1962, 39–43, quotation on 43.

10. Ariès 1962, 133.

11. Ariès 1962, 111–19.

12. Higonnet 1998, 28; Valentine 1996a.

13. Stannard 1974, 460–62.

14. Stannard 1974, quotation on 461; Sunley 1955, 159–62 on change on religious conversion.

15. Calvert 1992, 156, on "made and not born," quotation on 33, 27 on "upright child"; cf. Sunley 1955.

16. James, Jenks, and Prout 1998, quotation on 16.

17. Pollock 1983, 111–24.

18. See Plumb 1982, 289–90; see also Heininger 1982, 2–3.

19. Plumb 1982, quotation on 292.

20. Rousseau 1762; Higonnet 1998, quotation on 26.

21. Heininger 1982, 10–18 for this and the subsequent paragraph.

22. About children's commercial culture, toys, games, and literature, see Heininger 1982; on creating children's culture see Kline 1993, 82–97; see also Postman 1982; on the final quotation, see Heininger 1982, 19.

23. Heininger 1982, 19–21, for this and the subsequent paragraph.

24. Cowan 1983, 16–39, on women's "natural" place. See also Degler 1980, 52–65; Cott 1977.

25. On mothers' duty of domestic moralizing, see Cott 1977, 84–98, and Degler 1980, 86–110; on the "second shift" see Cowan 1983, 16–68; on the contemporary second shift see Hochschild 1989.

26. Douglas 1977; see also Hall and Davidoff 1987; on ministers' influence on women see Douglas 1977, 5–6.

27. See for instance Yellin and Van Horne 1994; Gordon 1988; Klaus 1993.

28. Cott 1977, quotation on 206.

29. Degler 1980, 66–85; Cott 1977, 63–100.

30. On compulsory schooling see Spring 1972.

31. Gordon 1988, 27–58; Platt 1977.

32. Gordon 1988, 27–30; Hawes, 1990, 39–40.

33. Gordon 1988, 92–95.

34. Klaus 1993.

35. About Julia Lathrop see Klaus 1993, 208–11; on maternalism see Sklar 1993, 45.

36. On the "male" model of infant care, see Klaus 1993, 210–11. On the ideology of "scientific motherhood" see Apple 1987; Klaus 1993.

37. On organized baby saving work, see Klaus 1993, 136–71; Sklar 1993; Apple 1987. On local "baby contests," see Klaus 1993, 136–71. On mothers' "need" of knowledge and education see Ehrenreich and English 1978; Apple 1987; Platt 1979, 75–100.

38. Klaus 1993.

39. On department stores, see Leach 1993b; Benson 1993. On department stores and women's wages, see Kessler-Harris 1982, 108–41; Leach 1984; Benson 1986. On ethnic and class distinctions in department stores, see Kessler-Harris 1982, 139–40; Benson 1986, 124–76.

40. Benson 1986, 227–82.

41. On accommodating consumer desire, see Benson 1986, 35. On the "consumption ethic," see Marchand 1985, 117–63; see also Campbell 1987.

42. Benson 1986, 124–76.

43. On fashion and enhancing women's independence see Wilson 1985; Simmel 1971b. For immigrant women's independence see Ewen and Ewen 1982, 43–56; Ewen 1985, 196–202; Peiss 1986.

44. Leach 1984, 332–34.

45. *System*, November 1915, 481–89; see also *System*, December 1915, 585–91.

46. On women's perspective on goods, see *Dry Goods Economist*, 16 December 1923, 13. For *Printer's Ink*, see 20 September 1923, 57–58; see also *Printer's Ink*, 14 June 1923, 130, 5 March 1925, 89–92, 18 February 1926, 3–5, 10 December 1931, 60; and *Printer's Ink Monthly*, February 1924, 52–53, June 1930, 31. On the persona of "the women," see Marchand 1985, 66–69, 84–87.

47. See Marchand 1985, 167–71; also see Frederick 1929.

48. Zelizer 1994, 48–63.

CHAPTER 3 *Merchandising, Motherhood, and Morality*

1. *Earnshaw's*, September 1917, 3, emphasis in original. As early as 1921, the publication had started taking on a substantial number of paid advertisements and in 1922 began paid subscriptions. It grew tenfold, from an average of approximately 250 pages yearly between 1918 and 1922, to over 2,500 total pages in 1924.

2. The *Infants' Department* was the only trade journal devoted exclusively to children's wear until 1926, when the *Children's Wear Review* (*CWR*) came on the scene. Unfortunately, no library, including the Library of Congress, holds more than a few scattered issues of *CWR* according to the *Union List of Serials* and to various inquiries of major libraries by the author. In 1965 Earnshaw's publication took over the *Review* and became *Earnshaw's Review*.

3. On cloth and gender roles and relations, Weiner and Schneider 1989; Cowan 1984, 26. For the increasing productivity of the clothing

industry in the early nineteenth century, Smith 1989, 9; Kidwell and Christman 1974, 47–53; Cowan 1984, 40–68.

4. On the influence of the sewing machine, Kidwell and Christman 1974, 27–28. On men's and boys' wear, Kidwell and Christman 1974, 55; Cowan 1984, 74. On women's wear, Kidwell and Christman 1974, 133. Bernard Smith (1989) explains this uneven development between men's and women's wear in terms of the differential ability of manufacturers to anticipate demand. The desire for fashion—i.e., regularized changes in design—along with low barriers to entry and easy style piracy (the copying of popular styles) delayed and slowed the development of the factory industry for women's apparel until the early twentieth century (see 179–205). It must be noted that the ready-made industry has never been a single entity but "rather an Industry of Industries, each with its own pattern of organization," including sweatshops, cottage industry, and the farming-out of work, as well as large-scale industrialized production (Kidwell and Christman 1974, 93).

5. For children's wear as a sideline to women's apparel, Walker and Mendelson 1967. *Babyhood* magazine was perhaps the first "national" (non-local) consumer publication devoted exclusively to motherhood and childrearing. It was published from 1884 to 1909 and then again from 1923 to 1934. For the influence of new periodicals on housewifery, Ehrenreich and English 1978.

6. The census measured only the manufacture of children's outerwear (e.g. coats, hats). The *Dry Goods Economist* most likely counted factories that manufactured all types of children's clothes.

7. In defining specialization the operative term for the Bureau of the Census is "primarily engaged" in the specialty. In manufacturing "primarily engaged" means having produced the items in the category at least three times more than the items in all other categories combined.

8. *Dry Goods Economist*, 19 November 1921, 225.

9. Robert and Helen Lynd found in their study of Muncie, Indiana (often regarded as "Middletown, U.S.A."), in 1924 that about four of five working-class wives spent two hours a month or less mending clothes, and much less time, if any at all, making clothes for anyone in the family (Lynd and Lynd, 1925, 165).

10. Palmer 1989, 167 n. 2; see also table 1 in the Appendix to this book. Domestic help became increasingly black and married, instead of white and single, beginning in the first decades of the twentieth century, according to Cowan (1983, 120). Married women preferred to work as day laborers rather than as live-in help. With the supply of servant labor

shrinking, they could ask for higher wages which priced their services out of the range of many families.

11. Palmer 1989, 13, emphasis in original; on school attendance, see *Historical Abstracts of the United States*, part 1 (1975), series H 412–432, 368.

12. For overall female labor force participation rates, *Historical Abstracts of the United States*, part 1 (1975), series D 29–41, 131–32; for married women's rates, *Historical Abstracts of the United States*, part 1 (1975), series D 49–60, 133.

13. Schlereth 1991, 29, on income.

14. Leach 1993b on department stores.

15. This publication underwent several name changes. *Infants' Department* changed its name in 1923 to the *Infants' and Children's Department*, in 1935 to *Infants,' Children's and Girls' Wear*, in 1965 to *Earnshaw's Infants' and Children's Wear Review* (when it merged with *The Infants' and Children's Review* in October), in 1978 to *Earnshaw's Infants'-Girls'-Boys' Wear Review*, and finally in 1983 to *Earnshaw's Review*. In chapters 4, 5, and 6 I will discuss the changing markets to which these changing names refer. Except for its first incarnation, the *Infants' Department*, I will refer to this publication as *Earnshaw's*.

16. Walker and Mendelson 1967 on absence of infants and children's departments; Huun and Kaiser 2001 on infants' clothing in the Sears catalogue; *Dry Goods Economist*, 28 March 1914, 11.

17. A buyer, not to be confused with a customer, is someone who is employed or contracted by retail or wholesale establishments to purchase lines of goods—in this case, infants' garments.

18. *Infants' Department*, September 1917, 3, emphasis in original.

19. *Infants' Department*, October 1917, 23–24, emphasis in original.

20. *Dry Goods Economist*, 19 November 1921, 231; *Journal of Retailing*, vol. 4, no. 1 (April 1928): 24.

21. *Infants' Department*, November 1921, 398; on mothers' view of babies' goods, see *Dry Goods Economist*, 18 May 1901, quotation on page 47. See also *Printer's Ink*, 10 April 1919, 93–94; and *Printer's Ink Monthly*, November 1923, 31–32, for other early revelations in trade publications about the potential of the children's market through appeals to mothers.

22. *Infants' Department*, January 1920, 97.

23. *Infants' Department*, March 1922, 561–63.

24. Kneeland 1925, 93.

25. On Baby Weeks see *Earnshaw's*, November 1927, 1833; on the following quotation, see *Earnshaw's*, December 1927, 5273–74.

26. *Infants' Department*, January 1920, 106.

27. For mothers as the basis of a separate department, see *Infants' Department*, January 1922, 484–85; for the quotations, see *Infants' Department*, October 1921, 374. See also "Service and Sympathy," *Infants' Department*, March 1919, 144; "A New Amendment," *Infants' Department*, September 1926, 5031–33.

28. On "secluded corner," see *Infants' Department*, December 1918, 69–70; see also *Infants' Department*, September 1921, 324; on the "desirability of these devices" see *Infants' Department*, May 1919, 178.

29. *Infants' Department*, August 1926, 4729, emphasis in original.

30. *Infants' Department*, September 1924, 2233.

31. See Miller 1998 on expressing love through consumption.

32. *Infants' Department*, January 1922, 490.

33. *Infants' Department*, May 1918, 134.

34. See *Historical Statistics of the United States, Colonial Times to 1970*, part 1 (1975), series B 136–147, 57; for Earnshaw's quotation see *Infants' Department*, November 1917, 37.

35. *Infants' Department*, November 1917, 38.

36. Klaus 1993, 208–43, on the Children's Bureau; 160–61 on nonpartisan attitude.

37. On "civilizing force" see Comaroff and Comaroff, 1997, chapter 4; on the latest medical and scientific information brought by babyhood and baby contests, see Klaus 1993, 144–54, 146–50, 164.

38. Apparently baby contests were a popular event despite the dismay of the bureau's first chief, Julia Lathrop, who expressed concern about the commercial and competitive atmosphere of baby contests to health officials. S. Josephine Baker, M.D., head of the New York City Department of Health, felt that baby contests would do more good than harm, if they stimulated the public's interest (Baker to Lathrop, 6 May 1914, Children's Bureau files, National Archives, Washington). In the same vein, Samuel Hamill, M.D., in charge of the "Baby Improvement Contest" in Philadelphia, informed Lathrop that there would be no interest in infant health in the "Italian Quarter" were it not for the contests (Hamill to Lathrop, 4 May 1914, Children's Bureau Files, National Archives, Washington).

Baby Week also turned out to be a popular idea for local merchants and women's magazines like *Woman's Home Companion*, as well as for mothers. In a clash with Gertrud B. Lane, managing editor of *Woman's Home Companion*, Lathrop objected to the magazine's close involvement with the Knoxville Conservation Exposition of 1913. Apparently, the *Companion* had sought to create its own scorecards and give its own prizes for the baby contests. By 1914 the magazine had turned over all correspondence to the bureau and bowed out of this level of involvement. (See Children's Bureau files 4-14-2-3-0, 4-14-2-3-1, 4-14-2-3-2, 4-14-2-3-3, correspondence between Lane and Lathrop in 1913, National Archives, Washington; see also Klaus 1993, 153.)

39. Cook 2000a.

40. Klaus 1993, 168.

41. *Dry Goods Economist*, 21 March 1914, 105

42. For using events as advertising, see Leach 1993a, 229–30; on slogans created for those events, see Klaus 1993, 167. Klaus gives other examples, like the Polk Sanitary Milk Company's leaflets, which attributed low infant mortality among its clients to using milk with "unquestioned purity" (1993, 166–67); also see Dupuis 2002.

43. Leach 1993a, 226–34.

44. *Infants' Department*, October 1919, 36.

45. *Infants' Department*, February 1922, 520.

46. *Infants' Department*, January 1918, 77, emphasis in original.

47. See *Infants' Department*, January 1918, 77, emphasis in original. Nurses became fixtures in many infants' and children's wear departments at this time and remained there until about 1950.

48. *Infants' Department*, May 1918, 148.

49. Cott 1977.

50. *Infants' Department*, February 1922, 521.

51. *Infants' Department*, March 1923, 1067–8, for this and subsequent quotation.

52. *Infants' Department*, February 1922, 519.

53. *Infants' Department*, March 1919, 147, emphasis in original.

54. *Infants' Department*, September 1921, 322.

55. *Parents*, May 1927, 38.

56. Similarly, in *Child Life* magazine in the 1920s and 1930s, a monthly feature called "Mothers' Service Bureau" featured various child-oriented goods. A response coupon could be clipped and sent in to the magazine to request additional information about the items.

57. *Printer's Ink*, 21 August 1930, 12.

58. For background, Leach 1993b, 263–97.

59. On the notion of "the feminine," see de Beauvoir 1945; Ehrenreich and English 1978; see also Laqueur 1990. On power and knowledge see Foucault 1978; Foucault 1979. On commodity logic see Baudrillard 1981; on ideology see Marx and Engels 1978 and Williams 1977.

60. Frazer 1922; Miller 1998. On gifts and exchange, see Appadurai 1986; Parry and Bloch 1989; Layne 1999.

CHAPTER 4 *Pediocularity*

1. Kaplan (1992, 209) perceptively notes a similar movement from adult to child in her analysis of films made in the 1990s, but marks that decade as the beginning of the shift. I argue that there are traces of it as early as the 1920s and that the child's perspective becomes institutionalized in retail practice by the 1950s.

2. Key 1993, 24–26; see Wolfenstein 1955, 171, on "fun morality"; deMause 1974, 52. In *Middletown* (New York: Harcourt, Brace, 1925), Robert and Helen Lynd found that stated parental attitudes toward children's desirable attributes were decidedly favoring "independence." One mother, for instance, states regarding her son, "We are trying to make our boy feel that he is entitled to his own opinion; we treat him as one of us and listen to his ideas" (144).

3. Higgonet 1998, 28.

4. Cross 1997, 89–91; on comic strip characters, 100–120. On radio, film, and fantasy toys, Kline 1993, chapters 3 and 4.

5. Cross 1997, 121–39.

6. See Slater 1997, 83–97, for a discussion of consumer culture, subjectivity, and choosing subjects.

7. Nasaw 1992; Nasaw 1985, 115–29, on working-class children's consumption in New York in the early twentieth century.

8. Market research on children began in earnest in the mid-1960s, see Cook 2000a; on customer vs. consumer cf. Williams 1999.

9. By 1930 only one in six boys and one in twelve girls had been gainfully employed. These were dramatic decreases since 1910 of over 50 percent for boys and 66 percent for girls; see Modell 1989, 79.

10. *Dry Goods Economist*, 24 March 1914, 107.

11. *System*, March 1915, 238–39.

12. *System*, March 1915, 240–41.

13. *Printer's Ink*, 9 February 1922, 121.

14. *Printer's Ink Monthly*, November 1923, 31. This same tripartite distinction—children as a *direct* market, as an *influence* market, and as a *future* market—has been analyzed in detail more recently by McNeal (1992).

15. *Printer's Ink Monthly*, November 1923, 32.

16. See Kline 1993; Seiter 1993; and Cross 1997 for discussions and analysis of the historical use of fantasy characters. See also *Printer's Ink Monthly*, June 1932, 40; *Printer's Ink*, 9 May 1935. Mickey Mouse, appearing first in 1929, had an estimated 300,000 clubs by 1931. According to one writer for *Earnshaw's*, many movie theaters sponsored these clubs,

and local merchants would donate prizes to the "girl or boy with the best school record, or some other exemplary achievement" (June 1931, 710). This writer defended against objections to these promotions: "There is no harm in promoting youthful interest in the higher education. It has always seemed to me to be singularly stupid on the part of educators not to find out first what the children really liked and wanted to do, and . . . link the favored pursuit or desire with the drudgery of study" (710). Here "education" is combined with consulting the child's pleasure to make defensible a children's market.

17. *Printer's Ink Monthly*, October 1930, 118.

18. *Printer's Ink*, 21 May 1931, 57.

19. *Printer's Ink Monthly*, April 1932, 65.

20. *Printer's Ink*, 12 October 1933, 70–72.

21. See also *Printer's Ink*, 18 August 1932, 68, 5 January 1933, 68–71, 2 May 1935, 85–90; *Printer's Ink Monthly*, May 1936, 9–10, and June 1936, 26–28.

22. Children were off limits to naked marketing; they were not off limits, however, to marketing mentality. An article in *Parents* magazine from 1926 suggests that parents use "business psychology" and "salesmanship" when the little ones are uncooperative (October 1926, 19–20). One suggestion is that mothers give an unpopular dish, like spinach, a name like "Babe Ruth's Home Run Plate," making the "consumption" of popular culture quite literal. Here the need to please and entertain joins forces with an approach to persuade the child, invoking a model of the child as a person like anyone else. The author, applying the "vacuum cleaner method (of selling) to spinach" asks, "Ever think of your child as a perfectly normal, intelligent human being who responds to flattery and every other form of salesmanship as you do?" (20).

23. *Printer's Ink Monthly*, October 1933, 53–54.

24. One article of hers summarized the findings "conducted by educators, librarians, children's book illustrators and the author's own surveys" about pictures and colors that children like. Among these findings are that familiar, realistic pictures and subjects which tell a story appeal to children. Girls reportedly show a greater preference for decorative illustration and for pictures of home and school life. Boys, on the other hand, like pictures which show action. Younger children prefer primary colors and, as they grow older, "develop a gradual preference for softer tints and tone." The research was conducted to assist the merchandiser in "artistically satisfying" the child by designing advertisements, books and illustrations which are "pleasing." *Printer's Ink Monthly*, March 1938, 39–40; see also *Printer's Ink*, 17 June 1937, 49.

25. Grumbine 1938, 32–33.

26. Grumbine 1938, 34–36.

27. Grumbine 1938, 39.

28. Grumbine 1938, 4–15.

29. Grumbine 1938, 11.

30. Grumbine 1938, ix. In terms of "education," Grumbine devoted an entire chapter to "Selling Children through Schools" with apparently little concern about "exploitation" (236–61). See Molnar (1996) for a more recent view of the incursion of commercialism into the classroom.

31. *Dry Goods Economist*, 2 July 1902, 7.

32. *Home Progress*, December 1912, 52–53.

33. DeMause considered the helping mode to be a phenomenon that arose after World War II. Chronologically, it is quite identifiable in the form of *advice* for parents or *beliefs* about the child as early as the 1920s; see deMause 1974.

34. *Children's Royal*, spring 1921, 40.

35. *Children's Royal*, spring 1921, 42.

36. The variability in size ranges is evident here. Note that the size range in 1920 for this writer was two to six years old; at other times and currently it is three to six years old.

37. *Dry Goods Economist*, 30 October 1920, 43.

38. *Ladies Home Journal*, January 1913, 64; *Delineator*, October 1921, 39; *Women's Home Companion*, January 1922, 65; *Women's Home Companion*, February 1925, 72. This concern remained prominent into the 1940s. See also "Cultivating Good Looks," *Parents*, February 1930, 22, 64; "Is Your Child Self-Conscious?" *Parents*, September 1936, 29, 61; "Forecasting Your Child's Looks," *Parents*, October 1942, 26–27, 122; "Good Taste and How it Grows," *Parents*, November 1942, 28, 40. Cures for children's "bowleggedness" and headgear to flatten a child's ears (if they stuck out too much) were advertised in women's and parents' magazines as early as the 1890s.

39. The young person's resentfulness of "babyish" clothes most likely refers to the sizing practices of the nascent clothing industry at that time: there existed little stylistic difference in ready-made garments for children between the ages of six and fourteen, and hence little means to make status distinctions based upon age. I will address changes in size ranges in some depth in chapter 5.

40. *Parents*, February 1927, 34.

41. *Parents*, April 1929, 21.

42. *Parents*, April 1929, 21.

43. *Parents*, April 1929, 58.

44. *Parents,* April 1929, 58 for this and the subsequent quotation on scant skirts.

45. On discounters and mail-order houses see Leach 1993b, 180–85. On leveling of class aspects in dress see Kidwell and Christman 1974; Marchand 1985; Leach 1993b. On taste and distinction see Bourdieu 1984.

46. *Babyhood,* February 1930, 33.

47. The psychological view of the importance of early experiences is evident in, and reinforced by, an anecdote about a man who as a child was dressed as Little Lord Fauntleroy (with long curls and ruffled shirts) and reportedly grew up with an "inferiority complex." *Babyhood,* February 1930, 34.

48. *Babyhood,* February 1930, 34.

49. *Earnshaw's,* October 1932, 843.

50. Marx 1972, 303.

51. *Oxford English Dictionary* (compact edition), 1989, 3340.

52. Jaffe and Rosa 1989, 4.

53. Jaffe and Rosa 1989, 5–6.

54. *Earnshaw's,* January 1934, 49.

55. *Earnshaw's,* February 1936, 70.

56. Having a separate infants' department and offering a variety of layettes were the first two stepping stones.

57. *Earnshaw's,* October 1937, 54.

58. *Earnshaw's,* October 1937, 54, 92.

59. *Earnshaw's,* October 1937, 92.

60. *Earnshaw's,* October 1937, 54, emphasis added.

61. Cook 1999. See also Higonnet 1998; Alexander 1994.

62. See Seiter 1993, 24; for instance, Margaret Mead's "South Sea Tips on Character Training," *Parents,* March 1932, 13.

63. Wolfenstein 1955, 168.

64. Wolfenstein 1955, 171.

65. On personality, see Stendler 1950. A child-rearing advice book of 1941 couldn't have stated Wolfenstein's thesis more directly: "The parent who is able to enter into the spirit of play with his child is sure to enjoy a priceless intimacy with his thought-life" (45).

66. Seiter 1993, 23.

67. Schlossman 1988.

68. Seiter 1993, 65. On the psychological understanding of childhood, see James and Prout 1990; James, Jenks, and Prout 1998. On the personality of the toddler in medical and psychological terms, see Rose 1990 and Armstrong 1987. For the "autonomous self" quotation, see Lears 1983, 9.

69. Child actors and performers were widespread in the vaudeville circuits from the late nineteenth century through the 1930s. However, the growth of the film industry effectively killed vaudeville by creating a star system which featured only a handful of key performers and actors on screen, rather than tens of thousands on stage.

70. Zelizer (1985) points out that one major exception to child labor laws, child actors, presented a paradox in that they had to work in order to portray the sentimental, priceless child on screen and stage (92–96).

71. *Pictorial Review*, June 1935, 20.

72. That toddlers became an object of social scrutiny and concern is suggested by an article in *Parents* in June 1937, which assured apparently concerned mothers that their toddler's "pot belly" was "normal" and would go away as the child aged, advising against subjecting the child to stomach-flattening exercises (28, 107).

73. Sidney Rosenau of Rosenau Bros. was appointed guardian for Shirley Temple in 1935 to act for her in matters regarding litigation. She was suing Lenora Doll Company for producing dolls in her likeness and advertised as Shirley Temple Dolls. *Earnshaw's*, August 1935, 76.

74. See "Dressing the Juvenile Film Star," *Earnshaw's*, November 1940, 31.

75. On conspicuous display, see Simmel 1971; Blumer 1969; and Davis 1992. See also Lynd and Lynd 1934. For the "must-have" Shirley Temple doll, see Cross 1997, 116–18.

76. See Berger 1972, esp. 45–47, for historical perspective on the self-reflexive female gaze.

CHAPTER 5   *Reconfiguring Girlhood*

1. These figures pertain only to independent specialty stores and do not include department store or chain store data. See table 2 in the Appendix.

2. On social changes related to changes in clock time, see Simmel 1978 [1900]; Thompson 1967; Zerubavel 1981; Hall 1983.

3. On the age range of family members, see Kett 1974, 10–11; see Chudacoff 1989, 96–97, for the increasing peer marriages; see also Gillis 1996, 81–87. Other instances of peer society, according to Chudacoff, are urban youth gangs, college fraternities and sororities, the Boy Scouts, and other adult, informal clubs (102–7). Peer society has been created and reinforced by technological advances such as sanitation, which prolonged lives, by institutional prerogatives such as old age pensions and formal retirement (107–16), and by popular literature and songs (138–

56). See Fass (1974) on the rise of peer society in the social context of colleges and universities.

4. Pleck 2001, 143–50 for the beginning of birthday celebrations; on birthday cards, see Chudacoff 1989, 132–37; see also Chudacoff 1989, 65, and Pleck 2001, 147, for the keeping of age statistics in urban areas.

5. Kett 1974, 18, on compulsory schooling. On systemizing the educational process, see Kett 1974, 13–18; Angus, Mirel, and Vinovkis 1988, 217–19; and Chudacoff 1989, 34–38; see also Ariès 1962, 189–240, on the lack of age grading in schooling before the nineteenth century.

6. On age-graded schooling, Chudacoff 1989, 37; on textbooks, Chudacoff 1989, 38, and Angus, Mirel, and Vinovkis 1988, 212.

7. An article in *Babyhood* in November 1902 expressed a common sentiment: "The child should learn to observe, to use its hands, its muscles, and its senses, before its memory, imagination, or reason is developed, for this is the natural order of events. Precocious thinkers, early book-worms, and children with remarkable memories, are liable to become common-place or unable to deal with affairs when they reach maturity" (361). For the social effects of age-graded schooling, see Chudacoff 1989, 36–37. On the negative attitudes toward precocity, see Kett 1978, S185; also see Rawlins 2002, 89–108.

8. Hacking 1990 discusses statistical conceptions of normality. See Foucault (1965) for a genealogy of the normal personality and Foucault (1978) and Chauncey (1994) for histories of normal sexuality. On social promotion, see Angus, Mirel, and Vinkovkis 1988, 228. Modell sees evidence of social promotion as early as the 1920s, Modell 1989, 79.

9. See Kline 1993; Seiter 1993; and Cross 1997 for different perspectives on the development of the toy industry in the United States and the relation between age-graded markets and age-graded toys.

10. The dimension of age has received the least attention from sociologists when it comes to examining the social meaning of clothing. With the notable exception of Susan Kaiser (see Kaiser and Chandler 1981, 1984; Kaiser and Khan 1980; Kaiser and Phinney 1983; Kaiser and Huun 2002, for example), few scholars mention age when addressing the social and cultural aspects of personal appearance (Simmel 1971; Bell 1945; Stone 1959; Blumer 1968; Rosencrantz 1967). Or, when mentioned, age is left to others to analyze (Davis 1992).

11. Recently, young girls' clothing styles like baby-doll dresses, pleated schoolgirl skirts, Mary Jane dresses, and ankle socks have gained popularity as adult women's wear. These scaled-up versions of children's wear have been denounced by some observers as "pedophilic fashion" (*New York Times*, March 27, 1994, sec. 9, p. 8) and described as "fun" by others

(*Newsweek*, 20 June 1994, 75). Young teen girls now work as professional models for adult clothing advertisements (*New York Times Magazine*, February 4, 1996), adding to the blurring of age and personhood found increasingly in publicly circulated images of children. This issue came to a head in 1995 when the FBI investigated whether the clothing designer Calvin Klein had used underaged models for some sexually provocative television commercials and print advertisements. See *Advertising Age*, September 4, 1995, and September 11, 1995, for a view of the advertising trade on the incident.

12. Jaffe and Rosa 1990, 285.

13. Paoletti and Kregloh 1989, 22–29.

14. Chauncey (1994) explains the historical emergence of "heterosexual-homosexual binarism" as a middle-class response to the perceived threat posed to manhood by publicly explicit and sartorially flamboyant "fairies" and "third-sexers" in the first four decades of the twentieth century. The timing of the practice of color-coding infants' garments by gender gives support both to Chauncey's chronology and to his argument in that middle-class parents may have been eager to indicate their child's sex clearly. See Kaiser and Huun 2002.

15. Kidwell and Christman 55; for a contemporary discussion on this matter, see "Denim Inequity," *Washington Post*, 30 July 1996, section E, page 5.

16. All discussion of clothing expenditure for 1918–19 is derived from "Cost of Living in the United States," Bureau of Labor Statistics, table C, May 1924.

17. An underwaist is a cotton garment with a fitted, sleeveless top which buttons down the front, used mostly in the early twentieth century. It was made with buttons around the waistline to attach to underwear bottoms and suspender garters.

18. The U.S. Census of Retail did not begin until 1929. Children's wear did not become a category in the U.S. Census of Manufacture until 1937.

19. Unfortunately, subsequent surveys of household expenditures did not record the items and ages of children with as much detail as the 1918–19 study, which disallows systematic comparison. See Jones 1945, tables 26 and 27, pp. 139–77.

20. Changing nutritional practices combined with regular athletic activity in schools apparently have contributed to the changing body dimensions of American children. The actual physical fit of children's clothing underwent a change to such an extent that manufacturers welcomed U.S. government efforts to standardize the actual measurements used to construct children's clothes (see Alene Burt, "Standardizing Size

Measurements for Children's and Infants' Wear," *Bulletin of the National Retail Dry Goods Association*, March 1938, 130–31). In the late 1930s, funds from the Works Progress Administration supported a large-scale project to measure 150,000 children. As reported in the *Bulletin of the National Retail Dry Goods Association*, height was the primary measure. Three ratios—height and girth of hips, height and weight, height and girth—were thought to accommodate approximately 90 percent of the size variation in the clothing of the nation's children (May 1939, 25). See, from the U. S. Division of Trade Standards, publication numbers TS-4000 (infants, babies, toddlers, and children), TS-4093 (girls), TS4216 (boys). Also available is *Miscellaneous Publication No. 366*, "Body Measurements of American Boys and Girls for Garment and Patterns Construction," U.S. Dept of Agriculture, Bureau of Home Economics, 1939.

21. Jaffe and Rosa 1989, 5; quotation on page 254.

22. Jaffe and Rosa, 1989, 5.

23. *Earnshaw's*, November 1937, 31.

24. *Earnshaw's*, November 1937, 31.

25. See Demos 1979 and Cowan 1983 on children's household duties in the eighteenth and nineteenth centuries. On the Supreme Court decision see the report in *Earnshaw's*, December 1936, 54.

26. *Earnshaw's*, January 1923, 986.

27. See, for instance Modell 1989, 36–39.

28. *Babyhood*, June 1924, 238.

29. *Earnshaw's*, January 1935, 54.

30. Lynd and Lynd 1925, 138–41; Lynd and Lynd 1937, 169–71; on the rise of non-chaperoned dating at this time, see Fass 1977, 191–98.

31. The origin and growth of the teen are discussed in chapter 6.

32. *Earnshaw's*, October 1934, 31, for this and the previous quotation.

33. On children's space in the department store, see Leach 1993a, 215; for the "checking" service offered by department stores see Benson 1986, 82–91; on commercial space around children's space, see Leach 1993a for details.

34. *System*, March 1915, 240.

35. *Dry Goods Economist*, 29 May 1920, 81.

36. *Dry Goods Economist*, 7 February 1920; quotation on page 89.

37. Little Lord Fauntleroy was the title character of a book by Frances Hodgson Burnett in 1886 who sported long curly hair and velvet clothes with fluffy collars.

38. In a similar vein, see also *Dry Goods Economist*, 29 May 1920, 81.

39. These sales clerks in urban department stores at this time were most likely working class (Benson 1986). It is difficult to tell whether the

advice given them for dealing with children indicates a potential class difference in the treatment and view of children during this time, or whether a more general sales persona was being inculcated—or both. For the quote concerning clerks' treatment of children, see *Dry Goods Economist*, 9 August 1919, 45, emphasis in original; for quote of the manager of L. S. Ayers & Co., see *Dry Goods Economist*, 19 November 1921, 231.

40. This girl represents a forerunner of the "tweener" or "tween-ager," who is "'tween" childhood and adulthood. See chapter 6.

41. *Earnshaw's*, May 1926, 4366.

42. *Bulletin of the National Retail Dry Goods Association*, October 1939, 72, for this and subsequent quotations on the design of Saks's children's floor.

43. *Bulletin of the National Retail Dry Goods Association*, October 1939, 73, for this and the subsequent quotation on color schemes in the children's department; see also *Earnshaw's*, January 1942, 47, for another description of child-apportioned fixtures.

44. *Earnshaw's*, October 1930, 1472–73.

45. See, for instance, *Earnshaw's*, May 1930, 724–28.

46. On the opening of a juvenile floor in the Depression, see *Earnshaw's*, September 1936, 48; for those who did not open such a floor, see *Earnshaw's*, January 1940, 66.

47. *Earnshaw's*, June 1935, 62.

48. *Earnshaw's*, May 1932, 67.

CHAPTER 6   *Baby Booms and Market Booms*

1. By 1938, more than 50 percent of all births took place in hospitals, a percentage which is skewed in favor of whites (Green 1992, 121).

2. *Printer's Ink Monthly*, November 1941, 51.

3. *Printer's Ink Monthly*, November 1941, quotation on 51–52.

4. Levy 1988, 50.

5. *Oxford English Dictionary* (compact edition, 1989), 248–49.

6. An economic "boom" accompanied the demographic boom and, despite recessions in 1949 and 1959–61, incomes increased steadily for about twenty-five years. The median family income in the United States was $13,540 in 1949. It grew to $19,300 by 1959, an increase of 42.5 percent (all values in 1984 dollars; see Levy 1988, 47). The growth continued, registering a median family income of $26,700 in 1969 (38.3 percent higher than in 1959) and peaked in real value in 1973 at $28,200 (Levy 1988, 56–66).

7. On named generations of the twentieth century, see Howe and

Strauss *13th Gen* (1993). The other side of the equation, that babies *cost* money for the family, was rarely mentioned during the prosperous era. But see an article in *Ladies Home Journal* in July 1944 which asked, "Can you afford a baby?" (104, 130). Although such discussions were rare, the connection between children and money became increasingly operative at this time.

8. *Earnshaw's*, January 1942, 74.

9. The decrease in child mortality did not stop business interests from using child welfare as a way to draw attention to themselves or their product. *Parents* magazine, for instance, staged a luncheon for 350 children on Child Welfare Day at the New York World's Fair (*Parents*, November 1939, 34).

10. An increasing number of children did not dissuade women from seeking paid employment. Married women in particular entered the work force in larger numbers, doubling their rate of work force participation. In 1940, married women's labor force participation rate was 15.6 percent; by 1960 it had jumped to 31.7 percent (see figure 3 in the Appendix). The rate of married women with children in the work force also rose comparably during roughly the same period. In 1948, 12.7 percent of married women with children aged seventeen or younger were gainfully employed; by 1967, the figure was 26.2 percent. See series D 63–74, p. 134, *Historical Statistics of the United States Colonial Times to 1970*, part 1 (1975).

11. *Earnshaw's* reported that the Dallas Apparel Mart immediately became a central player in the industry as two thousand buyers were attending four seasonal markets a year by 1968 (April 1968, 62–63).

12. See *Earnshaw's*, December 1951, 52–53; *Earnshaw's*, November 1958, 70–71.

13. Shortages due to the war effort were felt by children's wear merchants and customers in late 1944 and into 1945 (see *Earnshaw's*, August 1944 and November–December 1944). The biggest concern expressed was, understandably, in the lack of children's underwear and diapers. These problems pale in comparison with those faced by the British, who not only fought the war on their own soil but also were at war earlier than the United States (Guppy 1978, 67–149).

14. See *Stores*, January 1957, 29, for segregation of teen and subteen merchandise in 1951; see also Walker and Mendelson 1967, 8–9.

15. *Earnshaw's* July, 51–52; *Stores*, January 1957, 44.

16. I have found no studies on the history or emergence of baby showers as a routine, gift-giving occasion. The *Reader's Guide to Periodical Literature* only sporadically includes "baby showers" as a separate cate-

gory, at least since 1937. A few articles on the subject can be found under "Entertaining."

17. *Stores*, January 1957, 29.

18. Walker and Mendelson 1967; see also *Stores*, January 1957, 36.

19. *Earnshaw's*, February 1956, 75.

20. See *Earnshaw's*, May 1952, 116–17; July 1952, 52.

21. Another indication that the consumption of children's clothing was increasing, perhaps at a greater rate than the birth rate, is that few women were likely to sew infants' and children's clothing at home (*Family Economics Review*, October 1957, 24); see also *Earnshaw's*, September 1960, 49.

22. *Earnshaw's*, January 1960, 82–83.

23. "Family Stores," so named by the Census of Retail, carry apparel for all ages and is thus the only category where children's and the 7–14 (i.e., "girls' ") ranges may be counted.

24. For example, see *Earnshaw's*, April 1951, 79; *Earnshaw's*, October 1952, 110; *Earnshaw's*, August 1956, 115; see also Walker and Mendelson 1967, 8–12.

25. But see *Stores*, September 1955, 44, and February 1964, 23.

26. G. Stanley Hall 1904; on the characteristic of "adolescence" in the transitional period, see Elder 1987 and Coleman 1974, 112–22; see Troen 1987 for institutionalized adolescence in the early twentieth century; see also Palladino 1996, 3–15.

27. On the school as an institutionalized home for teenagers, see Gordon 1984. On engendered youth culture of adolescence, see Coleman 1974; Parsons 1959. Parsons 1959, 314–15, quotation on 315.

28. Riesman 1950.

29. *Parents*, April 1931, 21.

30. On girls' self-presentation, see Palladino 1996, 22; on the reinforced centrality of beauty, see 23–33.

31. *Business Week*, 8 June 1946, 72.

32. See *Earnshaw's*, April 1936, 46–47, for the survey on "successful teen girl buyers"; quotation on 50.

33. *Earnshaw's*, April 1937, 48.

34. *Business Week*, 8 June 1946, 72.

35. Palladino (1996) outlines some of the various versions of teenager-hood extant in the early 1940s. Subcultural lingo, comparatively open sexuality, and freedom of swingers, bobby-soxers, and hepcats worried many parents and schoolteachers (49–61).

36. One early report from 1937 discusses the use of "student" advisors for teen shops. The article, clearly directed to the high school–aged,

college-bound girl market, discusses the use of "college girl" clerks to help *mothers* determine the "correct attire" for school (*Earnshaw's*, August 1937, 61).

37. *Business Week,* 8 June 1946, 72–74.

38. See, for instance, *Earnshaw's*, May 1953, 79; *Earnshaw's*, November 1954, 86; *Earnshaw's*, January 1955, 146.

39. *Earnshaw's*, September 1942, 43, for this and the subsequent quotation about the style-conscious teen.

40. *Earnshaw's*, September 1942, 87.

41. *Earnshaw's*, June 1947, 209, for this and the subsequent quotation about high school days.

42. Fashion shows for high school girls were being held at or sponsored by retail departments as early as the '30s (*Earnshaw's*, April 1936, 46–47). They are reported in *Earnshaw's* in many large and small cities from Washington to Cincinnati to Scranton, Pennsylvania, to Sacramento, reaching their apex apparently in the late '50s and early '60s. Personal testimonial given to the author indicate that they are still held today in some communities like Tallahassee.

43. Wilson 1985, 42–45.

44. *Earnshaw's*, April 1951, 78.

45. *Earnshaw's*, July 1951, 64, emphasis in original.

46. *Earnshaw's*, October 1952, 58.

47. *Earnshaw's*, April 1953, 109.

48. *Earnshaw's*, February 1951, 106.

49. Earnshaw's, April 1953, 105, 134.

50. Clothing design was not the only enterprise for which teens' views were sought. One store, Raphael Well & Co. of San Francisco, polled local high school girls regarding their preferences for the layout, design, and contents of a planned clothing store (*Earnshaw's*, May 1947, 51).

51. *Earnshaw's*, September 1950, 135.

52. *Earnshaw's*, May 1953, 154.

53. *Earnshaw's*, November 1954, 86, for this and the subsequent quotation on teens telling mothers what they want.

54. On the rejection of "teen" and "young junior," see *Earnshaw's*, May 1954, 65.

55. *Stores,* January 1957, 29.

56. *Earnshaw's*, April 1944, 103.

57. "$10 Billion Power," *Life,* 31 August 1959, 78–85.

58. Some of the most successful promoters of youth culture have not been age-peer members. For instance, Colonel Tom Parker, Elvis Presley's agent, was about twenty years his elder. Ed Sullivan's television

show launched many rock 'n' roll bands and careers, though Sullivan was far from being a teen.

59. *Parents,* April 1956, 90.

60. See the "Teen-Agers' Preferences in Clothes," *Journal of Home Economics,* December 1950, 801–2; *Stores,* March 1951, 28; *Stores,* March 1952, 54; *Stores,* February 1957, 33.

61. On "fun worshippers," see *Newsweek,* 11 December 1961, 88; see Gilbert's book (1957) on the youth market. For a sardonic look at this teen marketing pioneer, see the *New Yorker,* 22 November 1958, 57ff., and 29 November 1958, 57 ff. See also Palladino 1996, 109–15.

62. Ford 1960, 10–12.

63. See *Earnshaw's,* June 1949, 139, for "toned down" versions of teen dresses for girls; on the new size category, see *Earnshaw's,* March 1961, 48; on subteen styles, see *Earnshaw's,* June 1949, 135.

64. *Earnshaw's,* January 1955, 83.

65. *Earnshaw's,* January 1955, 83, emphasis in original.

66. *Earnshaw's,* December 1955, 70.

67. *Earnshaw's,* December 1955, 70, 72.

68. See *Earnshaw's,* May 1949, 136; *Earnshaw's,* April 1953, 134; *Earnshaw's,* March 1956, 54, 79.

69. *Earnshaw's,* May 1954, 65; *Earnshaw's,* August 1956, 64; *Earnshaw's,* October 1959, 48; see also *Stores,* January 1957, 40.

70. Bourdieu 1984.

71. *Earnshaw's,* July 1959, 81, emphasis in original.

72. *Earnshaw's,* November 1957, 55.

73. *Earnshaw's,* July 1956, 111.

74. On peer pressure of teens, see *Earnshaw's,* January 1958, 88; on "charm classes," see *Earnshaw's,* June 1958, 119, and *Earnshaw's,* August 1959, 48–49.

75. *Earnshaw's,* 1956, 64; quote in *Earnshaw's,* November 1960, 72.

76. *Earnshaw's,* February 1958, 37.

77. Unsure of how the study was conducted, I cannot comment on the generalizability of its findings. See *Earnshaw's,* September 1960, 86.

78. *Earnshaw's,* September 1960, 63.

79. *Earnshaw's,* September 1961, 76.

80. On developing a new size between subteen and teen, see *Earnshaw's,* March 1961, 28; on the preteen dilemma, see, for instance, *Earnshaw's,* May 1979, 58, and July 1986, 70.

81. *Earnshaw's,* August 1967, 127.

82. On the beginning of producing brassieres, see *Earnshaw's,* March 1954, 95; see *Earnshaw's,* January 1956, 130, for the "beginning bra";

about new styles and problems brought by the beginning bra, see *Earn-shaw's*, January 1960, 115; see also Ewing 1978, 165–82.

83. In an advertisement in *Earnshaw's* in September 1969, Teenform boasted: "Sixteen years ago, nobody ever heard of a nine year old wearing a bra, no less a panty girdle. Today, the world's finest retailers and a thriving industry thank Teenform for understanding and developing the 9 to 15 year old into a seasoned, eager-to-buy multimillion dollar customer!" (21).

84. " Boys and Girls: Too Old Too Soon: America's Subteens Rushing toward Trouble." *Life*, 10 August 1962, 54.

85. Concerns about "dating," while clearly a public, parental concern in the twentieth century (Fass 1977), did not surface in the national periodical press until the later 1940s, and not significantly until the mid-'50s. The *Reader's Guide to Periodical Literature* cited only two articles for the period 1942–43 on "courtship." These were parent-directed to the extent that they addressed the parental assessment of courtship and marriage (see *Good Housekeeping*, June 1943, 27; *Ladies Home Journal*, March 1942, 32). By the mid-'50s, dating and sex were widely discussed in the periodical literature; many articles were also presented from the child's (teen's and preteen's) point of view.

86. *Life*, 10 August 1962, 59; for the subsequent quotation, 60.

CHAPTER 7 *Concluding Remarks*

1. See Langer 2002, for a similar understanding of the place of sentiment in market relations.

2. Werland 1999 on children divorcing their parents. In Article I of the UN Convention on the Rights of the Child (1989), the child is defined as "every person under 18, unless national law grants majority at an earlier age" (UN Convention 1991, 50–52).

3. Hart 1991, 55. See also Cohen and Naimark 1991; Wilcox and Naimark 1991.

4. Alwin 1988, 42; Alwin 1990, 352–58; on materialism see Easterlin and Crimmins 1991; see also Jacobson and Mazur 1995.

5. Demo 1992 correlates changes in desired characteristics of children with changes in maternal employment.

6. Pollock 1999 on frozen dinners; MacArthur 2001 on pizza; *Restaurants and Institutions* 1993, 1994, on dining out; Hays 1996 on intensive mothering; Miller 1998 and Miller 2001 on mothers alleviating guilt with purchases.

7. According to Denise Fedewa, vice president and planning director

at Leo Burnett, an advertising firm based in Chicago, "Moms have loosened nutritional controls . . . They now believe there are so many battles to fight, is fighting over food really worth it?" (Pollack 1999, 16; see also McNeal 1992, 65–70; Guber and Berry 1993, 19–37).

8. On children's nagging-strategies, see Hendrick 2002, 3D, and Guber and Berry 1993, 2; see Underhill 2000 for ways that merchandisers position goods to entice children to make requests; for children's influence on big-ticket household items, see McNeal 1992, 63–87; McNeal 1999.

9. Whitman 1994; see also *Parents,* October 1990, 108, for advice to parents on how to curtail children's "natural" tendencies to want everything—they are now increasingly said to have been "born to shop" unless trained otherwise.

10. Flusser 1992, 9–10.

11. Revelli 1993, 3, emphasis added in first quote; see also Aria 1987.

12. Kunkle and Roberts 1991 on the triumph of free-market principles and the underlying model of the child implied in children's television legislation; see Cook 2000c and Jacobs 2002 on the Columbine tragedy.

13. For instance, see Senator Joe Lieberman's press releases and speeches on the issue of video game violence; for Federal Trade Commission reports, see www.ftc.gov/opa/2000/09/youthviol.htm.

14. Kincheloe 2002; see also Kenway and Bullen 2001.

15. On acknowledging children's voices in consumption, see Kenway and Bullen 2001 and Chin 2000. For a more general discussion of children's active engagement in commerce, see Zelizer 2002.

16. See Watson 1997; Yan 1997; Davis and Sensenbrenner 2000 for descriptions of children's consumption in contemporary China.

Bibliography

I. ACADEMIC REFERENCES

Adler, Patricia A., and Peter Adler. 1998. *Peer Power: Preadolescent Culture and Identity*. New Brunswick, N.J.: Rutgers University Press.

Alanen, Leena. 1994. "Gender and Generation: Feminism and the 'Child Question.'" In *Childhood Matters*, ed. Jens Qvortrup, Marjatta Bardy, Giovannia Sgritta, and Helmut Wintersberger, 31–42. Aldershot: Avebury.

Alexander, Victoria A. 1994. "The Image of Children in Magazine Advertisements from 1905–1990." *Communication Research* 21, no. 6:742–65.

Althusser, Louis. 1971. "Ideology and Ideological State Apparatuses." In *Lenin and Philosophy and Other Essays*, trans. Ben Brewster.

Alwin, Duane F. 1988. "From Obedience to Autonomy: Changes in Traits Desired in Children, 1924–1978." *Public Opinion Quarterly* 52:33–52.

———. 1990. "Cohort Replacement and Changes in Parental Socialization Values." *Journal of Marriage and the Family* 52 (May): 347–60.

Angus, David L., Jeffrey E. Mirel, and Maris A. Vinovskis. 1988. "Historical Development of Age Stratification in Schooling." *Teachers College Record* 90, no. 2:211–36.

Appadurai, Arjun. 1986. "Introduction: Commodities and the Politics of Value." In *The Social Life of Things*, ed. Arjun Appadurai, 3–63. Cambridge: Cambridge University Press.

Apple, Rima D. 1987. *Mothers and Medicine*. Madison: University of Wisconsin Press.

Aria, Barbara. 1987. *Kid Style*. New York: 2M Communications.

Ariès, Philippe. 1962. *Centuries of Childhood: A Social History of Family Life*. New York: Vintage.

Baudrilliard, Jean. 1981. *For a Critique of the Political Economy of the Sign*. St. Louis: Telos.

Beales, Ross W., Jr. 1985. "In Search of the Historical Child: Miniature Adulthood and Youth in Colonial New England." In *Growing Up in America: Children in Historical Perspective*, ed. Ray Hiner and Joseph M. Hawes, 7–26. Urbana: University of Illinois Press.

Becker, Howard S. 1982. *Artworlds*. Berkeley: University of California Press.

Beem, Margery. 1926. "A Word from the Ultimate Consumer." *Infants' and Children's Department* 10, no. 8:4729.

Belk, Russell W., Melanie Wallendorf, and John F. Sherry, Jr. 1989. "The Sacred and Profane in Consumer Behavior: Theodicy on the Odyssey." *Journal of Consumer Research* 16:1–38.

Bell, Quentin. 1976. *On Human Finery*, 2d ed. New York: Schocken.

Benson, Susan Porter. 1986. *Counter Cultures: Saleswomen, Managers, and Customers in American Department Stores, 1890–1940*. Urbana: University of Illinois Press, 1986.

Berger, John. 1972. *Ways of Seeing*. London: BBC.

Blumer, Herbert. 1969. "Fashion: From Class Differentiation to Collective Selection." *Sociological Quarterly* 10:275–91.

Book House for Children. 1956. *In Your Hands: The Parents' Guide Book*. Lake Bluff, Ill.: Book House for Children.

Bourdieu, Pierre. 1984. *Distinction*. Cambridge: Harvard University Press.

Buckingham, David. 2000. *After the Death of Childhood*. Cambridge: Polity.

Calvert, Karin. 1992. *Children in the House: The Material Culture of Early Childhood, 1600–1900*. Boston: Northeastern University Press.

Campbell, Colin. 1987. *The Romantic Ethic and the Spirit of Modern Consumerism*. Oxford: Basil Blackwell.

Carrier, James G. 1997. *Meanings of the Market*. Oxford, N.Y.: Berg.

Chauncey, George. 1997. *Gay New York*. New York: Basic Books.

Chudacoff, Howard P. 1989. *How Old Are You? Age Consciousness in American Culture*. Princeton: Princeton University Press.

Cohen, Cynthia Price, and Hedwin Naimark. 1991. "United Nations Convention on the Rights of the Child." *American Psychologist* 46 (January): 60–65.

Coleman, James S. 1974. *Youth: Transition to Adulthood*. Chicago: University of Chicago Press.

Comaroff, Jean, and John Comaroff. 1997. *Of Revelation and Revolution*. Vol. 2. Chicago: University of Chicago Press.

Cook, Daniel Thomas. 1995. "The Mother as Consumer: Insights from the Children's Wear Industry, 1917–1929." *Sociological Quarterly* 36:505–22.

———. 1999. "The Visual Commodification of Childhood: A Case Study from a Children's Wear Trade Magazine, 1920s–1980s." *Journal of Social Sciences* 3, nos. 1–2:21–40.

———. 2000a. "Childhood Is Killing 'Our' Children: Some Reflections on the Columbine Shootings and the Agentive Child." *Childhood* 7, no. 1:107–17.

———. 2000b. "The Other 'Child Study': Figuring Children as Consumers in Market Research, 1910s–1990s." *Sociological Quarterly* 41, no. 3:487–507.

———. 2000c. "The Rise of 'the Toddler' as Subject and as Merchandising Category in the 1930s." In *New Means of Consumption*, ed. Mark Gottdiener. Lanham. Md.: Rowman & Littlefield.

———. 2002a. "Interrogating Symbolic Childhood." In *Symbolic Childhood*, ed. Daniel T. Cook, 1–14. New York: Peter Lang.

———, ed. 2002b. *Symbolic Childhood*. New York: Peter Lang.

Corsaro, William. 1997. *The Sociology of Childhood*. Thousand Oaks, Calif.: Sage.

Cott, Nancy. 1977. *The Bonds of Womanhood*. New Haven: Yale University Press.

Cowan, Ruth Schwartz. 1983. *More Work for Mother*. New York: Basic Books.

Cross, Gary. 1998. *Kids' Stuff*. Cambridge: Harvard University Press.

Davis, Deborah S., and Julia S. Sensenbrenner. 2000. "Commercializing Childhood: Parental Purchases for Shanghai's Only Child." In *The Consumer Revolution in Urban China*, ed. Deborah Davis. Berkeley: University of California Press.

Davis, Fred. 1992. *Fashion, Culture and Identity*. Chicago: University of Chicago Press.

Davis, Susan. 2001. "Shopping." In *Culture Works*, ed. Richard Maxwell. Minneapolis: University of Minnesota Press.

deMause, Lloyd. 1974. "The Evolution of Childhood." In *The History of Childhood*, ed. Lloyd deMause, 1–74. New York: Psychohistory Press.

Demo, David H. 1992. "Parent-Child Relations: Assessing Recent Changes." *Journal of Marriage and the Family* 54 (February):104–17.

Dennis, Jeffery P. 2002. "The Heterosexualization of Boyhood." In *Symbolic Childhood*, ed. Daniel T. Cook, 211–26. New York: Peter Lang.

Douglas, Ann. 1977. *The Feminization of American Culture*. New York: Avon.

Douglas, Mary. 1966. *Purity and Danger: An Analysis of the Concepts of Pollution and Taboo*. New York: Praeger.

Douglas, Mary, and Baron Isherwood. 1979. *The World of Goods*. New York: W. W. Norton.

"Do You Know Where Your Children Are?" 1999. *U.S. News and World Report*, 3 May, 16.

Dupuis, E. Melanie. 2002. *Nature's Perfect Food: How Milk Became America's Drink*. New York: New York University Press.

Durkheim, Émile. 1915. *The Elementary Forms of the Religious Life*. New York: Free Press.

Easterlin, Richard A., and Eileen M. Crimmins. 1991. "Private Materialism, Personal Self-fulfillment, Family Life, and Public Interest: The Nature, Effects and Causes of Recent Changes in the Values of American Youth." *Public Opinion Quarterly* 55:499–533.

Ehrenreich, Barbara, and Deirdre English. 1978. *For Her Own Good: 150 Years of the Experts' Advice to Women*. New York: Doubleday.

Elder, Glennard Holl. 1974. *Children of the Great Depression: Social Change in Life Experience*. Chicago: University of Chicago Press.

Elkind, David. 1981. *The Hurried Child Growing Up Too Fast Too Soon*. Reading, Mass.: Addison-Wesley.

Englehardt, Tom. 1986. "The Shortcake Strategy." In *Watching Television*, ed. Todd Gitlin, 68–110. New York: Pantheon.

Ewen, Elizabeth. 1985. *Immigrant Women in the Land of Dollars*. New York: Monthly Review Press.

Ewen, Stuart, and Elizabeth Ewen. 1982. *Channels of Desire: Mass Images and the Shaping of American Consciousness*. New York: McGraw-Hill.

Ewing, Elizabeth. 1978. *Dress and Undress*. New York: Drama Book Specialists.

Fass, Paula S. 1977. *The Damned and the Beautiful: American Youth in the 1920s*. Oxford: Oxford University Press.

Featherstone, Mike. 1991. *Consumer Culture and Postmodernism*. London: Sage.

Flusser, Marilise. 1992. *Party Shoes to School and Baseball Caps to Bed: The Parents' Guide to Kids, Clothes and Independence*. New York: Simon and Schuster.

Ford, E. A. 1960. "Organizational Pattern of the Nation's Public Secondary Schools." *School Life* 42 (May): 1–14.

Forty, Adrian. 1986. *Objects of Desire*. London: Thames and Hudson.

Foucault, Michel. 1965. *Madness and Civilization*. New York: Vintage.

——. 1978. *The History of Sexuality: An Introduction*. New York: Vintage.

——. 1979. *Discipline and Punish*. New York: Vintage.

Frank, Thomas. 2000. *One Market under God: Extreme Capitalism, Market Populism, and the Economic Democracy*. New York: Doubleday.

Frazer, James. 1922. *The Golden Bough*. New York: Macmillan.

Frederick, Christine. 1929. *Selling Mrs. Consumer*. New York: Business Bourse.

Gilbert, Eugene. 1957. *Advertising and Marketing to Young People*. Pleasantville, N.Y.: Printer's Ink Books.

Giroux, Henri. 1998. "Nymphet Fantasies: Child Beauty Pageants and the Politics of Innocence." *Social Text 57*, no. 4 (winter):31–53.

——. 1999. *The Mouse that Roared*. Lanham, Md.: Rowman and Littlefield.

Gordon, Linda. 1988. *Heroes of Their Own Lives: The Politics and History of Family Violence*. New York: Penguin.

Green, Harvey. 1992. *The Uncertainty of Everyday Life, 1915–1945*. New York: Harper Collins.

Grumbine, E. Evalyn. 1938. *Reaching Juvenile Markets: How to Advertise, Sell, and Merchandise through Boys and Girls*. New York: McGraw-Hill.

Guber, Selina S., and Jon Berry. 1993. *Marketing to and through Kids*. New York: McGraw-Hill.

Hacking, Ian. 1990. *The Taming of Chance*. Cambridge: Cambridge University Press.

Hall, Catherine, and Lenore Davidoff. 1987. *Family Fortunes*. Chicago: University of Chicago Press.

Hall, Edward T. 1983. *The Dance of Life: The Other Dimension of Time*. New York: Anchor.

Hart, Stuart N. 1991. "From Property to Person Status: Historical Perspective on Children's Rights." *American Psychologist* 46, no. 1:53–59.

Hawes, Joseph M. 1990. *The Children's Rights Movement*. Boston: Twayne.

Hays, Sharon. 1996. *The Cultural Contradictions of Motherhood*. New Haven: Yale University Press.

Heininger, Mary Lynn Stevens. 1984. "Children, Childhood, and Change in America, 1820–1920." In *A Century of Childhood, 1820–1920*, ed. Heininger, 1–33. Rochester, N.Y.: Margaret Woodbury Strong Museum.

Hendershot, Heather. 1998. *Saturday Morning Censors*. Durham: Duke University Press.

Henrick, Bill. 2002. "Nagging Their Parents Snags Kids the Products They Want." *Atlanta Journal Constitution*, 17 June, 3D.

Higonnet, Anne. 1998. *Pictures of Innocence*. New York: Thames and Hudson.

Hochschild, Arlie, with Anne Machung. 1989. *The Second Shift*. New York: Avon.

Holloway, Sarah L., and Gill Valentine, eds. 2000. *Children's Geographies: Playing, Living, Learning*. New York: Routledge.

Howe, Neil, and William Strauss. 1993. *13th Gen*. New York: Vintage.

Huun, Kathleen, and Susan B. Kaiser. 2002. "The Emergence of Modern Infantwear, 1896–1962: Traditional White Dresses Succumb to Fashion's Gender Obsession." *Clothing and Textiles Research Journal* 19, no. 3:103–19.

Jacobs, Mark. 2002. "The School Shooting as a Ritual of Sacrifice." In *Symbolic Childhood*, ed. Daniel Thomas Cook, 169–82. New York: Peter Lang.

Jacobson, Michael F., and Laurie Ann Mazur. 1995. *Marketing Madness: a Survival Guide for a Consumer Society*. Boulder: Westview.

Jaffe, Hilde, and Rosa Rosa. 1990. *Childrenswear Design*. New York: Fairchild Publications.

James, Allison, Chris Jenks, and Alan Prout. 1998. *Theorizing Childhood*. New York: Teacher's College Press.

James, Allison, and Alan Prout, eds. 1990. *Constructing and Reconstructing Childhood*. London: Falmer Press.

Jenks, Chris. 1996. *Childhood*. New York: Routledge.

Jones, Alice Hanson. 1945. *Family Spending and Saving during Wartime*. Washington: Government Printing Office.

Kaiser, Susan B., and Jean S. Phinney. 1983. "Sex Typing of Play Activities by Girls' Clothing Style: Pants versus Skirts." *Child Study Journal* 13, no. 2:115–32.

Kaiser, Susan B., and Kathleen Huun. 2002. "Fashioning Innocence and Anxiety: Clothing, Gender, and Symbolic Childhood." In *Symbolic Childhood*, ed. Daniel Thomas Cook, 183–208. New York: Peter Lang.

Kantrowitz, Barbara, and Pat Wingert. 1999. "The Truth about Tweens." *Newsweek*, 18 October, 62–71.

Kaplan, E. Ann. 1992. *Motherhood and Representation*. London: Routledge.

Kenny, Mary Lorena. 2002. "Orators and Outcasts, Wanderers and Workers: Street Children in Brazil." In *Symbolic Childhood*, ed. Daniel Thomas Cook, 37–63. New York: Peter Lang.

Kessler-Harris, Alice. 1982. *Out to Work: A History of Wage-Earning Women in the United States*. New York: Oxford University Press.

Kett, Joseph. 1974. "History of Age Groping in America." In *Youth: Transition to Adulthood*, ed. Coleman et al., 9–29. Chicago: University of Chicago Press.

Key, Ellen. 1909. *The Century of the Child*. New York: G. P. Putnam's Sons.

Kidwell, Claudia B., and Margaret C. Christman. 1974. *Suiting Everyone: The Democratization of Clothing in America*. Washington: Smithsonian Institution Press.

Kincheloe, Joe L. 2002. "The Complex Politics of McDonald's and the New Childhood: Colonizing Kidworld." In *Kidworld: Childhood Studies, Global Perspectives and Education*, ed. Gaile S. Cannella and Joe L. Kincheloe. New York: Peter Lang.

Kinder, Marsha, ed. 1998. *Kids' Media Culture*. Durham: Duke University Press.

Klaus, Alisa. 1993. *Every Child a Lion: The Origins of Maternal Health Policy in the United States and France, 1890–1920*. Ithaca: Cornell University Press.

Kline, Stephen. 1993. *Out of the Garden: Toys and Children's Culture in the Age of TV Marketing*. London: Verso.

Kneeland, Natalie. 1925. *Infants' and Children's Wear*. Chicago: A. W. Shaw and Co.

Kopytoff, Igor. 1986. "The Cultural Biography of Things: Commoditization as Process." In *The Social Life of Things*, ed. Arjun Appadurai, 63–91. Cambridge: Cambridge University Press.

Kunkel, Dale, and Donald Roberts. 1991. "Young Minds and Marketplace Values: Issues in Children's Television Advertising." *Journal of Social Issues* 47, no. 1:57–72.

Laqueur, Thomas. 1990. *Making Sex: Body and Gender from the Greeks to Freud*. Berkeley: University of California Press.

Langer, Beryl. 2002. "Commodified Enchantment: Children and Consumer Capitalism." *Thesis Eleven*, no. 69 (May): 67–81.

Layne, Linda, ed. 1999. *Transformative Motherhood*. New York: NYU Press.

Leach, William. 1984. "Transformations in a Culture of Consumption: Women and Department Stores, 1890–1925." *Journal of American History* 71, no. 2:319–42.

———. 1993a. "Child-World in the Promised Land." In *The Mythmaking Frame of Mind*, ed. J. Gillbert et al., 209–38. Belmont, Calif.: Wadsworth.

———. 1993b. *Land of Desire: Merchants, Power and the Rise of a New American Culture*. New York: Pantheon.

Lears, T. J. Jackson. 1983. "From Salvation to Self-Realization." In *The Culture of Consumption*, ed. T. J. Jackson Lears and Richard Wightman Fox, 3–38. New York: Pantheon.

———. 1994. *Fables of Abundance: A Cultural History of Advertising in America*. New York: Basic Books.

Levy, Frank. 1998. *Dollars and Dreams*. New York: W. W. Norton.

Lieberman, Joe. Speeches. www.senate.gov/member/ct/lieberman/ general.

Lies, B. Eugenia, and Marie P. Sealy. 1928. "Planning a Department Store Layout." *Journal of Retailing*, April, 24.

Lury, Celia. 1996. *Consumer Culture*. New Brunswick, N.J.: Rutgers University Press.

Lynd, Robert S., and Helen M. Lynd. 1929. *Middletown: A Study in Contemporary American Culture*. New York: Harcourt, Brace.

———. 1937. *Middletown in Transition: A Study in Cultural Conflicts*. New York: Harcourt, Brace.

Lynott, Patricia Passuth, and Barbara J. Louge. 1993. "The 'Hurried Child': The Myth of Lost Childhood in Contemporary Society." *Sociological Forum* 13, no. 3:471–91.

MacArthur, Kate. 2000. "McDonald's Revisits Pizza with New Happy Meal Test." *Advertising Age* 71, no. 9:28.

McNamee, Sara. 1998. "Youth, Gender and Video Games: Power and Control in the Home." In *Cool Places*, ed. Tracey Skelton and Gill Valentine, 195–206. London: Routledge.

McNeal, James. 1992. *Kids as Customers*. New York: Lexington.

———. 1999. *The Kids' Market: Myths and Realities*. Ithaca, N.Y.: Paramount Market.

Marchand, Roland. 1985. *Advertising the American Dream, 1920–1940*. Berkeley: University of California Press.

Marx, Karl. 1978. "Commodities." In *The Marx-Engels Reader*, ed. Robert C. Tucker, 301–29. New York: W. W. Norton.

Marx, Karl, and Frederick Engels. 1978. "The German Ideology." In *The Marx-Engels Reader*, ed. C. Tucker, 146–200. New York: W. W. Norton.

Mauss, Marcel. 1979. "A Category of the Human Mind: The Notion of Person; the Notion of Self." In *The Category of the Person*, ed. Miachael Carrithers, Steven Collins, and Steve Lukes, 1–25. Cambridge: Cambridge University Press.

Miller, Anita. 1999. "They're Home Alone." *Newsweek*, 29 November, 62–71.

Miller, Daniel. 1997. "How Children Grow Mothers in North London." *Theory, Culture and Society* 14, no. 2:67–88.

———. 1998. *A Theory of Shopping*. Cambridge: Polity.

———. 2001. *The Dialectics of Shopping*. Chicago: University of Chicago Press.

Modell, John. 1989. *Into One's Own: From Youth to Adulthood in the United States, 1920–1975*. Berkeley: University of California Press.

Modell, Judith. 1999. "Freely Given: Open Adoption and the Rhetoric of the Gift." *Transformative Motherhood*, ed. L. Layne, 29–64. New York: New York University Press.

Molnar, Alex. 1996. *Giving Kids the Business: The Commercialization of America's Schools*. Boulder: Westview.

Nasaw, David. 1985. *Children of the City*. New York: Oxford University Press.

———. 1992. "Children and Commercial Culture." In *Small Worlds: Children and Adolescents in America, 1850–1950*, ed. Elliot West and Paula Petrik, 14–25. Lawrence: University Press of Kansas.

Oakley, Ann. 1993. "Women and Children First and Last: Parallels and Differences between Women's and Children's Studies." In *Childhood as a Social Phenomenon*, ed. Jens Qvortrup, 51–69. Vienna: European Centre.

Oldman, David. 1994. "Adult-Child Relations as Class Relations." In *Childhood Matters*, ed. Jens Qvortrup, Marjatta Bardy, Giovannia Sgritta, and Helmut Wintersberger, 43–58. Aldershot: Avebury.

The Oxford English Dictionary, 1989. 2d ed. New York: Oxford University Press.

Palladino, Grace. 1996. *Teenagers*. New York: Basic Books.

Palmer, Phyllis M. 1989. *Domesticity and Dirt: Housewives and Domestic Servants in the United States, 1920–1945*. Philadelphia: Temple University Press.

Paoletti, Jo B., and Carol L. Kregloh. 1989. "The Children's Department." In *Men and Women, Dressing the Part*, ed. Claudia Kidwell and Valerie Steele, 22–41. Washington: Smithsonian Institution Press.

Parry, Jonathan, and Maurice Bloch, eds. 1989. *Money and the Morality of Exchange*. Cambridge: Cambridge University Press.

Parsons, Talcott. 1959. "The School Class as a Social System: Some of Its Functions in American Society." *Harvard Educational Review* 29, no. 4:297–318.

Platt, Anthony. 1977. *The Child Savers*. Chicago: University of Chicago Press.

Pleck, Elizabeth. 2001. *Celebrating the Family*. Cambridge: Harvard University Press.

Plumb, J. H. 1982. "The New World of Children in Eighteenth-century England." In *The Birth of a Consumer Society*, ed. Neil McKendrick, John Brewer, and John Plumb, 286–315. Bloomington: Indiana University Press.

Pollack, Judann. 1999. "Foods Targeting Children Aren't Just Child's Play." *Advertising Age*, 79, no. 9 (March): 16.

Pollock, Linda. 1983. *Forgotten Children: Parent-Child Relations from 1500–1900*. New York: Cambridge University Press.

Postman, Neil. 1982. *The Disappearance of Childhood*. New York: Laurel.

Qvortrup, Jens. 1987. "Introduction." *International Journal of Sociology* 17, no. 1:1–26.

———. 1990. "A Voice for Children in Statistical and Social Accounting: A Plea for Children's Right to be Heard." In *Constructing and Reconstructing Childhood: Contemporary Issues in the Sociological Study of Childhood*, ed. Allison James and Alan Prout, 79–98. New York: Falmer.

Qvortrup, Jens, ed. 1993. *Childhood as a Social Phenomenon*. Vienna: European Centre.

Rawlins, Roblyn. 2002. "'Long Rows of Short Graves': Sentimentality, Science, and Child-Saving in the Construction of the Intellectually Precocious Child, 1870–1925." In *Symbolic Childhood*, ed. Daniel Thomas Cook, 89–108. New York: Peter Lang.

Revelli, Clare. 1993. *Baby and You: A Fun-Filled Guide to Discovering Your Baby's Very Own Style*. New York: Pocket Books.

Riesman, David. 1950. *The Lonely Crowd*. New York: Doubleday.

Rose, Jacqueline. 1984. *The Case of Peter Pan*. Philadelphia: University of Pennsylvania Press.

Rose, Nicholas. 1990. *Governing the Soul*. London: Routledge.

Rousseau, Jean-Jacques. 1762. *Emile*.

Rubenstein, Ruth. 2000. *Society's Child*. Boulder: Westview.

Schlereth, Thomas J. 1991. *Victorian America: Transformations in Everyday Life, 1876–1915*. New York: Harper Collins.

Schlossman, Steven. 1988. "Perils of Popularization: The Founding of *Parents* Magazine." *Monographs of the Society for Research in Child Development* 50, no. 4:65–77.

Schneider, Jane, and Annette B. Weiner. 1989. "Introduction." In *Cloth and Human Experience*, ed. Annette B. Weiner and Jane Schneider, 1–29. Washington: Smithsonian Institution Press.

Seiter, Ellen. 1993. *Sold Separately: Mothers and Children in Consumer Culture*. Bloomington: Indiana University Press.

———. 1999. "Power Rangers at Preschool: Negotiating Media in Child Care Settings." In *Kid's Media Culture*, ed. M. Klinder, 239–62. Durham: Duke University Press.

Shorter, Edward. 1975. *The Making of the Modern Family*. New York: Basic Books.

Simmel, Georg. 1971a. "Fashion." In *On Individuality and Social Forms*, ed. Donald N. Levine, 294–323. Chicago: University of Chicago Press.

——. 1971b. "The Metropolis and Mental Life." In *On Individuality and Social Forms*, ed. Donald N. Levine, 324–39. Chicago: University of Chicago Press.

——. 1978. *The Philosophy of Money*. Trans. Tom Bottomore and David Frisby. Boston: Routledge and Kegan Paul.

Sklar, Kathryn Kish. 1993. "The Historical Foundations of Women's Power in the Creation of the American Welfare State, 1830–1930." *In Mothers of a New World: Maternalist Politics and the Origins of Welfare States*, ed. Seth Koven and Sonya Michel, 43–92. New York: Routledge.

Slater, Don. 1997. *Consumer Culture and Modernity*. Cambridge: Polity.

Slater, Don, and Fran Tonkiss. 2001. *Market Society: Markets and Modern Social Theory*. Malden, Mass.: Basil Blackwell.

Smith, Bernard. 1989. "A Study of Uneven Industrial Development: The American Clothing Industry in the Late 19th and Early 20th Century." Ph.D. diss., Yale University.

Spigel, Lynn. 1998. "Seducing the Innocent: Childhood and Television in Postwar America," 110–35. In *The Children's Culture Reader*, ed. Henry Jenkins. New York: NYU Press.

Stannard, David E. 1974. "Death and the Puritan Child." *American Quarterly* 26 (December): 456–76.

Steinberg, Shirley, and Joe L. Kincheloe, eds. 1997. *Kinderculture: The Corporate Construction of Childhood*. Boulder: Westview.

Stendler, Celia B. 1950. "Psychologic Aspects of Pediatrics: Sixty Years of Child Training Practices." *Journal of Pediatrics* 36:122–35.

Stone, Lawrence. 1977. *The Family, Sex and Marriage in England, 1500–1800*. New York: Harper and Row.

Strandell, Harriet. 2002. "On Questions of Representation in Childhood Ethnography." In *Symbolic Childhood*, ed. Daniel Thomas Cook, 17–36. New York: Peter Lang.

Sunley, Robert. 1955. "Early Nineteenth-Century American Literature on Child-Rearing." In *Childhood in Contemporary Cultures*, ed. Margaret Mead and Martha Wolfenstein, 150–60. Chicago: University of Chicago Press.

Thompson, E. P. 1967. "Time, Work-Discipline and Industrial Capitalism." *Past and Present* 38:56–97.

Thorne, Barrie. 1993. *Gender Play*. New Brunswick, N.J.: Rutgers University Press.

Troen, Selwyn K. 1987. "The Discovery of the Adolescent by American Educational Reformers, 1900–1920: An Economic Perspective," 414–25. In *Growing Up in America*, ed. Harvey J. Graff. Detroit: Wayne State University Press.

"UN Convention on the Rights of the Child: Unofficial Summary of Articles." 1991. *American Psychologist*, January, 50–52.

Underhill, Paco. 2000. *Why We Buy*. New York: Touchstone.

U.S. Bureau of Labor Statistics. 1924. *Cost of Living in the United States*. Washington: Government Printing Office.

Vann, Richard. 1982. "The Youth of Centuries of Childhood." *History and Theory* 21, no. 2:279–98.

Valentine, Gill. 1996a. "Angel and Devils: Moral Landscapes of Childhood." *Environment and Planning D: Society and Space* 14:581–99.

——. 1996b. "'Children Should Be Seen and Not Heard: The Production and Transgression of Adults' Public Space.'" *Urban Geography* 17, no. 3:205–20.

——. 1999. "'Oh Please, Mum. Oh Please, Dad': Negotiating Children's Spatial Boundaries." In *Gender, Power and Household*, ed. Linda McKie, Sophia Bowlby, and Susan Gregory. New York: St. Martin's.

Walker, Herbert S., and Nathaniel Mendelson. 1967. *The Children's Wear Merchandiser*. New York: National Retail Merchant's Association.

Watson, James, L. 1997. "McDonald's in Hong Kong: Consumerism, Dietary Change, and the Rise of a Children's Culture." In *Golden Arches East: McDonald's in East Asia*, ed. James L. Watson. Stanford: Stanford University Press.

Werland, Ross. 1999. "Being 18 Doesn't Guarantee Liberation." *Chicago Tribune*, 4 July, Family Section.

Whitman, Cynthia. 1994. *"The Answer is No": Saying No and Sticking to It*. Los Angeles: Perspective.

Wilcox, Brian L., and Hedwin Naimark. 1991. "Children's Rights around the Globe." *American Psychologist* 46, no. 1 (January): 49.

Williams, Raymond. 1977. *Marxism and Literature*. Oxford: Oxford University Press.

Wilson, Adrian. 1980. "The Infancy of Childhood: An Appraisal of Philippe Ariès." *History and Theory* 19, no. 2:132–53.

Wilson, Elizabeth. 1985. *Adorned in Dreams*. London: Virago.

Winn, Marie. 1985. *The Plug-In Drug*. New York: Viking.

Wolfenstein, Martha. 1955. "Fun Morality: An Analysis of Recent American Child-Training Literature." In *Childhood in Contemporary Cultures*, ed. Margaret Mead and Martha Wolfenstein, 168–78. Chicago: University of Chicago Press.

Yan, Yunxiang. 1997. "McDonald's in Beijing: The Localization of American." In *Golden Arches East: McDonald's in East Asia*, ed. James L. Watson. Stanford: Stanford University Press.

Yellin, Jean Fagan, and John C. Van Horne, eds. 1994. *The Abolitionist*

Sisterhood: Women's Political Culture in Antebellum America. Ithaca: Cornell University Press.

Zelizer, Viviana A. 1985. *Pricing the Priceless Child: The Changing Social Value of Children*. New York: Basic Books.

———. 1994. *The Social Meaning of Money*. New York: Basic Books.

———. 2002. "Kids and Commerce," *Childhood* 9, no. 4:375–96.

Zerubavel, Evitar. 1981. *Hidden Rhythms*. Chicago: University of Chicago Press.

II. NONACADEMIC JOURNALS AND MAGAZINES

Advertising Age
    4 September 1995.
    11 September 1995.

Babyhood
    7 February 1920, 89.
    November, 1920, 361.
    "Summer Vogue for Toddlers." June 1924, 238.
    "Correct Dress for Children." February 1930, 33.

Bulletin of the National Retail Dry Goods Association (BNRDGA)
    Alan Burt. "Standardizing Size Measurements for Children and in Wear." March 1938, 130–31.
    Green, Betty. "Will Your C Dept. Get Its Share of the Fairs?" May 1939, 24–25.
    "Two New Children's Floors." October 1939, 72.

Delineator
    Babley, Mary E. "Your Child's Right to Beauty." October 1921, 39.

Dry Goods Economist (DGE)
    "Getting Baby's Trade: It Can Be Done by Making a Direct Appeal to Mothers." 21 March 1914, 105, 107.
    "Store Arrangement: Plan for Store 96x118." 28 March 1914, 11.
    "Selling to the Young Girls." 9 August 1919, 45.
    "Clothing Widows That Won Prizes in Contest Just Closed." 7 February 1920, 87.
    " 'Little Men' Want to Be Recognized." 7 February 1920, 89.
    "Appeal to Boy and Sell to Parent." 29 May 1920, 81.
    "And Now the Child Is Recognized as Fashion Factor." 30 October 1920, 43, 89.

"How Grouping Children's Goods Reduces Sales Resistance." 19 November 1921, 231.

"Wonderful Industry for American Baby Built Up in Last 60 Years." 19 November 1921, 225.

"Reflecting the Old Spirit of Christmas and a New Spirit of Service." 15 December 1923, 13.

"A Twixt-and-Tween Section." 1 May 1926, 4366.

January 1920, 97.

March 1922.

Earnshaw's Infants and Children's Merchandiser

"Amusing Children While Mother Shops." April 1920, 165–66.

"Babies on the Air." November 1927, 1757–59.

"Stop—Says the Layette." December 1927, 5273–74.

"'Haas Brothers' Bambino Shop." May 1930, 724–26.

"Baby's Own Shop." October 1930, 1472–73.

June 1931, 710.

Hawn, Ruth. "Unity in Children's Merchandising." May 1932, 67.

"A Model Wardrobe for a Young Girl." October 1932, 845–46.

Krauch, Flora. "What about Toddlers?" January 1934, 48–49, 56.

"Alene Burt . . . Discusses the Girls' Wear Department." October 1934, 31, 59.

"Dresses in the Girls' Department." January 1935, 54.

"Columbia Pictures Renew Their Contrast." June 1935, 62.

"Sidney Rosenau Appointed Guardian for Shirley Temple." August 1935, 76.

Krauch, Flora. "Toddlers." February 1936.

"Coats-Hats Separated in 10–16 Range." April 1936.

"Wanamaker Opens a New Juvenile Floor Stressing Individual Shops." September 1936, 48.

December 1936, 54.

Krauch, Flora. "The Second Stepping Stone." August 1937.

"Catering to Toddlers." October 1937, 54, 92.

Krauch, Flora. "The Fourth Stepping Stone." November 1937.

"Popularity Contest Brings Good Results." January 1940.

"All Daytton Designs Girls' Coats." November 1940, 31.

"Dressing the Juvenile Film Star." November 1940, 30.

January 1942, 48, 50.

January 1942, 74.

Blank, C. L. "Floor for Youth Pays." January 1942, 47.

"Powers Push the Teen Shop." September 1942, 43.

April 1944, 103.

May 1947, 51.

"Teens Are Important People." June 1947, 125, 209.

May 1949, 136.

June 1949, 139, 135.

Grant, Marie. "Our Customers Are Teenagers." September 1950, 135.

Thomas, C. "Kerr's Courts Teens." February 1951, 106.

April 1951, 79.

"Your Impressionable Teen Customers." April 1951, 78.

July 1951, 64.

"United Council Shows for Spring." December 1951, 52–53.

Clepper, Patrick M. "Customer Psychology Is a Sales Stimulant for Emporium Trade." May 1952, 110.

Vossen Amy. "Supermarket Merchandises Up-to-12 Boys' Wear and Girls' Apparel." May 1952.

April 1953, 105, 109, 134.

May 1953, 79.

Schneider, Virginia. "All Schaefer's Teen Council Functions for Pogue's." May 1953, 154.

March 1954.

Marr, O. J. "Good Sub-teen Selections Are a Scission Specialty." May 1954, 65.

Willinsky, Harriet. "How to Promote Children's Business on a Fashion Basis." May 1954, 65.

"Teen Fun Pays Off." November 1954, 86, 106.

January 1955, 146.

Breen, Mildred. "What Is the Retailer Doing for the Sub Teen?" January 1955, 116.

Reimann, Marge. "Dual Purpose Costumes Please the Sub-teen." December 1955, 70.

January 1956.

Youman, Irene L. "How to Fit a Sub-teen's Bra?" January 1956.

February 1956, 75.

"More Sub-Teen Space Holds Them Longer." March 1956, 54.

August 1956, 64.

August 1956, 115.

Schneider, Virginia. "Sub-teen Space Holds Them Longer." January 1958, 88–89.

Hudson, Walter. "When Sub-teens Say 'It's Time to Take Inventory.'" February 1958, 24.

November 1958, 70–71.

"Survey Indicates Importance of Playwear in Gift Purchase." July 1959, 51.

August 1959, 48–49.

January 1960.

"How Subteen Dollars Are Spent for Christmas." September 1960, 86.

"Retail Ads That Sell Subteens." November 1960, 72.

March 1961, 28.

Dechter, Martin. "Subteens . . . How They Grew?" March 1961, 48.

Paturis, Cleo. "Are Subteen Dresses Becoming Too Sophisticated?" September 1961, 76.

Albert, Helen R. "The Cosmetic Whirl . . . How It's Reaching Children." August 1967.

April 1968, 62–63.

September 1969, 21.

May 1979, 58.

"Ton Sur Ton: Selling Lifestyle." July 1986, 77.

Infants Department

"How Mr. Leason Doubled the Business." October 1917, 23–24.

November 1917, 37, 38.

Yandell, Nellie. "Selling Infants' Wear to Daddy." January 1918, 77.

"The Department Store As an Educational Factor." May 1918, 148.

"Secluded Layette Room for Prospective Mothers." December 1918, 69–70, 134.

March 1919, 144.

March 1919, 147.

May 1919, 174.

"Ethics in Selling Infants' Wear." October 1919, 36.

January 1920, 106.

September 1921, 324.

"The Creed Service." September 1921, 322.

Earnshaw, G. F. "Who Really Buys Infants' Wear." October 1921, 374–79.

November 1921, 398.

Earnshaw, G. F. "These Who Dwell In Cuter Darkness." January 1922, 490.

Mabel, R. "Helps and Hints for Those Who Sell." January 1922, 484–85.

"A Bankable Asset." February 1922, 519–20.

March 1922, 561–63.

"Winning the Store's Most Important Customer on Her First Trip."
March 1923, 1067.

September 1924, 2233.

Beem, Margery. "A World from the Ultimate Consumer." August
1926, 4729.

September 1926, 5031–33.

Ladies Home Journal

Burtis, Edith M. "How Can I Dress My Boy Different from Others?"
January 1913, 64.

March, 1942, 32.

July 1944, 104, 130.

Parents

Cundiff, Esther M. "Good Taste in Children's Clothing." February
1927, 34.

May 1927, 38.

Ripperger, Henrietta Sperry. "Train Your Children's Taste in
Clothes." April 1929, 21, 58–60.

"Cultivating Good Looks." February 1930, 22, 64.

"The Adolescent and His Clothes." April 1931, 21.

March 1932, 13.

"Is Your Child Self-Conscious." September 1936, 29, 61.

Cundiff, Esther M. "What Shall They Wear to School?" October
1936, 38.

"Toddlers Are Made That Way." June 1937, 28, 107.

November 1939, 34.

October 1942, 26–27, 122.

"Good Taste and How It Grows." November 1942, 28, 40, 72.

"Mothers' Looks." April 1956, 90–91.

"Curing the 'Gimmes.'" October 1990, 108.

Printer's Ink

"Winning the Child's Good-Will by Plussing the Sale." 9 February
1922, 121.

"Helpfulness: The Big Idea in Advertising to Women." 14 June 1923,
130.

"Johns-Manville Tests Out an Appeal to Women." 20 September
1923, 57.

Heath, W. R. "When Salesmen Sell to Women." 5 March 1925, 89–92.

Stanton, Warren M. "Mothers Laugh." 21 August 1930, 12.

Collins, James H. "All about Women: For Advertisers Only." 18 February 1926.

"The Overdone Mother Appeal." 21 August 1930, 12.

"Cutouts for Children." 21 May 1931, 56–57.

Dunn, Elizabeth. "A Man Would Say It That Way." 10 December 1931, 60.

"Children Are Joiners." 18 August 1932, 68–69.

"If It's Free the Kids Will Like It." 5 January 1933, 68–71.

"Advertising to the Child to Reach the Parent." 12 October 1933, 70–72.

"Children's Club as Sales Aid." 2 May 1935, 85–90.

Muller, Charles G. "Don't Overlook the Sons and Daughters of Mr. & Mrs. Consumer." 9 May 1935.

Grumbine, E. Evalyn. "Advertising to Children." 17 June 1937, 49.

Printer's Ink Monthly

Davis, Louis Taylor. "What a Housewife Wants in Copy." February 1924, 52–53.

"Making the Smile: A Female Sales Factor." June 1930, 31.

Howell, Wilbur F. "With Designs upon the Next Generation." October 1930, 118.

"Specially Designed Package for Children." April 1932, 65.

"Why General Foods Likes the Comic Strip." June 1932, 40, 70.

Stevens, S. W. "Psychology Offers New Approach to Marketing Problems." October 1933, 53–54.

May 1936, 9–10.

Grumbine, E. Evalyn. "Juvenile Clubs and Contests." June 1936, 26–28.

——. "Pictures and Colors Children Like." March 1938, 39–40.

"Boom in the Baby Market." November 1941, 51–52.

Stores

"Teen-Age Market." March 1951, 28.

"Teen-Age Registries." March 1952, 54.

July 1952, 52.

January 1957, 36, 44.

Castaldi, Joseph. "Modern Merchandising in Infants' and Children's Wear." January 1957, 29.

"Surveys & Shows." February 1957, 33.

January 1960, 82, 83.

" 'Fashion' Ousting 'Classics' in Children's Wear." February 1964.

September 1995, 44.

System

28 March 1914, 11.

Clark, Neil M. "The 'Knee-high' Customer." March 1915, 237–44.

"Ninety-Housewives Tell Why They Buy." November 1915, 481–89.

"Why Women Buy." December 1915, 581–91.

January 1920, 97.

7 February 1920, 89.

29 May 1920, 81.

19 November 1921, 225.

16 December 1923, 13.

Women's Home Companion

"Dressing the Well-Dressed Children." January 1922, 65.

Cades, Jazel Rawson. "Good Looks: Let Your Child Have Her Chance to Be Beautiful." February 1925, 72.

Other Publications

"Body Measurements of American Boys and Girls for Garment and Patterns Construction." Miscellaneous publication no. 366. Bureau of Home Economics, U.S. Department of Agriculture, 1939.

"Child-Friendly Restaurants Aren't Kidding Around." *Restaurants & Institutions*. 1 September 1994, 112.

Children Royal. Spring 1921, 40–42.

"Denim Inequity." *Washington Post*. 30 July 1996.

"Food for Tots." *Restaurants & Institutions*. 15 March 1993, 131, 134.

"The Fun Worshippers." *Newsweek*. 11 December 1961, 88.

Good Housekeeping. June 1943, 27.

"Home Sewing." *Family Economic Review*. October 1957, 24.

"A New $10-Billion Power: The U. S. Teen-age Consumer." *Life*, 31 August 1959, 78–85.

New Yorker. 22 November 1958, 77.

New Yorker. 29 November, 1958, 57.

New York Times. 27 March 1994, section 9, p. 9.

New York Times Magazine. 4 February 1996.

Ober, Grace. "Clothing as Expression." *Home Progress*, December 1912, 52–53.

Owen, Hortense. "Hollywood's in the Nursery Closet Now." *Pictorial Review*, June 1935, 20.

"Teen-age Market: It's 'Terrif.' " *Business Week*. 8 June 1946, 72–74.

"Teen-agers' Preferences in Clothes." *Journal of Home Economics*. December 1950, 801–2.

"Wash Hot, Shrink Well." *Newsweek*. 20 June 1994, 75.

Index

Italic page number refers to an illustration, italic "f" to a figure, italic "t" to a table

movies: child actors in, 91–94, 170 nn. 69–70; pediocularity in, 166 n. 1; star system in, 170 n. 69; violence in, 148

Munsingwear, 142

nagging, by children, 146–47, 180 n. 9

Nannette Manufacturing Company (New York City), 92

Nasaw, David, 70

National Baby Week, 56

National Congress of Mothers, 34–35, 55–56

New Look, 133

Newsweek, 136

New York market, 124–25

normality, 99–100

ostentation, 80

Palladino, Grace, 128, 129

Palmer, Phyllis, 45–46

Paoletti, Jo B., 101

Paramount, 92–93

parenting, 25–26, 67, 146, 149. *See also* motherhood

Parents (formerly *Children, the Magazine for Parents*), 61–62, 81, 82, 89, 90–91, 128–29, 142, 167 n. 22, 175 n. 9

Parsons, Talcott, 128

pediocularity: adults' vs. children's tastes, 81, 82–83; anecdotes and, 72–73, 75; autonomy and, 77, 88; change to, 66–70, 166 nn. 1–2; child psychology and, 75–76, 90–91, 167 n. 24 (*see also* childrearing); childrearing and, 89–94; children as consumers, 70–78, 96, 146, 166–67

n. 16, 166 n. 14, 167 n. 24; children as customers, 70, 115, 150; in children's wear, 96; girls' perspective (*see* girlhood); innocence and, 68, 69; marketing to children and, 75, 167 n. 22; markets and, 68–69; ostentation and, 80; in package design, 74–75; promotions and, 75, 76; self-expression and, 77, 82, 83; taste, beauty, simplicity, and functionality in, 78–85; toddler as merchandising category, 85–94, 170 n. 72; of toys, 69; vanity of girls, 79–80, 94

peer society, 98, 128, 130, 131, 136–37, 143, 170–71 n. 3

pensions, 170–71 n. 3

permissive parenting, 67

personality, 91, 99, 147–48

Pessel, Helen, 142

Philbrick, John, 99

Piaget, Jean, 91

pizza, 146

play, 90

Plumb, J. H., 29

Polk Sanitary Milk Company, 165 n. 42

Pollock, Linda, 25–26, 29

pollution vs. purity, 10

portraits of children, 24–25

Powers (Minneapolis), 131, 132

precocity, 99, 171 n. 7

prestige, in high school, 128

preteens and subteens, 112, 127, 137–43, 179 n. 83

Printer's Ink Monthly, 62, 73–75, 122–23

profane vs. sacred value of children, 7–13, 16, 151, 158 n. 13

profits, 126

Daniel Thomas Cook is an assistant professor of advertising, and
a research assistant professor at the Institute of Communications
Research, at the University of Illinois, Champaign-Urbana.

*Portions of this book have appeared in the following previously published
articles:* "The Mother as Consumer: Insights from the Children's Wear
Industry, 1917–1929," *Sociological Quarterly* 36 (1995): 505–22. Kind
permission granted by the University of California Press. "The Other
'Child Study': Figuring Children as Consumers in Market Research,
1910s–1990s." *Sociological Quarterly* 41, no. 3 (2000): 487–507. Kind
permission granted by the University of California Press. "The Rise of
'the Toddler' as Subject and as Merchandising Category in the 1930s."
In *New Forms of Consumption: Consumers, Culture and Commodification,*
ed. Mark Gottdiener. Lanham, Md.: Rowman & Littlefield, 2000. Kind
permission granted by Rowman and Littlefield. "Spatial Biographies of
Children's Consumption." *Journal of Consumer Culture* 3, no. 2 (2003).
Kind permission granted by Sage Publications. "Agency, Children's
Consumer Culture and the Fetal Subject." *Consumption, Markets and
Culture,* June 2003. Kind permission granted by Taylor and Francis.

Library of Congress Cataloging-in-Publication Data
Cook, Daniel Thomas.
The commodification of childhood : the children's clothing industry
and the rise of the child consumer / by Daniel Thomas Cook.
p. cm.
Includes bibliographical references and index.
ISBN 0-8223-3279-5 (cloth : alk. paper)—ISBN 0-8223-3268-X (pbk. :
alk. paper) 1. Childhood—United States—History. 2. Adolescence—
United States—History. 3. Child consumers—United States—History.
4. Teenage consumers—United States—History. 5. Children's clothing
industry—United States—History. 6. Mother and child—United
States—History I. Title.   HQ792.U5C673 2004   305.23—dc22
2003016060